ISBN 978-0-266-06407-7
PIBN 10951684

The

FARM CREDIT SYSTEM

...a history of financial self-help

by W. Gifford Hoag

THE INTERSTATE
Printers & Publishers, Inc.

Danville, Illinois

The Farm Credit System

Library of Congress Catalog Card No. 76-026777

Reorder No. 1853

FOREWORD

This history of the cooperative Farm Credit System is dedicated to the thousands of people over the years who had the courage to tackle the impossible. It is dedicated to those who persisted in working to make their dreams and visions, and those of others, come true—whether for a span of a few years or a lifetime—and looked upon it all as a labor of love, regardless of the personal sacrifices or monetary rewards. It is dedicated to those who had faith in themselves and in each other and were willing to pull together as a team.

It is dedicated to those who hammered out and battled to protect the basic principles that were to make the System a successful model of self-help that has inspired others at home and abroad to adopt some of those principles to solve other problems. It is dedicated to those who caught the visions of others and pitched in to work toward their accomplishment.

The people to whom this history is dedicated include representatives from many groups. These groups include farmers, ranchers and growers, member-directors, management and employees of the local credit associations, Farm Credit Banks, and the Farm Credit Administration. They include farm, ranch, and cooperative organization leaders; Congressional leaders; educators; farm communicators who spread the word; and investors in the System's securities issued to raise the lending funds.

A large proportion of the farmers to whom this book is dedicated started with, or at some time were reduced to, very little—sometimes only a few hundred dollars of net assets—but persisted through the adversities of weather, waves of pests and diseases, and years of little or no monetary returns, to build successful farm businesses of their own, their marketing and farm supply cooperatives, and the Farm Credit System. They stuck with it "no matter what."

Farmer-directors had to have faith in their fellow farmers to continue to finance them through their years of economic adversity.

They also had to learn the skills of policy-making in the fields of lending, finance, management, marketing, member relations, and public relations. Management in local associations, district banks, and the supervisory agency also had to have faith in farmers and had to develop new skills.

The list of people to whom this history is dedicated is lengthy. Because of the difficulty in deciding where to stop, few are mentioned in the text, but their unnamed contributions are hereby recognized and appreciated.

Many people have had a hand in designing, developing, and adjusting the System over the years. For example, under the leadership of E. A. Jaenke, Governor from 1968 to 1974, the System's basic legislative charter was comprehensively revised and recodified, and, with the strong approval of Congress, the System's authorities were expanded to better meet the modern needs of rural America. It fell to his successor, W. Malcolm Harding, to continue further implementation of the Act and thereby expand and improve the System's ability to serve.

However, the chief dedication of this history logically goes to W. I. Myers, second Governor of the Farm Credit Administration—1933 to 1938—the chief architect who, drawing on the ideas of many farm, System, and Congressional leaders, conceived and drew up the blueprints for the modern System in 1933 and outlined its basic principles. He also provided inspiring leadership to win approval and adoption of those plans from farm organizations, cooperatives, Congress, System officials and directors, as well as a host of farmers who were then or later became its members.

The greatest tribute to Myers is that decades later System leaders espoused as their own most of the basic principles he stood for and so lucidly and convincingly taught. Proof of Myers' greatness is that he enthusiastically supported the changes in operating methods, alterations, and additions found necessary over the years as merely needed fine tuning and modern application of those original basic principles. Leaders without broad vision resist change. Myers intentionally designed a dynamic, ongoing System that could and would adapt or adjust to the ever-changing needs of farmers, ranchers, and their cooperatives because they are the member-owners of the System as well as its borrowers.

W. Gifford Hoag

February 1976

ACKNOWLEDGEMENTS

It has been my good fortune to know and have as friends hundreds of people in the Farm Credit Administration, the cooperative Farm Credit System, and other cooperatives. They have contributed to my knowledge and understanding of the Farm Credit and cooperative family that made my writing of this history possible. I hope they consider themselves duly recognized because I cannot mention every one of them.

In addition to those mentioned in the Foreword, long-time friends B. Ben Sunbury, Executive Assistant to the Governor, and H. T. "Bill" Mason and Jon F. Greeneisen, successive Deputy Governors and Secretaries to the Federal Farm Credit Board, urged me onward.

The people who lived through the early days of Farm Credit and helped shape its course, who were kind enough to let me interview them to get the needed background for starting the project, included former FCA Governors W. I. Myers, F. F. Hill, and I. W. Duggan; their deputies A. T. "Art" Esgate; Fred Gilmore, who also served as Vice President of the Federal Land Bank of Omaha; J. D. "Doug" Lawrence, who was also President of the Columbia Bank for Cooperatives; Rufus Clarke, who also at various times served as President of each of the four Farm Credit institutions at Columbia; Harold Miles, who also was Secretary of the Production Credit Corporation of Wichita. Others interviewed included James R. Isleib, former Land Bank Commissioner who later served for many years on the Farm Credit Board of Wichita; John Eidam, President of the Omaha Bank for Cooperatives; and Fred Merrifield, General Agent and President of the Bank for Cooperatives at Wichita.

I am particularly indebted to the members of the History Advisory Committee who guided and encouraged me throughout the project and dutifully read three drafts of the manuscript. The chairman of this Committee was Gordon Cameron, President of the Farm Credit Banks of Springfield. Others on the Committee were Aubrey

Johnson, Fiscal Agent of the Farm Credit Banks, former Deputy Governor of FCA, and Vice President of the Federal Intermediate Credit Bank of St. Paul; Lloyd Ullyot, former President of the St. Paul Bank for Cooperatives; Kenneth Naden, President of the National Council of Farmer Cooperatives; Jon F. Greeneisen; and Carroll Arnold, Director of Information of FCA and previously Director of Information for the Farm Credit Banks of New Orleans, who served as Secretary of the Committee and assisted with the publication of the final product.

Others who were kind enough to read my first rough draft and give me valuable criticism and suggestions were W. I. Myers; Art Esgate; Russell C. Engberg, former Director of Research and Information, whose career dated back to the Federal Farm Loan Board and included service as Director of Research for the Farm Credit Banks of Omaha; C. T. "Terry" Fredrickson, current Director of the Supervisory Division; W. N. Stokes, Jr., former President of the FICB of Houston and previously President of the Bank for Cooperatives there; Bill Mason; Frank ImMasche, former member of the Credit Research Division whose career started with the Federal Farm Board; William H. Johnson, former Director of Information for the Baltimore Banks and early Secretary of the PCC; and C. Maurice Wieting, retired Vice President-Information of the Ohio Farm Bureau Federation and former Director of Information of the National Council of Farmer Cooperatives, who diligently gave me suggestions on almost every page. Ronald H. Erickson, Assistant Director of Information, checked my final draft in detail. Many other members of the Farm Credit Administration staff provided me with many details and checked various parts of the manuscript.

And most of all, I am indebted to my wife, Diane, who not only lived through all my days of indecision, urged me on, and researched many details at the Library of Congress but who also typed the various drafts and caught many of my mistakes enroute.

But with all this help, any errors of omission or judgment are my own.

W. GIFFORD HOAG

CONTENTS

WHAT IS THE FARM CREDIT SYSTEM?

Farmers and ranchers obtain more than one-third of their financing from the user-owned and controlled cooperative Farm Credit System. Their marketing, farm supply, and business service cooperatives obtain about 65 percent of their borrowed funds from it. Other users of the System include open seas fishermen, nonfarm rural home owners, and businesses providing on-farm services. Users of the System were borrowing well over $30 billion from it annually by the mid-1970s.

The Farm Credit System is organized on a district basis. Each of the 12 Farm Credit Districts has a Federal Land Bank, a Federal Intermediate Credit Bank, and a Bank for Cooperatives operating under a single policy-making board of directors known as the Farm Credit Board for that district. In addition, a Central Bank for Cooperatives, owned by the district Banks for Cooperatives, is located in Denver, Colorado. Its board of directors is made up of appointees from the 12 district boards, plus one director appointed by the Governor of the Farm Credit Administration with the approval of the Federal Farm Credit Board.

The Federal Land Banks make long-term first mortgage loans through more than 500 local Federal Land Bank Associations. These farmer-owned Associations in turn own the Land Banks. The Banks also lend to nonfarm rural home owners.

The Federal Intermediate Credit Banks provide loan funds to more than 400 local farmer-owned Production Credit Associations. Farmers, ranchers, and farmers of the sea borrow from these associations for seasonal operating purposes and to finance capital expenditures for periods up to 7 years. The Intermediate Credit Banks also provide funds for farm loans to about 100 other lenders, including agricultural credit corporations and commercial banks.

The Banks for Cooperatives provide financing for facilities and operating loans to more than 3,000 marketing, farm supply, and business service cooperatives that own the Banks. The Central Bank for Cooperatives participates with them in giving loans to the larger cooperatives as a method of spreading the risk. This Bank also serves all the other Banks of the System by operating a money desk that transfers funds from Bank to Bank.

Farmers and ranchers elect the boards of directors of their local Federal Land Bank Associations and Production Credit Associations, as well as the boards of directors of the cooperatives that own the district Banks for Cooperatives. These three groups of boards of directors represent their members in selecting two members each on the district Farm Credit Board. The seventh director is appointed by the Governor of the Farm Credit Administration. The local and district boards determine policies and appoint top management for their organizations.

The System is supervised and examined by the Farm Credit Administration—an independent government agency whose expenses are paid for by the banks and associations of the System. Farm Credit Administration policies are made by the 13 member Federal Farm Credit Board. This Board also appoints the Governor of the Farm Credit Administration, who is its chief administrator. Board members are appointed by the President of the United States—subject to Senate confirmation—after he considers the three nominees made by the boards of directors of the FLBAs, PCAs, and the cooperatives that own and use the Banks for Cooperatives in each Farm Credit District.

The 13th member of the Federal Board is appointed by the Secretary of Agriculture as his representative. All Presidential appointments since the Board was established in 1953 have been from the nominees made by boards of directors elected by farmers. Thus farmer-members, through their local farmer-elected board of directors, are represented on the policy-making board for the System's national supervisory agency.

The System, in cooperation with groups of security dealers and dealer banks, obtains most of its lending funds by selling securities through a joint fiscal agent in New York City.

The 37 Farm Credit Banks in the mid-1970s established Farmbank Services in Denver, Colorado. This organization operates the Farmbank Information and Research Service and also provides services in such fields as management training and public communications when the Banks find phases of such programs can be developed more effectively or efficiently on a joint rather than an individual bank or district basis.

PART ONE

Significance to Farmers
and the Economy

The various parts of the cooperative Farm Credit System were authorized by Congress over a 17-year period—1916 to 1933—to meet extremely pressing needs of farmers, ranchers, and their cooperatives. In overly simplified terms, these needs can be summed up as having a dependable source of adequate credit, on terms suited to the particular needs of agriculture, from lenders who understood their problems.

The Land Banks and their affiliated associations came into being by Congressional law in 1916,[1] because farmers had an urgent need for more and better long-term mortgage financing. Money was scarce in most rural areas, and when lenders could be found, costs usually were high. Every few years mortgages had to be renewed or refinanced. There was the ever-present danger that renewals or a new lender would not be available.

Congress established the Federal Intermediate Credit Banks in 1923[2] as wholesalers of funds from investment centers in recognition of farmers' and ranchers' needs for operating credit for periods of more than 30, 60, or 90 days and the frequent shortage of funds in rural America. The need had become acute as a result of the 1921 general business recession which triggered the farm depression of the mid-1920s that merged into the general depression of the 1930s. The Intermediate Credit Banks were authorized to discount farmers' notes for commercial banks, agricultural credit corporations, and livestock loan companies. They were also authorized to make credit available to cooperatives, but only on farm products they held in storage.

---

[1] Federal Farm Loan Act.
[2] Agricultural Credits Act.

In the financial crisis, climaxing in 1933, the Government came to the assistance of the Land Banks[3]—along with many other financial and business organizations through such organizations as the Reconstruction Finance Corporation—and requested them to take on the responsibility of stemming the tide of farm foreclosures sweeping the country. At the same time the Production Credit Associations and the Banks for Cooperatives were organized.[4] Even the former inadequate supply of short-term credit had dried up. Financial organizations of all kinds were stocked with frozen assets. Hundreds of commercial banks, especially in rural areas, had gone bankrupt and closed their doors. Many others were faced with that possibility. Insurance companies that normally made loans to farmers were loaded with loans of all kinds that could not be repaid. All types of lenders were making frantic efforts to collect loans to pay their own expenses rather than making new loans. Merchants, dealers, and individuals were trying to collect credit advanced to farmers in order to pay their bills. Farms were being sold for unpaid taxes in an effort to pay teachers and provide other local services.

In such circumstances, the organizations making up the Farm Credit System played a vital role in the lives of farmers and the economy as a whole. Under varying conditions in the years that have followed, the System has had changing but increasingly significant roles in the agricultural and general economies of the Nation.

---

[3] Emergency Farm Mortgage Act.
[4] Farm Credit Act of 1933.

Chapter 1

FARMERS AS FINANCIERS

"Neither a borrower nor a lender be. . . ." So goes Polonius' long-quoted advice to his son. American farmers and ranchers for generations tended to follow that fatherly advice, whenever possible, based on many bitter experiences of relatives, friends, or neighbors. But starting in World War I—with the early funding of a national credit system they were eventually to own—more and more of them began being numbered among those who have proven there are exceptions to *both* ends of Shakespeare's ancient axiom. Farmers and ranchers became *both* borrowers and lenders. Over a period of 60 years, farmers and ranchers by the hundreds of thousands have built a system of credit institutions that has become one of the most respected borrowers on Wall Street and in other financial markets—surpassed only by the Federal Government itself.

This cooperative Farm Credit System, now owned and controlled by farmers, lends the money to those very same farmer-owners. Thus, farmers lend money to themselves at an ever-expanding rate—by the mid-1970s more than $30 billion a year. As organized groups, they do so while maintaining the best of relationships both as borrowers and lenders, rather than engaging in the endless squabbling Polonius implied, even though a very small minority fail to carry out all the provisions of their contracts on time. It is all made possible by the faith built and buttressed by an enviable record of repayment by farmers to their lending System and by their System to the investors who buy its securities. No member of this cooperative Farm Credit System has ever missed a scheduled payment of principal or interest on its securities, even in the years of the Great Depression of the 1930s, although at that time, like most businesses, it had some help from the Government.

For more than 20 years, the Farm Credit System has been generally recognized as the largest cooperative organization in the world. It is also one of this country's largest financial organizations.

When David Rockefeller, chairman of the board of one of the Nation's largest banks—Chase Manhattan—visited W. Malcolm Harding, current Governor of the Farm Credit Administration, he was amazed to learn that the farmer-owned, farmer-controlled, and farmer-operated Farm Credit System was doing almost as much business as his bank with its worldwide network. It might have reminded him that his grandfather came out of a small farming town in New York State to found an oil empire that sprouted into a financial empire and many other businesses.

Focus on People Rather Than Profits

The cooperative Farm Credit System has been highly successful dollarwise. But even more importantly, it has been highly successful peoplewise. It has been instrumental—the catalyst supplying much of the financial power—in helping farmers increase the food and fiber supply for more and more consumers on this earth at a reasonable cost.

Thus, the Farm Credit System has been and still is a vital force in improving the well-being of all the people in the United States, as consumers, plus millions of other people throughout the world. It passes the acid test of any institution—it serves the public interest. It also serves the interests of its owner-users—farmers.

In this whole process, farmers, ranchers, and other users of the System have benefited as people in many ways, many of which contribute to a better standard of living. However, the benefits do not end there. Farmers have learned the advantages of democratically controlled and operated organizations by actually using and running them. They also have learned the realities of economics, finance, and good business management.

The number of farmers and their cooperatives using the System—with some interruptions—has kept growing in the face of declining numbers from which the System can draw its members. By the mid-1970s farmers and ranchers and their cooperatives, plus commercial fishermen and rural home owners, were borrowing a total of $30 billion a year and had outstanding $30 billion in loans. The total credit made available to farmers and their cooperatives over the entire period of the System's operation adds up to more than $250 billion. The System has an accumulated net worth from actual stock investments of its borrowers and net worth reserves set aside from earnings totaling more than $4 billion.

Many people rightfully point to the fact that, except for the 1920s and the Great Depression of the 1930s, when large losses were taken by the Land Banks, the System has operated over a period when the general price level was usually on the rise. This made it easier for farmers to pay their loans than they might have expected to do when the loans were originally made, and it also tended to hide possible mistakes. However, farmers have also gone through many testings of their ability to cope with the elements and periods when farm prices went down while costs continued their upward climb. The Farm Credit System has had a good record of sticking with its members as long as they were doing a good job and there was any hope that they might be able to pay off their debts eventually.

The major early partner in this enterprise—the United States Government—had the original faith in farmers as borrowers and lenders and gradually sold out its interest to farmer-borrower-owners of the System, according to the original visionary and optimistic plan. The importance of this achievement to the development of a highly efficient farming industry, and its critically important effects on the American economy, will be explored. Beyond that, we will trace the hammering out and development of the basic principles that have successfully transformed a visionary experiment into a well-respected member of the financial community—through trial and error and learning from those experiences. This cooperatively owned and operated System has remained devoted to serving the interests of its member-borrowers at the lowest possible cost consistent with building and maintaining a sound financial foundation. Many of the basic principles and practices pioneered by the cooperative Farm Credit System are applicable for use in solving other national and international problems. This has already been proven by their adaptation to other situations at home and abroad.

Chapter 2

FARM EFFICIENCY MAKES HIGH STANDARD OF LIVING POSSIBLE

With all its problems, the United States has the highest standard of living in the world. There are many people with low incomes whose standards of living cry for improvement, but there also are very few people who are actually starving. The United States is one of the few countries of the world that is a net exporter of food. Food is one of its major exports without which the United States would not have the exchange needed to buy essential imports of scarce but important raw materials, not to mention much-desired finished goods. Since World War II, the United States also has given away huge quantities of food and has supplied technical assistance in the field of agricultural production to the hungry, starving people in a host of lesser developed countries. In addition, representatives of many nations of the world have given much study to the U.S. Farm Credit System in their search for ways of increasing their agricultural production.

American education, research, natural resources, invention, ingenuity, technology and industrial know-how, and many other factors, have had much to do with the high standard of living in the United States. However, most of the tremendous industrial output has been made possible only because the United States has made even more spectacular advances on the food and fiber production fronts. It is the people released from the task of raising food and fiber who have made possible the production of an ever-increasing variety of other goods and the provision of more and more services—such as radios, television sets, cars, a wide variety of home equipment—in addition to everything from the processing of ready-to-cook dinners to space exploration.

Increases in land under cultivation have *not* been a major reason for rapid increases in farm production. In fact, in 1920 there were 6.5 million farmers and ranchers who were operating 959 million acres of land. They had 106 million Americans to feed and clothe. By the mid-1970s, 2.8 million farmers were using only 13 percent more land to supply a U.S. population that had more than doubled. They also were producing more food and fiber to bring farm exports close to equaling the value of the nation's huge, expensive imports of oil.

It is significant that over the last 28 years production per man-hour in farming has increased much more rapidly than in industry— 5.8 percent annually in farming compared to only 3.5 percent for manufacturng.[1] In view of agriculture's being so deeply involved with the biological laws of nature, such a record is even more significant, if not surprising.

For example, farming is highly dependent on the weather, and that factor remains uncontrollable. The best agricultural science has been able to do in that direction is to try to adapt to possible weather hazards. It has done so by such means as breeding varieties that can mature more quickly and withstand lack of moisture, cold weather, and high temperatures. Development of overhead irrigation systems, even in normally humid areas, has lessened dependence on rainfall. But too much moisture in the spring can still delay cultivation and planting. Late frosts in the spring or early frosts in the fall can still put large dents in farm production. The best farmers can do is to try to work around such uncontrollable hazards.

Rapidly increasing farm production per man and per acre in the United States has been due to a combination of many factors. These include research; invention; better educated farmers; mechanization; highly developed technology; better adapted, higher producing crop varieties; and efficient, production-bred livestock. But most important of all has been the farmers' ability to develop a host of important skills, from the ability to manage complex businesses to mastering the practical application of such arts and sciences as engineering and mechanics, genetics of plants and animals, entomology, plant pathology, chemistry, veterinary medicine, to careful and wise financial planning and many other abilities in between. In general, it has been a survival of the fittest. Those who could not master such tremendous assignments sought out less demanding fields of endeavor and sold out to those who could and to those who needed more land to make the most efficient use of their heavy investment in labor-saving machinery and equipment that could also accomplish needed tasks more quickly and at the optimum time in the production cycle.

---

[1] Economic Research Service, USDA, estimates for period 1947 to 1974.

A Many-Member Team

Many organizations have been involved in contributing to this outstanding record of progress achieved by farmers.

The Land Grant colleges have been an important factor. They have contributed a wide variety of ongoing research and teaching of future farmers, agricultural scientists, and farm-related businessmen. The agricultural research of the U.S. Department of Agriculture has made important contributions along with other USDA programs.

The Extension Service supported by Federal, state, and county governments, working in close harmony with the Land Grant colleges, spreads the word on how best to apply the results of current research and vital breakthroughs to operating farmers.

Other important members of the dynamic agricultural team pressing for a more effective farming effort included vocational agriculture teachers in the high schools and inventors, innovators, and scientists employed by manufacturers of farm machinery, equipment, fertilizers, herbicides, pesticides, and fungicides. They also included plant breeders employed by seed companies to supplement the research work of the Land Grant colleges and the U.S. Department of Agriculture.

The strong, innovative farm supply, marketing, and business service cooperative organizations gradually built by their farmer-owners have been of ever-growing importance in increasing farm efficiency. They have been a driving force in obtaining for farmers the highest quality farm supplies and services possible. They have brought electrical power to a large portion of the nation's farms. They have improved many phases of the processing, marketing, and merchandising of farm products. By cutting costs and returning the savings to their farmer-users, cooperatives not only have increased the incentive for farmers to move forward in doing their very best to improve their productive ability, but they have also been a vital factor in making farmers' money go as far as possible.

One measure of cooperatives' overall effectiveness is that by 1976 7 farmer cooperatives appeared on *Fortune* magazine's list of the 500 largest industrial corporations—4 of them ranked between 100 and 200. Five other cooperatives were included in *Fortune's* list of the second 500. However, cooperatives were still far outranked in number and size by privately owned corporations engaged in the food processing and distribution business and those in the farm supply business—providers of farm inputs. *Fortune* listed 20 industrials in the food business ahead of the largest cooperative with Kraftco ranked as number 33 with sales of \$4.9 billion leading the list.[2] Non-cooperative companies in the food business accounted for 62 of *Fortune's* 500 largest industrials.

Farm Investments Skyrocket

Practically every technological advance in agricultural production has required each farmer, rancher, and his cooperative to spend and invest more and more money to adopt. The rising demands for funds could not be met out of past savings of individual farm operators. Farmers' needs to borrow money have leaped forward, with the speed often spurred on by inflation. Farmers, once they were convinced they should adopt new methods, had to have a ready supply of funds to buy new equipment. They had to have money to finance the purchase of more land to use the new equipment efficiently. They had to have the money to build new buildings to house their ever-increasing line of machinery. They needed more and more money to buy higher producing livestock, more fertilizer, better seed and feed, and more chemicals.

Farmers, while waiting for crops and livestock to be ready for market, also needed to borrow money to pay increasing labor and family living costs. There has been a never-ending demand for increased capital investment to substitute for labor. Annual production costs have spiraled too, pushed by more and more purchased inputs and rising prices.

Not only have farmers needed an ever-increasing supply of borrowed money—farming investments per man in the mid-1970s were \$98,540 compared to \$55,344 per worker in industry[3] and cash farm production costs soared with improved technology—but they also have needed the funds on terms particularly suited to farming and at the lowest possible cost. The ready availability of credit on terms suited to farm needs—in which the cooperative Farm Credit System has been the pacesetter—is generally recognized as having been a major factor in making it possible for farmers to move rapidly forward in enlarging and improving the efficiency of their businesses.

Farmer cooperatives also have needed ever-increasing amounts

---

[2] Cooperatives ranked as follows: 135, Farmland Industries with \$1.51 billion sales; 141, Associated Milk Producers, \$1.48 billion; 154, Agway, \$1.33 billion; 180, Land O' Lakes, \$1.12 billion; 239, Gold Kist, \$815 million; 359, CF Industries, \$468 million; and 438, Dairylea Cooperative, \$355 million.

[3] Economic Research Service, USDA, estimates for 1975 (industry figure is unofficial preliminary estimate).

of money for expanding and improving facilities and equipment, for working capital, for the processing and orderly marketing of increasingly large amounts of farm products, and for providing larger quantities of a larger number of farm supplies.

Before the Banks for Cooperatives started in business to finance farmer cooperatives, a large number of such organizations were still relatively small, new, or weak in many areas. Many farmers' cooperative efforts had failed. Usually, failure was due to poor management, undercapitalization, or lack of understanding and support from farmer-members. Although some commercial banks were financing the better established, stronger cooperatives, most local banks were at best skeptical of the idea that farmers could own, control, and run cooperatives.

The Banks for Cooperatives, balancing the proper amounts of understanding, financing, and counseling, began to demonstrate to local banks that cooperatives could be good credit risks. More of them cautiously began to lend money to cooperatives. Loans from Banks for Cooperatives thus played an important part in moving farmers toward more successful cooperation.

Chapter 3

FARM CREDIT SYSTEM AN ESSENTIAL LINK

Today, the Farm Credit System supplies about one-third of the credit used by farmers directly and 65 percent of the financing they require for their cooperatives. More than $30 billion a year is being pumped into rural America from investors all over the world. The cooperative Farm Credit System has made these funds available over the years promptly when, where, and as needed on terms specifically tailored to fit the needs of individual farmers and their cooperatives. And that financing has been and is supplied at reasonable rates that reflect the current wholesale cost of money in the Nation's money markets. Thus, the cooperative Farm Credit System and the increased farm income that it has helped generate has been and is an essential link in the chain driving the farming industry to greater and greater production efficiency.

The timely availability of credit from the System, in any amounts farmers needed and could handle wisely and safely, put its member-borrowers in the enviable position of being able to adopt new methods promptly after they had been developed and proven out.

The importance of the availability of an adequate supply of credit in expanding farm production was explained by Secretary of Agriculture Earl Butz at the swearing in of W. Malcolm Harding in 1974 as the new Governor of the Farm Credit Administration. He pointed out that there is little new land to develop—and thus increased production to meet the rising demand for food must come from improved technology and the credit which makes its adoption possible.

System Has Benefited All Farmers

But the benefits of the cooperative Farm Credit System have not and do not stop at the line fences of the farmer and rancher members or at the walls of the cooperatives which use it. Farmers and their cooperatives who have used other sources of credit also have benefited from it in many ways.

13

Other lenders have kept close track of the agricultural credit specialists in the Farm Credit System—and from time to time have hired some of them. The System has inspired other lenders, by example, to have more confidence, first of all, in the ability of capable farmers and ranchers and well-managed and operated cooperatives to use credit wisely and to repay their loans when due.

Other lenders have tended to adopt many of the loan terms and innovations the System developed to meet the specific needs of farmer and cooperative borrowers. In the field of pricing—interest rates—they also have been influenced by the System. The forces of competition have pushed them to keep in mind the rates at which their customers could borrow from the Farm Credit System.

The Temporary National Economic Committee of Congress, which made an exhaustive study of the Nation's economy in 1941, referred to the operations of the Farm Credit System as an excellent example of regulation by competition. The System's influence on the economy has continued to increase over the years.

System Has Brought in Outside Money

However, probably even more important than the effects of competition has been the System's contribution in increasing the total supply of credit to the agricultural industry. Except for the farm mortgage lending of some large life insurance companies, which have competing outlets for their investment, most other non-Farm Credit System sources of credit are dependent on the local supply of funds. These sources of credit tend to expand and contract their loan funds with the ups and downs of the business cycle.

On the other hand, the Farm Credit System increased the total supply of credit available in rural America, in good times and bad, by bringing in a continuing flow of funds from outside investors in quantities needed by farmers. By doing so, it has reduced the pressure on local lenders to spread available loan funds to all farmers in their territory. Without the availability of such outside funds, interest rates to farmers generally would have tended to skyrocket—especially in "tight money" periods. Local lenders might well have been forced to ration credit to farmers either indirectly, by means of even higher interest rates, or directly, by dropping less favored customers. "Outside money" to supplement local capital was of tremendous importance—especially in earlier years—in the "newer" regions like the far western and intermountain states, as well as in the South, because these areas were particularly short of capital and were thus traditionally high credit cost areas. "Livestock development got special advantages since PCA credit supplemented local bank funds to meet cyclical credit crises."[1]

At times, some casual observers of the agricultural scene have questioned whether too much of the Nation's financial resources were flowing to farmers, particularly in times when a "tight money" policy was being used as a brake on inflation. Such observers tend to overlook the fact that agricultural credit is largely used to keep up or expand production and thus in itself is counter-inflationary. True, there are opportunities for speculation in agriculture. However, the Farm Credit System endeavors to avoid lending for speculative purposes even in times of a plentiful supply of funds.

So long as institutions are run by human beings there will always be exceptions to all rules to point at; however, the System's record in avoiding lending for speculative purposes generally has been considered relatively good by those who have kept in close touch with its operations. In times of inflation and "tight money" policies, the System has been very careful to avoid lending for speculative projects.

System Not Only for Large Farmers

The emphasis up to this point on the significance of the cooperative Farm Credit System to the development and maintenance of today's efficient and highly productive agricultural industry might lead to the conclusion that the System is only interested in financing large farmers and large cooperatives.

The System has not forgotten nor overlooked the fact that most of today's larger, more efficient family farm operations are the descendants of the relatively small farm operations and small beginning cooperatives financed by the System in its earlier years. There are many examples of farm families who first borrowed a few hundred or a few thousand dollars in the 1930s who now have net worths of a quarter million or more dollars and who borrow proportionately.

In fact, in those earlier years of the System it was the smaller farmers who first came to it for financing. Many of the large operators of that day, being conscious of the Government capital invested in the System, or being somewhat skeptical of the credit cooperative idea, proudly asserted they could qualify for credit elsewhere. From the System's standpoint its early lending to larger farmer-borrowers

---

[1] Pointed out by W. I. Myers in October 13, 1975, letter to the author.

was engaged in, at least to some extent, as a means of providing the System with income to offset the higher cost of handling small loans.

An extreme example of the need for more income was cited in the late 1930s by one southern Production Credit Association secretary-treasurer, Robert Darr, now President of the Federal Land and Intermediate Credit Banks of Columbia. He said the number of his farmer-members was growing rapidly—then about 1,000—but each loan, which averaged only $150, put him further from the goal of paying the PCA's expenses out of operating income. The income from such small loans was less than the expense of handling them. The difference had to be made up from the PCA's interest income from the Government-owned capital, then invested in bonds.

The System continues to make a large number of loans to relatively small farmers. The latest figures show that about 30 percent of Land Bank loans are for $25,000 or less and 52 percent of Production Credit Association loans are for $10,000 or less. Measured in today's dollars and with today's mechanized farms, these are relatively small loans.

Financing Part-Time and Younger Farmers

The System also has a continuing good record of financing part-time farmers. The latest studies show that about 30 percent of the loans by Production Credit Associations and about one half the loans made by the Land Banks are to finance part-time farmers. Many of these part-time farmers are getting started in farming and supplementing their farm income by off-the-farm jobs. Others are older farmers who are gradually getting out of farming. They also include business and professional people who own or buy farms as an investment.

Many of the Associations and Banks in the System also proudly point to their records of helping young farm families get started in farming. They look forward to the opportunity to help them gradually build their businesses into larger operations. Some of the Banks and Associations have developed formal plans designed to finance more young farm families. Such plans are in recognition of how difficult it is to get started in farming today because of the high price of land and big investments that need to be made in farm machinery and livestock. These plans are based on endeavoring to select young people who demonstrate potential management capability even though their equities are relatively small.

Services Not Limited to Loans

The Farm Credit System over the years has long had a reputation of endeavoring to design its loans to fit farm and cooperative credit needs. It also has counseled and advised its borrowers on an informal, voluntary basis. As a result, many borrowers have prospered through the wise use of credit in their businesses. Since the Depression years, a relatively small number have had to liquidate their businesses. As one observer points out, except for those caused by personal reasons such as illness, such liquidations represent the System's failure to get the job done in those particular cases. Especially in more recent years, the System has developed more and more financially related services tuned to the members' needs. These services are reported in more detail in Chapter 18.

Adapting to Changing Needs

Financing agriculture—farmers, ranchers, and their cooperatives—has been an exciting business over the last 60 years. It has been a period of rapid change. The System has survived periods of inflation, recession, and depression, shifts from war-time economies to peacetime economies, and back again. Sometimes food and other items were scarce. And at other times there seemed to be no prospect for anything beyond mounting surpluses and depressed farm prices. Farmers have often been squeezed by declining farm prices and rising farm costs. In some years droughts or floods were combined with low farm prices to cause devastating effects on farmers' incomes and net worths. Farmers and their cooperative Farm Credit System have frequently had to change their plans. However, the System has been able to stand by a high proportion of its members and help them work out of their financial problems.

Farming and agribusiness have changed rapidly and drastically over these 60 years. In 1916, farmers who succeeded were chiefly those who worked the hardest themselves and got the most work out of their families. The power available on farms in 1916 was mostly horse and mule power plus man, woman, and child power. Today, with almost all farms electrified—with a big assist from the rural electric cooperatives, especially in the more sparsely settled areas—and with 17 million horses and mules replaced by nearly 5 million tractors and other power equipment, management ability and financing have become crucial elements for success.

Average farm size has increased to 387 acres in 1975 from 152 acres in 1933 and from 148 acres in 1920. But averages are particularly misleading when it comes to farm size. One family with little outside labor can operate a 1,000-acre or more, modernly equipped wheat farm in the plains states or the Palouse area of Washington State. On the other hand, only a small number of acres are needed for large-scale poultry or cattle feeding operations that involve considerable amounts of hired labor. Certain types of large-sized fruit, vegetable, and dairy operations take a relatively small number of acres.

Farm assets and debts have also risen rapidly. By the mid-1970s, the U.S. Department of Agriculture estimated average assets per farm at $212,000 compared with $5,970 in 1935. Average debt per farm had risen to $32,500 from $1,493 in 1933.

But these changes on farms and ranches tell only part of the story. The increased farm efficiency also has benefited consumers greatly. Today, the average consumer has to spend only about 17 percent of his family income for food compared to 24 percent in 1933—the highest was just under 26 percent in 1947 when prices were decontrolled following World War II. Consumers in the United States spend a lower percentage of their income for food than in any other country in the world. In the Soviet Union, food takes 38 percent of the consumer's dollar. In Spain it is 33 percent, in Sweden 27 percent, and in Mexico 42 percent.

The cooperative Farm Credit System over this 60-year period has had to adapt its policies and operations to such ever-changing conditions—and sometimes the adjustments seemed to come too slowly. Yet over much of the period the System, by providing adequate credit on terms suited to farmers' needs, has been a major factor in making change possible and in speeding up the very rate of change itself.

Chapter 4

SYSTEM BUILT STRONG CAPITAL BASE

By the mid-1970s, the completely farmer- and user-owned co-operative Farm Credit System had a net worth of about $4.5 billion. If they were still alive, this would have completely confounded the critics, who in 1916 and years later were certain farmers could not run their own credit business and that the government would lose its $9 million investment in capital stock authorized by Congress to start the 12 Federal Land Banks. These Banks were to become the cornerstone of the cooperative Farm Credit System. This record has certainly also far outstripped the dreams of the most optimistic supporters of the original Federal Farm Loan Act of 1916 and those who supported the legislation of 1923 and 1933 that rounded out the System.

The original Government capital stock in the Federal Land Banks was replaced by farmer-owned stock in the Land Banks by 1932. However, in that year, at the bottom of the Great Depression, Congress authorized a new investment in capital stock of $125 million in an effort to stem the great wave of farm foreclosures. Other Government investments in the paid-in surplus of the Land Banks and the capital of the Federal Intermediate Credit Banks, the Production Credit System, and the Banks for Cooperatives brought the Government investments in the Farm Credit System to a peak of $638 million in 1939. In addition, the Government had $200 million invested in the capital stock of the wholly Government-owned Federal Farm Mortgage Corporation organized on an emergency basis in 1933 to finance high-risk mortgage loans which the Corporation made through the Land Banks and Associations.

By 1947 the Land Banks were able to retire all their Government capital, and by 1968 the entire System had repaid the last of its Government-owned stock. In addition to repaying all its stock to the U.S. Treasury, the Federal Farm Mortgage Corporation had paid $150 million in dividends.

By the mid-1970s the completely cooperative Farm Credit System had more than $32 billion in loans outstanding. Farmer-members of the Federal Land Bank Associations had more than 470,000 loans outstanding. Over 525,000 farmers were members of Production Credit Associations. And more than 4,000 farmer cooperatives were member-owners of the Banks for Cooperatives.

The building of strong institutions, however, is important chiefly for what they can do for people or a nation. Forrest F. Hill, consultant to the Ford Foundation, its former Vice President for Overseas Operations and early Governor of the Farm Credit Administration, pointed this out recently. He said that the main difference between highly developed and lesser developed countries is that over a period of time the developed countries have built strong institutions that can serve people by helping to solve their problems and meet their needs—like cooperatives, universities, and churches. The lesser developed countries do not yet have the strong institutions to serve them.

Farmer-members of the System, with Government encouragement and assistance, have built an organization to serve their credit and related needs on a continuing but ever-changing basis. In the process the System has helped and is continuing to help serve the needs of all farmers, thus benefiting the overall economy and the general public. And by so doing, the System has accomplished and is still accomplishing the general objectives Congress had in mind when it authorized the Government's encouragement, support, and early investments in the capital of the System,[1] even though it has probably been of greater service and use than even its most visionary founders could have foreseen.

Of course, the System has had its share of mistakes, problems, and differences of opinion. The Public Relations, Advertising, and Training Committee of the Federal Intermediate Credit Banks—F. Vernon Wright, Chairman; George M. Anderson and T. R. McGuire[2]—commented on this in the introduction to W. N. Stokes, Jr.'s "Credit to Farmers." Recalling the history of the Intermediate Credit Banks and Production Credit Associations, the Committee said:

> Each objective, goal, function was brought . . . by a

---

[1] Myers pointed out in October 13, 1975, letter that such Government investments—interest-free—provided financial strength necessary to obtain lending funds at low interest rates.

[2] Presidents of the New Orleans, Berkeley, and St. Louis Federal Intermediate Credit Banks, respectively.

long process of devoted and dedicated effort, work, and action by many people. These years were marked by many false starts, errors aplenty, and some controversy. But always present was unity of purpose. Many times men moved down different channels, but always toward common goals.

Although he was referring to the 50th anniversary of the Federal Land Banks, the words of President Lyndon Johnson still sum up the significance of the entire cooperative Farm Credit System. In a letter to Robert B. Tootell, then Governor of the Farm Credit Administration, he said in part:

> The Farm Loan Act, through the Federal Land Banks and local associations it provided, opened the door to modern farming and ranching operations throughout the country . . .
> Over the years these Banks have pioneered, innovated, set standards, and provided leadership in the wise use of credit. The effect on the American economy is immeasurable . . .
> . . . the Farm Credit System constitutes a unique partnership of farmers, the financial community and the Government, based on the best traditions of our democratic society and dedicated to agricultural progress.
> . . . people everywhere . . . have just cause to recognize the important part which the productive use of credit has played in developing the agricultural strength of this Nation.

Governor Tootell quoted the late Clifford Hope of Kansas, who had served as Republican Chairman of the House Agriculture Committee, as follows:

> Of all the farm legislation we enacted during my long years in Congress, I am proudest of my part in passing the acts dealing with the Farm Credit System because I believe they helped farmers more than any other legislation we enacted.

One of the highly important keys to success of the cooperative Farm Credit System has been its good fortune to have bipartisan support from Congress and the Executive branch of the Government at most times in its history—and at all times when crucial issues were involved.

But that bipartisan support did not just happen.[3] Congress has long recognized the importance of an adequate supply of sound credit for farmers. It also has continued to be favorably impressed with the

---

[3] For details see "Bipartisan Support" in Chapter 10.

System's record of service to farmers provided on a nonprofit basis. It appreciated the strong financial stability farmers were building into the System. But Congress and the Executive branch undoubtedly have most appreciated the fact that with very few exceptions, the System and its officials have succeeded in studiously avoiding involvement in partisan politics. In such an atmosphere Congress has long been willing to consider on their merits most proposals for increasing the System's flexibility and usefulness and for modernizing it and removing no longer needed restrictions. With a few exceptions these proposed changes have been accepted even when some of them were opposed by other farm lenders.

PART TWO

Pioneering Innovations

Largely because the cooperatively owned and operated Farm Credit System has always endeavored to keep its focus on the individual credit needs of its borrower-members rather than on making a profit for its owners as investors, it has a continued history of pioneering innovative policies, methods, and loan terms. Admittedly, at times the System's leaders became too set in their ways and were content to continue traveling in well-worn ruts. But eventually, pressures from the user-owners of the System have jostled, jolted, or pushed old and/or new leaders back onto the modern road agriculture is traveling.

Other lenders to farmers, ranchers, and their cooperatives have tended to adopt or adapt many of the System's innovations to their own credit operations after the System has proven they work. Some of these innovations have been adapted for use outside the field of agriculture. These have varied from the use of amortized repayment plans introduced nationally by the Land Banks in 1917 to the relatively recent introduction of varying interest rates on loans as the cost of money fluctuates. Some of the System's innovations are discussed in Chapters 5, 6, 7, and 8.

Chapter 5

GOVERNMENT STARTING CAPITAL TO BE REPLACED BY USERS

Today the idea of the Government supplying the original equity capital for a financing organization and providing mechanisms for the users to gradually replace it by direct investment or through accumulated net worth reserves or surplus derived from their use of such organizations is almost taken for granted. It has been used by the following organizations:

	Date Organized	Date of Final Payment of Govt. Capital
Federal Home Loan Banks	1932	1951
Federal Deposit Insurance Corporation	1934	1948
Federal Savings and Loan Insurance Corporation	1934	1944
Export-Import Bank of United States	1934	1
Federal National Mortgage Association	1938	1970
National Rural Telephone Bank	1971	2

This was not always so. Congress first tried this idea in the cooperative Farm Credit System with the passage of the Federal Farm Loan Act of 1916 which established the Federal Land Banks. It has since used the same method in the other organizations making up the cooperative Farm Credit System as follows:

	Date Organized	Date Last Govt. Capital Repaid
Federal Land Banks	1916	1932, 1947
Federal Intermediate Credit Banks	1923 [3]	1968
Production Credit Associations	1933	1968
Banks for Cooperatives	1933 [4]	1968

---

[1] Has not yet paid back any of its Government capital.

[2] Has not paid back any Government capital; Government is still purchasing equities.

[3] Provision of plan to repay Government capital not adopted until 1956.

[4] Plan to repay Government capital revised in 1955 to make repayment attainable.

The Land Bank System Plan

The original plan adopted by Congress in 1916 provided that farmers who obtained Federal Land Bank loans would invest in stock amounts equal to 5 percent of their loans in the federally chartered local Federal Land Bank Associations to be organized by any 10 farmers who applied for Land Bank loans. These Associations, in turn, invested in like amounts of stock in the Land Banks. These Banks were then to use 25 percent of the capital supplied by farmers to pay off the Banks' Government-owned capital stock. This plan resulted in the complete repayment of the Government's investment by 1932.

However, by that time farmers had experienced a period of declining farm prices since 1921 that started the continuing precipitous decline of the Great Depression for the entire economy from 1929 onward. Hundreds of thousands of farmers were faced with foreclosures on their mortgages. As a desperate step to try to remedy the situation, Congress provided for the Government investment of $125 million in the capital stock of the Land Banks—compared to their original capital of $9 million.

In 1933, with the passage of the Emergency Farm Mortgage Act, Congress formally gave the Land Banks the job of refinancing the debts farmers owed to other creditors. That Act provided for the Treasury to invest in the paid-in surplus of the Banks, to enable them to grant extensions on their loans to farmers who were making every possible effort to meet the scheduled payments on their loans so they could be carried along until the prices of farm products recovered and returned to normal. These funds were also used to enable the Land Banks to defer farmers' payments of principal for 5 years in cases where they were not otherwise delinquent. Under that program the Government invested $189 million in paid-in surplus of the Land Banks in the 1933 to 1937 period.

Prices of farm products did recover and return to the 1910 to 1914 "parity"—and beyond during World War II—and with them farmers' and ranchers' income. As a result the value of the farms that the Land Banks acquired during the depression and drought years also went up. The Land Banks started repaying their Government capital. In fact, the Louisville and Houston Banks completed the job by 1940. The others soon did likewise—the last one by 1947. Thus, they met the goals of the System's founders.

The discovery of oil on many of the farms on which a few of the Land Banks retained a portion of the mineral rights when they

Federal Land Bank	Completed Repayment of Government-Invested	
	Capital Stock	Paid-in Surplus
Louisville	1940	1940
Houston	1940	1940
Springfield	1940	1945
New Orleans	1940	1945
St. Louis	1940	1945
Berkely	1940	1945
Spokane	1943	1945
Wichita	1944	1945
Omaha	1945	1945
Baltimore	1946	1946
Columbia	1946	1946
St. Paul	1947	1947

sold the surface rights following necessary forecloseures, during the Depression years, was an important factor in their financial recovery.

Repayment by FICBs Not Originally Provided

When Congress established the Federal Intermediate Credit Banks (FICBs) in 1923, it provided that these banks could discount farmers' notes financed by agricultural credit corporations, livestock loan companies and commercial banks, as well as make loans to co-operatives on warehouse receipts. Only a few of the organizations using this discount privilege were cooperatives. Thus, the Congress did not provide a plan for farmers to gradually replace the Government-owned capital.

With the passage of the Farm Credit Act of 1953, the Farm Credit Administration again became an independent agency after being part of the U.S. Department of Agriculture since 1939.[5] Congress directed that the newly created Federal Farm Credit Board propose plans to make the entire Farm Credit System completely farmer-owned.

Plan for User Ownership of FICBs Adopted

In 1956, the Board proposed and the Congress approved merging the Production Credit Corporations with the Federal Intermediate

---

[5] For a full discussion of these steps, see "Looking Ahead to Things to Come" in Chapter 28.

Credit Banks. This plan combined the supervision function of the Production Credit Corporations[6] with the money-raising functions of the Federal Intermediate Credit Banks in the merged organizations. The Farm Credit Act of 1956 also provided for the PCAs gradually providing capital to the Federal Intermediate Credit Banks and becoming their owners.[7] The Production Credit Associations' investments enabled the Banks to become completely farmer-owned by 1968.

Original BC Plan Had to Be Revised

In the case of the Banks for Cooperatives (BCs), there was a provision for supplying farmer-owned capital from their inception as provided for in the Farm Credit Act of 1933. However, there was a flaw in this provision. Although it required the borrowing cooperatives to invest in capital stock of the Banks equal to 5 percent of their loans as in the Federal Land Bank Associations and Production Credit Associations, it also stipulated that such stock should be paid off when the loans were repaid as in the case of the Federal Land Bank Associations and Federal Land Banks. Since most of the Banks for Cooperatives' loans were seasonal or for a short term of years, the Banks for Cooperatives had only been able to accumulate about $21 million in stock held by cooperatives in the 22 years of their operation up to 1955, which was supplemented by $88 million of net worth reserves in the form of accumulated surplus.

The Farm Credit Act of 1955 provided a program for the cooperatives borrowing from the Banks for Cooperatives to actually become their complete owners.[8] When this plan was in its nebulous stages in the late 1940s, an astute, long time FCA division director scornfully predicted it would take the borrowing cooperatives from 30 to 50 years to reach the goal of becoming complete owners of these Banks under any plan that could be devised. Time proved him wrong. The goal was reached in only 13 years—1968. One thing he overlooked was the coming increase in the dollar volume of loans. Another factor he did not anticipate was the determination of the System and its users to become completely farmer-owned. That same prophet

---

[6] These Government-owned organizations were established by the Farm Credit Act of 1933 to capitalize and supervise the local PCAs.

[7] For details of the plan, see "FICBs and PCCs Merged" in Chapter 14.

[8] For details of the plan, see "Drive for Farm Ownership Spurs Action" in Chapter 14.

doubted the Production Credit Associations would even start on a program to become the owners of the Intermediate Credit Banks, not to mention their ever completing the job.

PCA Pay-offs Varied from 11 to 35 Years

The Farm Credit Act of 1933 also provided for the Government to furnish the starting capital for the local Production Credit Associations (PCAs). However, it also provided that farmers would gradually replace this Government-owned stock by investing in Class B voting stock equal to 5 percent of their loans.

Accomplishment of the objective of complete farmer ownership of PCAs did not come easily or quickly in many areas of the country. The 5 percent stock investments in themselves were not large enough to do the job because, as volume grew, the PCAs needed more capital to support their loans. Thus, they had to build up net worth reserves from accumulated savings (earnings) and sell additional Class A—nonvoting—stock to their members.

In areas where loans were small in size or number, the first goal was to have them operate within their loan income rather than depend on their interest income from their capital stock that was invested in government bonds. Most PCAs reached this position in the early 1940s. Production Credit Commissioner C. R. Arnold of the Farm Credit Administration provided constant leadership in this endeavor and the drive toward complete farmer-member ownership. However, operating within their loan income required leadership and determined efforts on the part of the district Production Credit Corporation and—after merger—by Intermediate Credit Bank officials and within the local PCAs themselves. To accomplish such objectives took efficient operation, attracting more sound, larger-sized loans and keeping down losses.

To build up sufficient capital also required programs to convince farmers that it was important enough for them to completely own their PCAs so they would be willing to buy and hold more capital stock than the law required.

The first Association to reach the goal of complete farmer ownership was the Kewanee (Illinois) PCA in 1944. By 1947, 12 PCAs were completely farmer-owned and 112 others had reduced their Government-owned stock to $50,000 or less. One of the factors that had to be considered by many PCAs in paying off the last of their Government-owned stock was that this placed them in the position of having to pay income taxes and thus reduced their capacity to generate additional capital needed to support expanding loan volumes. The last three PCAs became completely farmer-owned in 1968.

Incentives for System Becoming Completely Member-Owned

A constant incentive to the cooperative Farm Credit System to complete the job of becoming entirely member-owned as quickly as possible was the desire to be freed from various governmental regulations and the always-lurking-in-the-wings threats of additional regulations or constraints.[9]

Congress Tried to Strike Fine Balances

Congress, in agreeing to set up this policy-making Board for the Farm Credit Administration as the System's supervisory agency, endeavored to strike fine balances. Farm leaders and Congress wanted to have this policy-making Board for the System's supervisory agency responsive to, and knowledgeable regarding, the credit needs of farmers in all parts of the country. Thus, it provided for appointment on a district basis. At the same time, it was striving to make sure that the Board made its decisions in line with the broad, best long-time interests of all farmers and ranchers and their cooperatives. Congress, in limiting Federal Board members to single 6-year terms, was encouraging them to take the broadest possible view in contrast to the particular interests or biases of leaders in their home districts. However, in the opinion of observers, some Federal Board members, being human, have at times tended to succumb to the temptation to remain popular at home, even though they are not eligible for reappointment.

Another fine balance that farm leaders and Congress apparently were trying to strike was between providing adequate or sufficient supervision to keep the System on the track it chartered for the System, and at the same time urging the Federal and district Farm Credit Boards to work toward the maximum feasible delegation of authority and responsibility to district and, in turn, to local boards of directors.

Act of 1971 Reflected Confidence of Congress

An indication that Congress was well satisfied with the balance

---

[9] For a further discussion of this subject, see "Act of 1953 Gave Further Impetus" and "Farm Credit System Unique in Supervision" in Chapter 13.

the various boards were achieving was that in passing the Farm Credit Act of 1971 it agreed to remove many long-standing restrictions, increased the System's flexibility, and considerably expanded the System's authority to broaden its services. In the process, Congress gave the Federal Board authority to make needed adjustments that it previously reserved to itself. It also gave more authority and responsibilities to district and local association boards of directors that had previously been reserved for Congress, or the Federal or district boards. In addition, it encouraged the Federal and district boards to further delegate their authorities—within appropriate guidelines they might establish—to the level as close to the borrower as possible commensurate with demonstrated ability. Congress greatly increased the System's flexibility and its ability to meet the rapidly changing needs of farmers, ranchers, and their cooperatives.

Other Incentives for Farmer-Ownership

However, there were real regulation threats that could be avoided by paying off all the Government capital in the Farm Credit System, such as those promulgated under the Government Corporation Control Act, by the Budget Bureau (now the Office of Management and Budget), the General Accounting Office, and the Treasury Department. The significance of these are discussed in more detail in "Relationships with Treasury Department," and "Relations with Budget Bureau," Chapter 21.

Another factor in the successful drive for complete farmer ownership of the cooperative Farm Credit System was that farmers, boards of directors, and employed officials of the System took more and more pride in their organization as the push to achieve complete farmer ownership brought it closer and closer to that ultimate objective. The System was also encouraged by the growing esteem and encouragement the System received from Congress and financial circles, at least partially as a result of progress toward that goal.

As the year 1968 drew to a close and the long-term goal of complete farmer ownership of the System approached, there was a determined team effort to grasp the opportunity at the earliest possible moment. The whole cooperative Farm Credit System became completely farmer-owned. The last Government capital in the Banks for Cooperatives, Federal Intermediate Credit Banks, and Production Credit Associations was repaid. When the goal was reached, there were appropriate celebrations as there had been over the years as individual banks and associations had reached their individual goals of retiring the last of their Government capital.

One of the benefits of this achievement became almost immediately apparent when, in February of 1969, the Federal Farm Credit Board Chairman, Loren Bice of Florida, merely informed incoming President Richard M. Nixon that the Board had chosen E. A. Jaenke as Governor of the Farm Credit Administration to replace retiring 15-year Governor Robert B. Tootell. The White House reportedly was surprised to learn that because the Farm Credit System was now completely farmer-owned, the Federal Board's appointment of the Governor no longer required Presidential approval.

Chapter 6

ESTABLISHING THE "AGENCY MARKET"
FOR SECURITIES

The Farm Credit System pioneered the development of the "agency market" for securities. The agency market consists of buyers of securities sponsored or owned wholly or partially by the Federal Government. This market was created, nurtured, and built by the Federal Land Banks and, starting in 1923, by the Federal Intermediate Credit Banks. The Banks for Cooperatives did not start selling securities until 1950.

Other financial organizations using the agency market now include the Federally chartered, user-owned Federal Home Loan Banks and the Federal National Mortgage Association. The latter is known as "Fannie Mae." The agency market proved to be such a good place to raise funds that Congress also authorized its use by so many wholly Government-owned organizations that at the Treasury Department's urgent request, Congress established the Federal Financing Bank in 1974 to coordinate the borrowing of such agencies.

Buyers of such securities include commercial banks, savings banks, insurance companies, pension and trust funds, individuals, state governments, large corporations with temporarily surplus funds, and even foreign buyers.

By the mid-1970s the cooperative Farm Credit System's annual sales of bonds in the agency market were over $22 billion.

The Congressional hearings that preceded the enactment of the Farm Loan Act establishing the Federal Land Banks in 1916 vividly and forcefully brought out that one of the most serious problems faced by farmers was the lack of adequate supplies of lending funds in most rural areas. Farmers were usually dependent on loans from local commercial banks, merchants, dealers, family members, or retired farmers.

Commercial banks in rural areas were dependent on depositors for loan funds. Since their depositors were largely farmers or people doing business with farmers, the demand for loans from farmers often were greatest just when farmers, their suppliers, and the marketers of their products were drawing down their bank accounts. Thus, local banks' lending funds were reduced just at the times when they were most needed. And few banks had sufficient funds to make real estate mortgage loans for periods even as short as 3 to 5 years. Farm incomes rarely were large enough to pay off mortgages in such a short time. Therefore, even when farmers were able to obtain mortgage loans, they had the uncertainty of not knowing whether their loans would be renewed or whether other loans would be available when their mortgage loans came due. Frequently, this put farmers at the mercy of unscrupulous lenders. Even honest and friendly lenders sometimes needed their money and had to call their loans. Disproportionately high interest rates, costly renewal fees, and at least threats of foreclosure were common occurrences.[1]

Increasing the Money Supply in Rural Areas

Farm leaders convinced farmers that much of the solution to these problems was to provide a mechanism for channeling part of the investment funds that accumulated in the Nation's financial markets to rural areas. Thus, Congress authorized the Federal Land Banks to pool farmers' mortgages for collateralizing long-term bonds they would sell to investors.

This concept, which later proved perfectly sound, had to be developed. Up until 1923, Land Bank bond sales were handled by the office of one of the members of the Federal Farm Loan Board—the supervisory agency for the Land Banks and their local Associations—plus the FICBs until the Farm Credit Administration was established in 1933. Each Land Bank issued its own bonds, but each was jointly liable for them. With Land Bank bond sales totaling about a quarter of a billion dollars in 1922, and being faced with the need also to sell the newly authorized Federal Intermediate Credit Bank debentures, the Banks named Judge Charles E. Lobdell to the dual post of fiscal agent and general counsel. Judge Lobdell, an original member of the Federal Farm Loan Board, had succeeded George W. Norris of

---

[1] W. N. Stokes, Jr., comments, "I believe you could eliminate 'threats.' Foreclosures were common. I knew one man in West Texas who left his son more than 50 good farms, all of which he acquired by financing some poor guy at 10% and on a one-year maturity basis—the foreclosure following at his first misstep. This was fairly common practice."

Philadelphia as the Land Bank Commissioner member of the board. Judge Lobdell maintained his office in Washington until he resigned in 1929. Then the Fiscal Agent's office was moved to New York City.

Challenges to Access to Investors

With the entire concept of the Farm Credit System built on having a ready access to the money markets of the Nation and channeling it to farmers in accordance with their needs, the System gradually has organized a dependable method of making this a reality. It has worked well. However, it has been tested and challenged on various occasions. The idea had to be abandoned temporarily four times in the first 20 years.

Treasury and Federal Reserve Bought Bonds in Early Emergencies

The first challenge came at the very beginning. With the Nation involved in World War I, the new Land Bank bonds came into competition with patriotic drives to sell the Treasury's Liberty Bonds. Congress authorized the Secretary of the Treasury to buy $100 million a year of Land Bank bonds for the fiscal years ending June 30, 1918, and 1919. These bonds were subject to repurchase by the Land Banks one year after the end of the war. The Land Banks repurchased their bonds on schedule.

The second challenge came in 1920, when the constitutionality of the Federal Farm Loan Act establishing the Land Banks was being tested in the courts.[2] Again the U.S. Treasury was authorized to come to the rescue by buying Land Bank bonds at the rate of $100 million a year in 1920 and 1921. The Land Banks used only $45 million of such funds.

At the peak of the stock market rise in 1929, when there was no market for bonds, the Federal Reserve Banks bought $9.5 million of Land Bank bonds at 5 percent. These were retired or refunded at 4.5 percent by the end of the year.

FFMC Helped in Depression

In the years of the Great Depression—1933 to 1935—investors, having learned from bitter experience, were generally leery of all

---

[2] For explanation of the case, see footnote 4, Chapter 9.

securities except those that were issued by the U.S. Government. In addition, the Land Banks were having trouble with their loan collections. Thus, the supply of investment funds generally was at a low point just at the time when the Government was calling on the Land Banks to help stem the tidal wave of farm foreclosures that were engulfing the country. At this point—1933—W. I. Myers, second Governor of the Farm Credit Administration, told the author in an interview that consideration was given to having the Intermediate Credit Banks raise loan funds for the Land Banks because their short-term debentures had attained such a good reputation among investors. Instead, this crisis was met by the Land Banks exchanging their consolidated bonds for those of the Federal Farm Mortgage Corporation (FFMC). The FFMC bonds were fully guaranteed by the Government. During this period the Reconstruction Finance Corporation (RFC) bought some Land Bank bonds and FICB debentures.

For a time—starting in late March 1934—the Land Banks were lending at such an increased rate that they required their new borrowers and their borrowers' previous creditors to agree to accept FFMC bonds instead of cash. This was done to avoid the necessity of selling such a large volume of bonds on Wall Street and in other financial markets. It was hoped that at least a portion of these bonds would be retained by farmers' creditors and thus be dispersed around the country rather than become a burden to the central investment markets.

Farm Credit Securities Stand on Own
Since Depression

This practice ended as soon as the rush of emergency refinancing for farmers who were threatened with foreclosure subsided. Prices of farm products were going up from their Depression lows. Investors lost some of their fear of the future of the general economy as well as of farmers' ability to repay their loans. Ever since, the Federal Land Banks have raised the bulk of their financing by selling their own bonds to investors.

Much more recent challenges to the concept of the System's free access to the money market included the Treasury's pushing the System into adopting guidelines for taking extra care to avoid speculative financing and urging farmers during the credit crunch of 1966 not to borrow at the then current high rates for purchases that could be deferred. The alternative was facing the possibility of allocation of funds. During that period, one Bank for Cooperatives' debenture issue was actually cut by a few million dollars by President Johnson—from $78 million to $75 million. But that emergency, too, passed. Fortunately, the combination of generous original estimates of needs for loan funds by some Banks for Cooperatives and the decline in demand for loans from the Banks for Cooperatives prevented this from becoming a serious problem.

Exempted from Federal Financing Bank

Another challenge was avoided when Congress agreed to exempt the Farm Credit System and the Federal Home Loan Banks—whose securities also carry no Government guarantee—from the use and controls of the Federal Financing Bank that was organized. The long-time favorable record of the Farm Credit System in the agency market and the System's record of voluntary consultation with the Treasury, through the Governor of the Farm Credit Administration, undoubtedly were important factors in the Treasury's willingness to make that exemption decision. Another important factor was the long-time efforts of the System and the Farm Credit Administration to get the Treasury to realize that it was essential to the Nation's economy for the System to have ready access to the money markets in order to keep a continuous, uninterrupted flow of adequate financing going out to farmers. To do otherwise would endanger the Nation's food supply and could well increase inflationary pressures by driving up food prices. Actually, most of the credit extended to agriculture, if speculative financing is eliminated, is counterinflationary.

Joint Liability Tested Early

Each of the three groups of banks in the Farm Credit System issue consolidated bonds and each Bank is jointly liable for bonds issued on behalf of the other Banks in the group. The joint liability feature has had to be used only once. In 1925, the Federal Land Bank of Spokane had to foreclose on so many farms that the Bank found it impossible to sell them fast enough to enable it to meet its scheduled bond interest payments. The other 11 Land Banks bought the Spokane Bank's real estate inventory and wrote it down on their books to a value of $1.00. They also appointed a commission to supervise the sale of the farms acquired by the Spokane Land Bank. By

1932 Spokane had repaid the other 11 Banks with interest and the commission was dissolved.[3]

Central Bank for Cooperatives
Floats First Issue

Until 1950 the Banks for Cooperatives had sufficient Government capital and earned net worth to handle all their financing without issuing securities, even though the Central Bank for Cooperatives had the authority to issue debentures from the time of its organization in 1933. When the Central Bank for Cooperatives was planning to enter the agency market, there was some fear that the combination of floating a new security and the widespread lack of understanding about the nature of cooperatives might hurt the sale of the Banks for Cooperatives' debentures. When the Banks' first issue was oversubscribed by 13 times the amount offered, there were many sighs of relief throughout the System.

The fine reception of these new securities was a tribute to the excellent reputations among investors that had been built by the Banks for Cooperatives' sister organizations—the Federal Land Banks and Federal Intermediate Credit Banks—and their Fiscal Agent. It was also a tribute to the educational campaign the Fiscal Agent had carried out in advance of the first issue. In 1955, with a change in the law, the 13 Banks for Cooperatives began issuing consolidated debentures.

The Banks for Cooperatives quickly moved to a position where they could obtain loan funds at rates comparable to those paid by the other parts of the Farm Credit System. And except in periods of extremely tight money, the System has only had to pay a small fraction of 1 percent higher interest rate than the Federal Government.

It is fair to recognize that the small margin of cost over U.S. Government securities may be partly because of the belief of some investors that the U.S. Government would not allow the Banks to fail despite the fact that none of the Banks' loans is insured by the Government nor are any of the bonds guaranteed. Whatever might occur in a period of financial catastrophe is not known, but in any event, it is the policy of the owners of the System to manage and capitalize

---

[3]"The Federal Land Bank System, 1917–1967, a Half Century of Service to Agriculture," Circular E-43, Farm Credit Administration, Government Printing Office, 1967, p. 13.

it conservatively so that the need for Direct Government assistance would not arise. In addition to the financial strength the System has built into its structure, it continues to monitor its lending practices to make sure its loans are sound.

Handling Actual Sales of Securities

The presidents of each of the three individual banking groups in the Farm Credit System meet as bond committees to determine—annually or semiannually—overall plans for financing their separate group's financing for the months ahead. They consider the probable needs of their group and decide on general guidelines for maturity patterns. Before each sale a subcommittee of three presidents for each group meets either in person or in a telephone conference with the Fiscal Agent, who has tested the market by discussions with a representative sample of dealers, to decide the actual maturity and pricing (interest rate to be paid). Such decisions are subject to approval of the Governor of the Farm Credit Administration, who consults with the Treasury to make sure the Government's plans for financing and those plans of other institutions using the agency market are given due consideration. While there was still Government capital investment in any of the Banks, the Treasury also had to approve each issue of the Federal Intermediate Credit Banks' and Banks for Cooperatives' securities.

Each year the Fiscal Agent provides a schedule of bond sales to a group of 190 security dealers. All these dealers have a previously approved top amount of bonds which could be allocated for any bond sale. The Fiscal Agent has the responsibility for allocations based on the performance record of the dealer.

Although the methods of handling sales have changed over the years, the basic idea of using a group of security dealers to handle bond sales goes back to 1917 when a syndicate of 93 dealers was organized and managed by a few large dealers headed by Alexander Brown and Sons of Baltimore. The first sale of Federal Land Bank bonds—for many years called Federal Farm Loan Bonds—of $24 million took six months to sell.[4] As the bonds became more popular in the market, as many as 800 bond houses participated in some sales in the 1920s.

---

[4] "Brief History of Financing of the Farm Credit Banks," Finance Division, FCA memorandum, March 1960.

Supplementary Financing

No matter how carefully the various Farm Credit Banks estimate their future needs for lending funds, they frequently find themselves either with surplus funds for temporary periods of a few days or more, or short of funds to meet the daily demands for loans. In order to make the most efficient use of funds within the entire Farm Credit System, the various Banks keep in daily contact with the money desk at the Central Bank for Cooperatives which arranges transfer of surplus funds from the individual Banks to those in need for additional funds. Originally, such activities were carried on through collaboration between the Farm Credit Administration and the Fiscal Agent. However, in recent years the large increase in such transactions has made it more appropriate to handle this function through the Central Bank for Cooperatives since it was already supplying the district Banks for Cooperatives with needed interim financing.

Credit Lines at Commercial Banks

Gradually over the years, the Farm Credit Banks have also built up sizable lines of credit with various larger commercial banks so that they can call upon those banks for temporary lending funds on a day-to-day basis when unanticipated needs arise. These arrangements usually include lines of credit with some of the largest banks in their respective districts, as well as large banks in the Nation's financial centers like New York City and Chicago.

The combination of intersystem lending of temporary surplus funds through the Central Bank for Cooperatives and the maintenance of adequate lines of credit at large commercial banks gives all parts of the Farm Credit System the ability to meet the needs of farmers, ranchers, and their cooperatives on practically a day-to-day basis without maintaining large and costly reserve supplies of cash. These arrangements enable the System to keep the number of idle dollars to a minimum and at the same time have money available as needs arise.

This sounds like a relatively simple process, but it takes much understanding, cooperation, and specialized "know-how," which at times are tested to the limit. For example, in the winter of 1973 the volume of loans of several of the Banks for Cooperatives unexpectedly increased about 50 percent in a few weeks, at a time when the rest of the System's loan volume was increasing rapidly. These Banks for Cooperatives, along with other heavy demands for credit, found their member cooperatives greatly affected by the huge Russian grain deal. With payment for sales of large quantities of grain to exporters delayed by the long backup of railroad cars streaming to port cities and waiting to be unloaded when they arrived, most of the local and regional grain cooperatives throughout the Midwest needed unheard-of amounts of credit.

To meet this large upsurge in demand, the Banks through the Fiscal Agent reopened some outstanding issues. In addition, the Central Bank for Cooperatives did an excellent job of finding temporarily idle funds in new and unexpected places to finance lending operations until the next bond sale. Just to make it more difficult, this operation came at a period of "tight money."

Farm Credit Investment Bonds for Members

Over a period of years, various people raised the question of how arrangements could be made for farmer-members of the Farm Credit System organizations to use their surplus funds to invest in the System. To them it seemed only logical that farmers and their cooperatives should have the opportunity, as members of this farmer-owned lending system, of paying interest to themselves when some of them had surplus funds to lend. The simplest and best way to make such arrangements—both from the farmer's and lender's standpoint—would be to allow farmer and co-op members of the System to establish savings accounts with their respective parts of the System. However, commercial banks and savings institutions jealously guard their established prerogatives. They strongly resist letting any other organizations have anything that resembles their low-cost lending funds in the form of deposit accounts.

After considerable discussion and planning, in 1971 the Federal Land Banks and the Federal Intermediate Credit Banks, in cooperation with the Farm Credit Administration, devised a Farm Credit Investment Bond that could be purchased by members of Production Credit Associations and Federal Land Bank Associations. This experimental program was barely underway—with moderate success appearing in the offing—when the sale of these Farm Credit Investment Bonds was greatly hampered by a limitation commercial banks and savings institutions succeeded in getting inserted in the Farm Credit Act of 1971. This provision made such bonds subject to the Federal Reserve System Regulation Q which, along with other restrictions, limits the interest rates payable on savings. It came right at a time when the general level of interest rates was approaching an all-time high. Thus, farmers had opportunities to invest their temporarily idle funds at much higher rates than their own Farm Credit System was allowed to pay, even though the System had to pay much higher rates on its newly issued securities. However, the Farm Credit Investment Bonds continued to be available to members and employees.

Making Regular Bonds Available to Members

Another method of enabling farmers to invest in securities of the System and thus help finance it was the development in 1969 of a program by various Intermediate Credit Banks and in 1970 by some Land Banks to make their regular bonds directly available to members of Production Credit Associations and Land Bank Associations. In 1974 the Banks for Cooperatives also made their securities available to members.

At various times of the year and under certain interest rate conditions, farmers have made use of this method of investing temporary surplus funds. There has been little interest among farmers in placing their funds in longer term obligations, probably because they usually anticipate a need for using them in their farm operations after a relatively short period.

Seeking Discount Notes to Add Flexibility

One of the major goals of the cooperative Farm Credit System is to provide credit to its users at the lowest possible cost. That, of course, requires obtaining the money that it loans at the lowest possible cost. In fact, the cost of borrowed money is by far the largest single cost of the System. With the System having about $25 billion outstanding in securities, the saving of $\frac{1}{10}$ of 1 percent on its interest bill would amount to $25 million a year in savings for farmers.

It is small wonder that as the loan volume has risen and the amount of borrowed money necessary to finance that loan volume has also increased, the effort and study of various groups within the System to find ways of saving farmers several million dollars a year has intensified. Several funding methods have been explored by various committees of the cooperative Farm Credit System.

In 1970 the report of the Commission on Agricultural Credit[5] included a recommendation that investigations be made of possible

---

[5] "The Farm Credit System in the '70s' The Report of the Commission on Agricultural Credit," Farm Credit Administration, Washington, D.C., 1970.

ways to supplement the System's financing and the feasibility of a single Farm Credit security to replace those of the three groups of banks. With the concurrence of the Federal Farm Credit Board, Governor E. A. Jaenke in 1970 enlisted a committee of financial specialists from outside the System to study the System's funding needs and to make recommendations thereon.[6] Among this committee's recommendations were those for issuing discount notes to obtain short-term funds and the adoption of a unified funding operation for the System by issuing "a single market instrument covering a range of maturities" in order to have fewer but stronger market entries by the System into a crowded capital market.[7]

These recommendations by the commission and the advisory committee gave further impetus to the work of committees within the System that were studying the System's funding operations.

Issuance of Discount Notes

Early in 1975, the banks decided as a result of these studies to start issuing discount notes on behalf of all 37 banks. Such notes can be sold for periods of 5 to 150 days to organizations that have temporary excess funds. By the end of the first year of this program, the System raised a total of $3.7 billion by selling these discount notes and had $406 million outstanding at the end of the year at an average annual rate of 5.48 percent.[8]

Prospects for Long-Term Farm Credit Bonds

Also flowing out of these intensive studies have come in-depth discussions, searching for answers to the technical problems involved in issuing Farm Credit Bonds on behalf of all 37 Farm Credit Banks. It has been recognized that if such a program is to be embarked upon,

---

[6] Members of the Committee were Darryl R. Francis, President, Federal Reserve Bank of St. Louis (former manager, Production Credit Associations at St. Joseph and Springfield, Mo.), chairman; Daniel H. Brill, Senior Vice President, Commercial Credit Company; Samuel Chase, Professor of Economics, University of Montana; Walter W. Cragie, Sr., President, Craigie Incorporated; Lester H. Empey, Senior Vice President, Wells Fargo Bank; Maurice A. Gilmartin, Jr., Partner, Chas. E. Quincey & Co.; John J. Larkin, Senior Vice President, First National City Bank; William E. Simon, Partner, Salomon Bros. (current Secretary of the Treasury); and Robert Stewart, President, Bank of the Southwest.

[7] "Financing the Farm Credit System," Report of the Advisory Committee on Finance, Farm Credit Administration, Washington, D.C., 1970.

[8] For comparative costs of bonds sold, see "Getting More Money at Lowest Possible Cost" in Chapter 30.

each group of Banks would assume the first liability before the other two groups would be called on for assistance in case an individual Bank was unable to meet its commitments to investors in such securities.[9] Also recognized is the desirability of each group of Banks adopting loss sharing plans and agreed upon financial ratios to trigger corrective action. As this is written, the System is seriously considering the joint issuance of Farm Credit Bonds in the 10- to 20-year maturity range on the recommendation of a nationally known consulting firm.[10] The firm pointed out that while each of the three groups of Banks has some need to sell bonds in this maturity range, their individual needs are too small to warrant the marketing of separate issues.

---

[9] No Bank has been in such a position since 1925 when the other Federal Land Banks assisted the Spokane Bank.

[10] McKinsey and Company.

Chapter 7

INNOVATIONS IN EXTENDING CREDIT

Throughout its history the cooperative Farm Credit System has continuously tried to find and adopt better ways of meeting farmers' ever-changing, specialized needs for credit. In the process it has discovered, devised, and introduced new methods, procedures, and loan terms that, when proven out, have been copied by others making loans to farmers.

No part of the System has had a monopoly on conceiving new ideas and methods. However, many if not most of the new ways of doing things have very naturally been proposed, devised, or at least pointed out, by the local Land Bank and Production Credit Association managers or boards of directors. They are the people who are closest to the borrowing farmers and thus have been acutely aware of the things that are needed or that would make for smoother operations.

Some observers of the System have pointed out that many of the improvements have come at the insistence of a local association which finally got the supervising district Bank—sometimes reluctantly—to allow it to try a new idea. If it worked, the Bank then spread the idea, even though the Farm Credit Administration, in its national supervisory position, might still look on with skepticism. When the idea proved successful on a district-wide basis, the Farm Credit Administration frequently picked it up and supported the originating Bank in spreading the idea at national conferences of Bank officials and in other ways.

In other cases, one or more district Banks have come up with solutions in response to the problems or needs expressed by the local Associations. In the case of the Banks for Cooperatives, the ideas for changes have come from either the borrowing cooperatives, an individual Bank, or a group of Banks in their national conferences. The Farm Credit Administration and the Federal Farm Credit Board, on occasion, have also played a part in finding answers to widely expressed System-wide needs for changes. Usually these have come in consultation with district Bank officers or district Farm Credit Boards.

Some of the more important innovations are mentioned in the following discussion.

Amortized Loans Introduced

Today, an amortized loan is an everyday phrase in the vocabulary of most mortgage lenders and borrowers. However, it has not always been so. Congress, at the insistence of farm leaders, specified in the original Federal Farm Loan Act that farm mortgage loans provided by the Federal Land Banks would be made on an amortized basis. The idea—imported from European credit systems—was practically unknown in most parts of the country. Up until that time—1916— farmers could only borrow on their mortgages for 3 to 5 years at best. Then the loans came due. All the principal was payable at one time. There was no provision for making installment payments on the principal amount of the loan. There was little chance that a farmer could accumulate enough money in 3 to 5 years to repay all the principal on his loan. As a result, farmers were faced with a continual need to refinance their mortgages. When a farmer mortgaged his farm, he hoped he could get the loan renewed or refinanced when it came due. But, he could never be sure. Thus, if he fell into the hands of an unscrupulous lender who wanted to take over his farm, and there were many of them, he might lose his farm if he could not find someone else to lend him the money. At best, even if he continued with the same lender for another 3 to 5 years, he had to pay a healthy renewal fee.

In contrast, the Federal Land Banks, through the locally organized Federal Land Bank Associations, began making loans for periods up to 40 years. Most of them ran between 20 and 35 years. These loans provided for annual or semiannual payments on the principal along with the interest. Thus, farmers who obtained such loans were gradually reducing their mortgage debts.

Amortized loans were soon provided on two bases. One is known in the System as the standard plan. It provides for total installment payments to be the same amount each time, with the principal portion of the payment increasing from year to year as the interest grows less. The Springfield Bank has provided a plan in which the principal portion of the payment remained the same. The total payment declined as the interest cost was going down because of the smaller amount of the principal that was still outstanding.

The Springfield plan has some advantages over the standard plan because it reduces the principal amount outstanding more rapidly and thus quickly makes the loan a sounder one from the standpoint of the lender and a safer one from the standpoint of the farmer. Another advantage is the fact that the borrower can see the results of his payments on his loan because each one grows smaller. On the other hand, the plan has some disadvantages in that the largest payments on the loan come in the early years when many farmers are just getting started and find it the most difficult to meet their mortgage payments. At first, the individual banks tended to use one plan or the other. However, over the years there has been a tendency for the various banks to use both plans, depending somewhat on the individual situation of the borrower.

In the early years, the Land Banks encouraged farmers to get out of debt. This was the natural instinct of farmers themselves. The bitter experiences of the Great Depression of the 1930s, on top of the farm depression of the 1920s, brought that objective into sharp focus for farmer-borrowers and the Farm Credit System alike. As an example of the prevailing winds of that era, this author wrote a Farm Credit Administration circular in 1935 entitled, "Helping Farmers Get Out of Debt." The human miseries and horrors of mass farm foreclosures, and hundreds of thousands of close misses, were memories and lessons long remembered by those who lived through that period. Trying to feed and clothe a family, not to mention pay debts, from 1-cent-a-quart milk checks, 40-cents-a-bushel wheat, 30-cents-a-bushel corn, 5-cents-a-pound cattle, 3-cents-a-pound hogs, or 5 or 6-cents-a-pound cotton made a generation of farmers at least gun-shy of future debt. The drive to get out of debt and to stay that way, if at all possible, took the higher farm price levels of the World War II and post war years of the 1940s and 1950s to slow down.

As time passed, farmers, the Land Banks, the rest of the Farm Credit System, and the Farm Credit Administration realized that in many cases it was not practical for the farmer to plan to get out of debt. He may well find that by reducing his mortgage he is only increasing the amount of short-term credit he has to use, which may at times be more expensive credit than that he can obtain on a mortgage loan.

In later years Congress has authorized variations of the amortized loan. In some cases, the Land Banks may agree to defer principal payments for the first few years while the farmer is getting established. The loan agreement may also include other provisions which modify the amortized loan idea.

Probably the ideal balance of credit between long-term and short-term, from the standpoint of the farmer, is to have the minimum amount of credit that he needs in any one year included in the mortgage loan, with the balance of the credit he needs provided by a production or seasonal loan, such as those loans provided by the Production Credit Associations. However, this balance is usually only approached in putting together loan packages.

In recent years some of the Land Banks have made arrangements to allow farmer-members to vary their loans upward through open-end mortgages and to let them reduce the size of their loans ahead of schedule. In such cases, the mortgage loan becomes somewhat similar to a line of credit on a production or seasonal loan from a Production Credit Association or a Bank for Cooperatives.

Pioneered in Spirit of Truth-in-Lending

The cooperative Farm Credit System had the truth-in-lending idea generations before the public outcry against lenders made it necessary for Congress to pass the Truth-in-Lending laws. The cooperative Farm Credit System found it only natural to be truthful in quoting costs of credit to its members. It is a principle that is closely tied to the idea of operating at cost and treating farmer-members equitably. When the Federal Land Banks were instituted, it was common practice for lenders to charge excessive fees merely for the privilege of obtaining a mortgage loan. And since mortgages were for only 3 to 5 years, these lending fees raised the real interest rate to much higher than was actually quoted by lenders and thus created considerable cost and expense for farmers.

Loan Fees Geared to Costs Involved

When the Federal Land Banks began operating during World War I, they eliminated the need for high-cost renewal fees by making amortized loans, whose principal payments were spread out over a period of 20 to 35 years. While the Land Banks do charge some other fees, they endeavor to relate them to the actual costs involved.

Over the years, these Banks have varied their practices in regard to charging lending fees. Of course, it is only equitable to its farmer-borrower-owners to charge fees for such direct costs as those for title examination, recording of mortgages, and appraisal of the security offered.

On the question of charging fees for costs that are more difficult to measure, the individual Land Banks have experimented rather widely. Loan application fees have generally been charged in proportion to the size or complexity of the loan. Sometimes these fees have been refunded or applied to the applicant's account if the loan is actually made. But in any case, the Land Banks have a good record of trying to allocate actual costs on an equitable basis.

Costs Reduced to Help Member-Borrowers

While not directly associated with the modern concepts of Truth-in-Lending, two other practices initiated by the Land Banks to help member-borrowers reduce their debts as rapidly as possible have helped reduce borrowers' total costs even though they reduce the lenders' income.

Because it costs money to put a new mortgage loan on their books, many lenders have long discouraged repayment of loans ahead of schedule. In a few cases, lenders did not permit any advance payments. In other cases they have and are still charging penalty fees for allowing advance payments. Not so the Land Banks. They have usually allowed member-borrowers to make advance payments on their loans at any time or even pay off loans entirely far ahead of schedule, without charging any penalty fees.

Future Payment Fund Started

Payments of installments ahead of schedule, while reducing interest charges, technically leave the farmer under the same danger of being in default if he has a bad year and cannot meet his next scheduled repayment. In the Depression years the Land Banks realized that in order to give farmers the maximum encouragement to set aside funds for use in bad crop or poor price years, farmers needed a plan that particularly suited their needs.

The Land Banks therefore devised a Future Payment Plan. Under this plan, a farmer can set aside any additional income he may have by putting such funds in a Future Payment Plan account with the Land Bank, with the understanding that such moneys will be available to meet future scheduled payment in any year when his income is curtailed. Transfers from his Future Payment Fund account to pay scheduled repayments will thus keep his loan in good standing. In order to encourage the farmer-member to set aside money for making future installment payments, the Land Banks agreed to credit the farmer's Future Payment Fund account with interest at the same rate he was paying on his loan, even though the Land Banks could borrow money at lower rates. In recent years, some of the Banks have credited interest to these accounts at rates less than those being charged on the loans.

The Production Credit Associations and the Banks for Cooperatives always have charged interest for the actual time each dollar was outstanding. This practice, combined with the idea of advancing loans only as actually needed and scheduling repayments to coincide with the availability of income, has been an important means of reducing interest costs.

It is ironic that the technicalities of complying with the generally much-needed latter-day Truth-in-Lending Act caused *added* costs and difficulties in applying them to the cost-cutting lending practices of Production Credit Associations and Federal Land Banks. Such added costs eventually have to be paid by the member-borrowers. Now, some of these costs have been reduced by amendments to the Act which exempt larger agricultural loans from the disclosure requirements of the Truth-in-Lending Act.

PCAs Introduced Line of Credit Idea

Before the advent of the Production Credit Associations, the institutionalized operating credit that was available to farmers was usually for only 30-, 60-, or 90-day terms that banks traditionally used in making short-term loans to other businesses. Such terms were not suited to the 3- to 6-month crop production and marketing seasons of farmers, controlled as they are by the biological processes. Such loan terms were even less suited to financing livestock enterprises which have even longer production cycles.

Theoretically, bankers would renew farmers' loans for additional 30- to 90-day periods when they came due. However, many farmers learned by bitter experience they could not always be sure of such renewals. If the local supply of a banker's lending funds was short, or the banker was nervous about declining prices of farm products, he had the privilege of not renewing the loan. Then the farmer had to find another lender, or be forced to liquidate some of his assets to repay his loan. In addition, farmers often had to obtain additional loans to harvest or market their crops.

Some PCAs Loaned on Budgeted Basis

Production Credit Associations, oriented as they were to adapting loan terms to the needs of their farmer-owner-borrowers, from their beginning tried to tailor the maturity of their loans to the time farmers would normally be marketing their products. This soon led to many Production Credit Associations setting up their loans on a budgeted basis. They worked with farmer-members to develop plans for complete seasonal production financing packages. Farmers were asked to estimate when they would need the money and when they would have the money to repay their loans.

With this information, the Production Credit Association could set up a budget that would schedule advances as each farmer needed them and schedule repayments at dates when he expected to have the money available for repayments from the sale of his products. These budgeted loans assured the farmer-borrowers a complete year's financing and reduced interest charges at the same time. Since they had to pay interest on each dollar only for the number of days it was outstanding, farmers found they did not have to pay interest on idle dollars. So credit costs went down.

Gradually, other more progressive private lenders began to see the benefits of such financing plans and set up similar arrangements for their farmer clients, either for the lenders' convenience, or for that of their borrowers. Some bankers may have made the change because they found such loans were easier to collect. Others may have changed to make sure they did not lose customers to the Production Credit Associations. Thus, PCAs by their very existence have helped many farmers and ranchers who have never used their services.

Budgeted Loans Led to Line of Credit

The idea of budgeted loans gradually grew into the practice of many PCAs extending seasonal lines of credit to their better borrowers who had demonstrated their ability to use credit wisely. Under such plans, the PCAs merely approve a total line of credit for the season or year. Then the member-borrower can have the money advanced as his needs arise, as long as the total amount outstanding does not exceed the amount the PCA has approved as the maximum for his line of credit.

The Banks for Cooperatives use similar lending practices in financing farmers' marketing, farm supply, and business service cooperatives.

Pioneer Intermediate Term Loans

Early in the history of Production Credit Associations, it became evident that farmers or ranchers who borrowed to finance major capital expenditures could not be expected to make full repayment of their loans in one season or year. Such financing included the purchase of foundation livestock, major farm improvements, and later, needed heavy farm equipment or machinery. However, PCAs and particularly their district and Washington supervisors, were loathe to abandon the idea of limiting all loans to a seasonal or yearly basis.

Even though PCAs had adopted a general policy of adapting loan terms to the needs of individual farmers and were critical of commercial banks for sticking to their traditional lending patterns, a compromise rationale soon developed. There were tacit or implied agreements by PCAs with their borrowers. It was understood that as long as they repaid that part of their loan that was used to finance seasonal operating expenses, plus a reasonable portion of that used to finance capital improvement items, the unpaid portion of their loans would be extended and included in the following year's financing. PCAs wanted to have the option of a yearly review of the situation rather than commit themselves to any financing for periods beyond 1 year, even though the law permitted loans to be made for periods up to 3 years.

This approach to the problem of capital financing worked relatively well because both farmer and lender understoood each other and had faith in each other's intentions. Farm Credit Administration Governor I. W. Duggan in the late 1940s had a study made of the need for providing farmers with intermediate term loans—up to 3 years—for financing their growing needs for capital improvements. Following the study, in many of his speeches he called attention to the growing need for intermediate term loans. However, his suggestions met with almost universal resistance. The Production Credit Associations, the supervising district Production Credit Corporations, the Intermediate Credit Banks that provided the PCA loan funds, and Governor Duggan's own Intermediate Credit Bank and Production Credit Commissioners in the Farm Credit Administration were all wedded to past concepts.

Intermediate Term Loans Initiated by PCAs

But after Duggan resigned in 1953 and the Federal Farm Credit Board had been assigned the job of making national policy, sentiment for a change in policy began to crystallize. Many PCAs, because of their close contact with farmer-members, began to recognize their needs for longer term loans. Eventually, the PCAs convinced some of the district banks and their boards of directors, and through them the Federal Board, that they should be allowed to make loans for capital investments for periods up to the 3-year limit provided in the law. As a result, the Federal Board allowed a limited number of PCAs in selected Farm Credit Districts to experiment with such loans. After a short trial period, all FICBs were allowed to authorize PCAs they supervised to make such loans. On the basis of the experience with such loans, the Federal Board in 1956 requested Congress to raise the limit on loans for capital purposes to 7 years. Being somewhat skeptical, Congress compromised by raising the limit to 5 years. However, in 1961 Congress went the rest of the way and raised the limit to 7 years.

Adjusting Overlap in Length of Loans

Since the Land Banks have the authority to make mortgage loans for as short a period as 5 years, there is a flexible overlap of 2 years with the lending authority of PCAs. Some of the PCAs and their Intermediate Credit Banks feel Congress should allow them to make loans for periods up to 10 years. Their reasoning is that major capital improvements and investments in huge, heavy equipment may take that long to pay for themselves.

The Federal Farm Credit Board has, by regulation, made some accommodation to this need and point of view, without opening wide the gates to Land Bank–PCA competition. It has allowed PCAs to make loans for periods up to 7 years with a balloon payment at the end. Such loans are made with the expectation of renewing the balloon portion of the loan if necessary. However, the amortization payments over the original 7-year period must be large enough so that if the balloon portion of the loan is extended, the loan can be fully repaid in not more than 10 years.

The intermediate term loan idea for farmers quickly spread to many commercial banks who convinced the Federal Reserve Board they should be allowed to make loans to farmers for periods up to 7 years. Thus, PCAs again benefited many farmers who were not using their services.

BCs Provide Loans for Varying Periods

The Banks for Cooperatives have always had the authority to

make loans for various lengths of time, depending on the type of financing being provided. Originally, loans were classified as operating capital and facility loans. The Intermediate Credit Banks made commodity loans secured by warehouse receipts from 1923 to 1935. At that time, the Banks for Cooperatives took over most of such financing. However, the Banks for Cooperatives discounted such loans with the Federal Intermediate Credit Banks until the Central Bank for Cooperatives began selling debentures in 1950.

Commodity loans backed by warehouse receipts usually were expected to be paid by the end of the marketing season. However, if the cooperative had a carryover of nonperishable commodities into another marketing year and the organization remained in good financial condition, the Bank for Cooperatives usually renewed the balance of the commodity loan. Until 1967, commodity loans were generally made at slightly lower interest rates than other types of loans. This was because they were considered to have less risk involved and often were more costly to the borrower to maintain the required warehousing arrangements. Cooperatives only had to invest 1 percent of their commodity loans in Bank stock.

Commodity Loans Extended to Cover Farm Supplies

Former FCA Governor W. I. Myers reported that in the late 1920s, as a Professor of Farm Finance at Cornell University and advisor to the Cooperative GLF Exchange, he tried to convince the Federal Farm Loan Board that the Intermediate Credit Banks should be allowed to make commodity loans to farm supply cooperatives as well as to marketing cooperatives. He said that the Board ruled farm supply cooperatives as ineligible for such loans. The Banks for Cooperatives were authorized to make such loans in 1937.

Cooperatives obtained operating loans from the Banks for Cooperatives for working capital to finance their operations usually on a seasonal basis. The Banks for Cooperatives had authority to make loans up to 20 years on the security of mortgages on facilities. However, in practice most such loans were made for 10 years or less to guard against obsolescence.

From time to time, the Banks for Cooperatives have adjusted the classification of loans. Most of the Banks for Cooperatives now classify their loans as seasonal or term loans for the purpose of setting interest rates. "Seasonal" loans, however, include both commodity loans and operating or working capital loans that are made for periods of 1 year or less. Term loans include working capital loans that are made for periods of more than 1 year and facility loans. Since the passage of the Farm Credit Act of 1971, there has been no fixed limit on the maturity of term loans.

Variable Interest Rates Controversial

Traditionally, the general level of interest rates in various categories was relatively stable. From time to time rates might vary, but they did so within a relatively narrow range. Starting in the last half of the 1960s, fluctuations began to swing over a considerably wider range.

Borrowers might find they had signed a longer term contract at a rate that later was one-fourth to as much as 1 percent higher than the then current rate. No one liked to find himself in such a position, but most people realized that was a chance they were taking.

But when rates began to fluctuate over a range of 2 or 3 or more percent within a few months, private mortgage lenders were caught in a squeeze. Dependent on savings deposit accounts for their long-term mortgage loan funds, they found themselves with a relatively large volume of low interest rate loans outstanding, while they had to raise the rates on savings deposits in order to retain those deposits or attract new ones.

By the mid-1970s a few private mortgage lenders began making loans under contracts that allowed them to raise their interest rates if the cost of the money they were lending went up. Many others were discussing the possibility.

This raised considerable opposition among their borrowers who naturally were wary of entering into loan agreements which would enable the lender to raise the rate during the life of the loan if the cost of money to the lender increased.

Variable Interest Rates Well Accepted Within Farm Credit System

This reaction on the part of nonfarm home buyers and commercial borrowers was quite different from that of farmers, ranchers, and their cooperatives when the various parts of the cooperative Farm Credit System first introduced the idea on a broad scale several years earlier, when they were faced with the dilemma of having to finance relatively large volumes of low interest rate loans with currently high-cost lending funds obtained by selling securities to investors.

Once its borrowers understood the System's reasoning, the idea had been relatively well accepted. However, this arose from the fact that the Farm Credit System's focus and its historical record of dealing with its member-borrowers was quite different from that of other lenders.

Conventional lenders are in business to get the highest possible return or profit on their money. On the other hand, the cooperative Farm Credit System is not in business to make a profit, but to supply credit to its members on an equitable basis and at the lowest possible cost. Although frequently overlooked by many borrowers, if there are any net margins left after paying the cost of borrowed money, paying operating costs and contributing to necessary reserves, they belong to the System's borrowers. Such net margins are distributed to borrowers either in the form of dividends on the stock they hold in proportion to their loans, or as patronage refunds in proportion to the amount of interest they have paid on their loans.

When the Banks for Cooperatives first started making variable rate loans to borrowing cooperatives as far back as 1953, they very carefully explained the situation to their borrowing cooperatives. They pointed out that in a rising interest rate market, if they had the ability to adjust the Banks' interest rates on outstanding loans, they would find it unnecessary to raise rates on current loans as fast and as high as if they had to estimate in advance the average cost of money over the life of the loan. Variable interest rate loans would remove the need to charge for that hazard. They also had previously established the reputation of lowering the billed interest rates on outstanding loans in a declining interest rate market. This made sense to most of the cooperative borrowers from the Banks for Cooperatives, particularly since they knew that as borrower-members any increased net to their banks would be returned to them in the form of patronage refunds.

In 1957, when Production Credit Associations first began to adopt the variable interest rates in making intermediate term loans to their member-borrowers, which carried over to operating loans in 1963, they carried on an educational campaign similar to that used by the Banks for Cooperatives. And the program was also relatively well accepted.

The Land Banks had followed the practice over a long period of years of voluntarily billing interest on outstanding loans below the rates written in the mortgage contracts whenever the average cost of their lending funds went low enough to make such action feasible. Up until the middle of the 1960s this, in effect, amounted to a lowering of the contract rate permanently. Each time the Land Banks announced such reductions in rates they received many headlines in the newspapers in agricultural areas. It was a practical demonstration of how a member-owned and controlled lending institution can benefit its user-owners. This record of reducing rates on outstanding loans whenever possible undoubtedly helped gain acceptance for the variable interest rate plan.

The concept was readily accepted by borrowers. As owners, they recognized that there was no point in the Banks' overcharging them. If, indeed, anyone felt he could get a better deal elsewhere, he had the privilege of paying the loan off at any time without penalty.

Point of Purchase Loans

In the late 1950s Herbert Knipfel, President of the St. Paul Bank for Cooperatives, with Andrew Lampen and Aubrey Johnson, then respectively President and Vice President of the Federal Intermediate Credit Bank of St. Paul,[1] studied the problem that farm supply cooperatives frequently had in managing, financing, and controlling their accounts receivable to determine whether they could devise a plan by which the Banks for Cooperatives and the Production Credit Associations could be mutually helpful.

The recurring accounts receivable problem of many farm supply cooperatives usually arose from their over-enthusiasm in obtaining business and making sales. Managers and boards of directors of these cooperatives found their receivables became too large because they were not kept current. Knipfel and other presidents of Banks for Cooperatives had long urged boards of directors of cooperatives to adopt definite credit policies and see to it that their managers enforced them. However, many boards and managers did not get these difficult jobs done.

So, the Bank for Cooperatives and the Federal Intermediate Credit Bank at St. Paul worked out a program by which Production Credit Associations could sign agreements with cooperatives—and later other dealers—under which the cooperative could make Production Credit Association loans, up to specified amounts, to their patrons when they bought farm supplies. The Federal Farm Credit Board authorized St. Paul to experiment with such plans in a few PCAs.

---

[1] Johnson in 1972 became Deputy Governor and Director of the Production Credit Service of the Farm Credit Administration. After an FCA reorganization in 1972, he served as Deputy Governor and Director of the Credit Service in charge of supervising the extension of credit for the entire Farm Credit System. In 1973 he was elected Fiscal Agent for all 37 Banks of the System.

These agreements usually called for the farm supply cooperative's giving some form of guarantee. But the farmer immediately became conscious that he in effect had a definite loan obligation to meet and the collection of such loans was in the hands of experienced credit people. In addition, the plans often involved having the PCA discuss the handling of credit with the manager and other personnel of the farm supply cooperative in order to help them avoid taking on poor credit risks.

Following the experimental period in the St. Paul district, the Federal Board authorized the use of such plans in other Farm Credit districts. The plan was opposed by the president of at least one Bank for Cooperatives. He didn't like the idea of his Bank financing cooperatives that had some of their collateral pledged for contingent liabilities under the cooperatives' guarantee. Knipfel and some other Bank for Cooperatives' officials looked on this program as a means of helping farmers strengthen their cooperatives by getting them to handle credit on a more businesslike basis. From the PCAs' point of view, it gave them an opportunity to serve more farmers relatively safely and the possibility of eventually financing the total operating and intermediate term credit needs of the farmers involved. The plans met with varying degrees of success, depending to a large extent on how well the PCA and the other cooperatives worked together as a team.

Chapter 8

COMMERCIAL BANKS—IMPORTANT TO FARMERS AND SYSTEM

Commercial banks have long played a highly important role as suppliers of credit to farmers and ranchers both as direct lenders and indirectly as suppliers of funds to others who finance them. Their indirect financing of farmers and ranchers includes being one of the suppliers of loan funds to the cooperative Farm Credit System as well as financing merchants and dealers. The latter group are also important suppliers of credit to farmers in connection with their sales of farm supplies, farm equipment, and other farming inputs.

In early 1976, the Federal Reserve Bank of Chicago pointed out to commercial banks that the combined total loans of the Land Banks and Production Credit Associations had surpassed the total of their mortgage and non-real estate loans to farmers.

By the mid-1970s, farmers had more than twice as much money borrowed from the Land Banks as they had in farm mortgage loans from commercial banks—up from a post-depression low of 14.8 percent of their total farm mortgage debt in 1953 to 30 percent. In this period commercial banks' farm mortgages increased about 5 times. However, their share of the total declined from 15.3 percent in 1953 to 11.8 percent in 1963, but by 1975 had increased to 13.2 percent. In this period life insurance companies and individuals continued to have increasing amounts of money invested in farm mortgages, but their share of the total declined because their investments did not rise as rapidly as the total farm mortgage debt.

Farmers' loans from Production Credit Associations increased more rapidly than commercial banks for a long period of years, when measured on a percentage basis, because of their smaller base amount. However, PCA loans did not register larger dollar increases than the banks until 1970, 1971, and 1975. By the mid-1970s, PCA loans accounted for 28 percent of farmers' non-real estate debt—up from 5 percent in 1940 and 13 percent in 1960. In this same period—1940 to 1975—the percentage held by commercial banks increased from 30 percent to 52 percent. Much of the increased share of the total of both PCAs and commercial banks was accounted for by declines in the percentage supplied by merchants, dealers, and individuals, even though the dollar amounts rose. The Extension Service had long pointed out to farmers such credit is usually very expensive credit.

PCA Participation in Commercial Bank Loans

With the passage of the Farm Credit Act of 1971, a new relationship between the PCAs and commercial banks was authorized. PCAs can now participate—become joint lenders—with commercial banks in making loans to farmers. In most parts of the country, commercial banks are still a highly important source of credit for farmers. However, as the size of individual farm operations has grown, it has been more difficult for many local banks to handle the financing of the larger farmers in their territory, because of their limited assets and net worths.

Some smaller banks in the rural towns of the United States have developed highly successful correspondent relationships with larger city banks that enable them to handle larger operating loans to farmers. A few banks have also used the Federal Intermediate Credit Banks either directly or by setting up agricultural credit corporations as subsidiaries of the banks and then discounting farmers' loans with the Federal Intermediate Credit Banks. Recognizing the responsibility of the Farm Credit System to find ways to best serve the largest number of farmers possible, the System asked Congress—when the 1971 Act was being considered—to give the Production Credit Associations the authority to participate with local commercial banks in their larger farm and ranch loans. Congress granted that authority. Some PCAs have made such arrangements with local commercial banks in their territories. So far, there is too little experience to tell how well this arrangement may work. But if PCAs and commercial banks work closely together to develop such relationships, PCAs will find an additional method of improving the total credit service available to farmers and ranchers.

Commercial Banks Supply Funds to System

Commercial banks, especially those in the larger financial markets of the Nation, have long been important buyers of securities issued by all three banking groups in the Farm Credit System. Usually they buy the shorter term bond issues. Thus, commercial banks have been helping to finance agriculture through farmers' credit cooperatives for many, many years.

In addition, the Farm Credit Banks have long used loans from commercial banks to supply their temporary needs for loan funds between bond sales.[1]

Federal Land Bank–Commercial Bank Relations

Historically, in most areas of the country, the Federal Land Banks have had relatively good relationships with the commercial banks. Many commercial banks for a long period of years have referred their farm customers to their local Land Bank Associations when they needed mortgage loans. In the Northeast, where savings banks are numerous and strong, they have been willing and able to handle a considerable volume of long-term mortgage loans. However, most commercial banks have not looked upon Federal Land Bank Associations and the Banks as their competitors, because they, in order to keep liquid, cannot make a large number of long-term mortgage loans.

The mortgage loans that commercial banks do make to farmers are usually for relatively short periods of time, unless they have arrangements with a life insurance company, as many have had over the years, by which the insurance company agrees to take over the loan after a short period of years. However, most life insurance companies have shown less interest in making farm mortgage loans in recent years. This has been particularly true when the general level of interest rates is relatively high. At such times, life insurance companies can find more profitable uses for their investment funds. However, many commercial banks hold farm mortgages which they have taken as added security on operating loans.

Earlier PCA–Commercial Bank Relations

The relationships between Production Credit Associations and commercial banks have varied considerably over the years. When

---

[1] For a more detailed discussion, see "Credit Lines at Commercial Banks" in Chapter 6.

Production Credit Associations were first organized, a large share of the local banking community welcomed them with open arms as a means of unfreezing their assets by bringing an additional supply of money into the community.

By the 1940s, some of the more progressive local banks looked upon Production Credit Associations as friendly competitors and started adopting many of the practices that PCAs had inaugurated. Over the years, many banks have hired agricultural credit specialists to work with farmers. Other commercial banks that were trying to get back into the farm lending business following the rather poor experience in the depths of the Depression began to preach the idea that Production Credit Associations were only supposed to have operated on a temporary basis. Therefore, they argued, since they were again ready to do business with farmers, the Production Credit Associations should liquidate and let them take care of the business. Commercial banks of this type also tried to label Production Credit Associations as Government organizations that had unfair tax exemptions.

In the early days of the System, it was not uncommon for some farmers to boast of their ability to borrow from their local commercial bank. In later years, some of these farmers have been coming to Production Credit Associations in greater numbers because they find their business has grown to such an extent that it is necessary for the local bank to handle their loans through a correspondent bank in a larger city. Some farmers do not particularly like this arrangement, because they feel their loans are being influenced by city people who do not understand their problems. They prefer doing business with a credit organization made up of specialists who are familiar with the local farming conditions.

The number of PCA members obtaining loans from their PCAs has grown continuously, even though the total number of farmers has gone down. In 1940, the number of PCA members was only 253,000, and PCAs accounted for only 5 percent of the total short-term farm financing. The number of PCA members had increased to 508,000 by 1960, and PCAs were accounting for 13 percent of the short-term credit. By the mid-1970s, the number of PCA members exceeded 520,000, and the percentage of the business accounted for by PCAs had risen to 28 percent. However, commercial banks nationally were still supplying about twice as much operating credit to farmers as that being supplied by Production Credit Associations when measured on the basis of national averages. The percentage of business handled by PCAs in some Farm Credit districts runs well over 50 percent of the total, while in others the percentage is less than 20.

Banks for Cooperatives–Commercial
Bank Relations

Some local bankers with broad vision have often welcomed the arrival of a new cooperative in their community, or the enlargement of an old one, as a means of improving the local economy, and that attitude has spread as bankers generally have become better acquainted with successful cooperatives. However, in earlier days many local banks were skeptical that farmers had the ability to run their own organizations. Many bankers did not understand how cooperatives operated and were therefore unable to properly finance cooperatives. Some bankers were not anxious to finance cooperatives because the competitors of a new or old cooperative happened to be valued customers or friends.

Gradually, the Banks for Cooperatives demonstrated to more progressive banks that cooperatives are frequently excellent credit risks. As a result, some city banks have welcomed or sought large cooperative accounts.

At one conference of presidents of Banks for Cooperatives, FCA Governor Robert B. Tootell asked how the interest rates of banks in their area compared with those of the Banks for Cooperatives. Several of the Bank presidents answered that the smaller cooperatives in their areas would have to pay somewhat higher interest rates at their local banks. But they reported that some city banks were offering to finance larger cooperatives on the basis of a fixed, small fraction of a percentage point below whatever interest rate the Bank for Cooperatives charged. (This has not been true in more recent "credit crunch" periods.) However, such inducements did not attract many cooperatives who appreciate borrowing from their own bank where they do not have to maintain minimum balances, share in the earnings by way of patronage refunds, and are assured of cooperative-oriented, specialized advice and counsel. They also like the idea of having a lender that they know will continue to work with them if times get tough.

One example of what advice and counsel from the Banks for Cooperatives can mean is a cooperative that for many years operated highly successfully and then was weaned away from a Bank for Cooperatives as its lending source by one of the largest banks in the Nation, on the promise of a slightly lower interest rate. Within a few years, that commercial bank came to the Bank for Cooperatives and asked it to take over the loan. With the encouragement of the commercial bank, the cooperative had made contracts with a large number of farmers to greatly expand their businesses, only to have the price of their product decline rapidly, thus putting the cooperative in a very poor financial condition.

Closer Ties Developed from Experience

Generally, the relationships between the Farm Credit System and commercial banks have improved with the passing years. The experience of their ever-growing business relationships has fostered mutual respect between them.

PART THREE

Basic Principles and Major
Guidelines Developed

In order to build a strong organization, its founders and later leaders must have or develop basic principles, guidelines, concepts, and methods to use in steering it. The cooperative Farm Credit System started with some unusual ideas. Some were developed or grew out of its experience. Some were borrowed or adapted from other successful organizations. Some that were used and tested in operation had to be dropped when they did not work in practice. Many were modified or adjusted to meet the changing needs of farmers, ranchers, and their cooperatives. Those that remained proved useful in building a dynamic organization.

Russell C. Engberg, former Director of Research and Information of the Farm Credit Administration,[1] points out that the framers of the original Farm Loan Act of 1916 deserve particular credit for incorporating in it four concepts that survived and became important blocks in the foundation of all permanent parts of the Farm Credit System. Those he lists are:

1. The cooperative form of organization borrowed from the German Landschaften societies.
2. The requirement that borrower-members had to contribute to the capital structure by investing in stock.
3. The obtaining of loan funds from the sale of securities in the in-

---

[1] Russell C. Engberg, an Iowa State graduate, came to the Federal Farm Loan Board from the Brookings Institution in 1928. After serving in several positions in the Farm Credit Administration he went to the Omaha Farm Credit Banks as Director of Research in 1938. He returned to FCA as Director of Research in 1945. He is the author of "Financing Farmer Cooperatives" . . . a study of the credit experience of the Banks for Cooperatives.

vestment markets—a deviation from the European credit societies
that depended on members' savings deposits.

4. The requirement that the Government capital be repaid from
   member investments in stock and accumulated earned net worth
   reserves.

Numbers 3 and 4 were discussed in Part Two as "Pioneering Innovations" that have since been adopted by other groups. Numbers 1 and 2 are
among those principles and concepts discussed in Chapters 9 to 18.

Chapter 9

COOPERATIVE NATURE OF SYSTEM
MAKES IT PEOPLE-ORIENTED

The cornerstone of the successful operation of the Farm Credit System was laid when farm leaders, in urging Congress to authorize the establishment of the Federal Land Banks and the then National Farm Loan Associations—now known as the Federal Land Bank Associations—insisted that farmers could run their own credit organizations. Those same leaders convinced Congress that it should give farmers who used the System a chance to own it.

How deep that conviction may have been, or how many doubts and misgivings various members of Congress might have had, can be judged by the fact that Congress included many safeguards and restrictions in the 1916 Act which enabled the System to get started. Since then, Congress has gradually modified or removed a large proportion of those restrictions as the needs arose and the System proved itself. Finally, in the Farm Credit Act of 1971, Congress gave farmers, through the representatives they select to make policies for local associations, district banks, and the supervisory agency—the Farm Credit Administration—broad authority and responsibility to adjust the policies and regulations of the System to meet the ever-changing needs of agriculture and rural America.

Prior to 1933, the Federal Farm Loan Board, the predecessor of the Farm Credit Administration, moved cautiously. At least in the early years it was very careful to see that as many actions as possible were approved in Washington. Those responsibilities and authorities that were given to the Federal Land Banks were carefully surrounded by tight limitations, restrictions, and regulations.

The plan which Henry Morgenthau, Jr.,[1] and W. I. Myers present-

---

[1] See "Leaders with Vision and Ability" in this chapter and "Developing Plans to Solve Farmers' Credit Problems" in Chapter 26 for more information on the role of Morgenthau.

ed to Congress for rounding out the Farm Credit System in 1933 gave much more responsibility and left more leeway to the boards of directors of the new organizations and to the Farm Credit Administration.[2] These new organizations were the local Production Credit Associations, their supervising Production Credit Corporations, and the Banks for Cooperatives.

When Myers became Governor of the Farm Credit Administration in late 1933, succeeding Governor Henry Morgenthau, Jr., he began programs to fully inform the membership of the Production Credit Associations, and what are now the Federal Land Bank Associations, about their organizations, their operations, and their finances. With the cooperation and strong support of his Production Credit Commissioner S. M. Garwood, his Deputy C. R. "Cap" Arnold, and Land Bank Commissioner Albert S. Goss, he stressed the role of the member-users in their credit cooperatives. Myers and his top staff felt that if a cooperative credit system was to be built and operated successfully, it had to have a well-informed and concerned membership that would elect the best-qualified directors. But they went far beyond that.

Myers and his top staff also saw the need for training boards of directors, loan committees, and local officials to exercise their greater responsibility and authority. They had the Farm Credit Administration staffers hard at work developing programs to discuss with the Land Banks and Production Credit Corporations to see that such training became a reality. In addition, they impressed on the district boards of directors the importance of picking highly qualified officers for the newly formed Production Credit Corporations and Banks for Cooperatives and suggested where they could find them.

In staffing the Farm Credit Administration itself, Myers and his colleagues sought the best-qualified people available for the key positions and then pressed them to do the same in recruiting their subordinates. Fortunately, in those Depression years, there were a large number of highly qualified people who were out of work, or, if they had jobs, whose salaries had been cut to such an extent that they were readily available even for some of the lower grade positions. Naturally, some of the people chosen did not live up to expectations, but there were enough good ones to keep the organization moving forward for many years.

Such attitudes instilled an *esprit de corps* in the Farm Credit Ad-

---

[2] For plan, see "Developing Plans to Solve Farmers' Credit Problems" in Chapter 26.

ministration and throughout the System. As Gordon Finley, then a membership relations specialist in the Farm Credit Administration, remarked after coming back from a field trip, "When we're traveling, people often ask who we work for. We admit that we work for the Government. But then we quickly go on to say: '*But*, I work for the Farm Credit Administration.'"

The importance of having well-qualified people in the System was emphasized by Cameron Garman, Treasurer of the Commodity Credit Corporation, in 1946. Earlier in his career as Assistant Deputy Production Credit Commissioner, he had helped the Production Credit Corporations develop membership and public relations programs for the Production Credit Associations. He said, "Anyone who looks at the organization chart of the Farm Credit System would say that it was so complicated that it could not possibly work. But it has. It is because the System has so many outstanding people. They make it work!"

That such programs had an effect on building strong, well-knit organizations was demonstrated by Albert G. Black who served as Governor of the Farm Credit Administration from 1940 to 1944. In his retirement address to employees of the Farm Credit Administration, Black said, "One thing I have learned from Farm Credit: An organization that knows where it is going has more effect on the man than the man has on the organization." This was particularly significant because Black had come to Farm Credit from the U.S. Department of Agriculture to restyle it in accordance with the personal ideas of Secretary of Agriculture Henry A. Wallace.

Thousands of People Helped Build System

The success of the Farm Credit System has been due to the ideas, sweat, devotion, and loyalty of thousands of people. Any recognition of such people would have to start with farmers themselves. They would include those members of the Federal Land Bank Associations during the Depression who got way behind on their loan payments, but stayed on their farms and eventually succeeded. It would include farmers whose staggering debt loads were refinanced by the Land Banks and who didn't give up in the face of low prices and drought years. These families had the courage and tenacity to stick with farming when it seemed almost impossible to get enough money to live on, not to mention paying off mortgages and other debts. Although thousands of farmers gave up, hundreds of thousands stayed on their farms and pulled through. Recognition should also go to those farmers who had the vision to organize and use their weak and struggling young farm supply, marketing, and business service cooperatives and build them into strong, efficient organizations to serve farmers in ever-increasing ways.

The farmer boards of directors of those associations—the newly formed Production Credit Associations and the bankrupt or nearly defunct Land Bank Associations—faced an almost impossible task of building a strong local underpinning for the Farm Credit System. Those who went around organizing Production Credit Associations frequently had difficulty in finding five farmers at well-attended meetings who had five dollars apiece to buy their first share of stock and thus become charter members.

Farmers and ranchers serving on the boards of directors of the local associations, then and in the ensuing years, had tough decisions to make not only in setting loan and other policies for their organizations but also in the making of individual loans. These farmer-directors were often troubled by the knowledge that their decisions were determining the future course of the lives of entire farm families—often their neighbors and friends.

Farmers and their cooperative leaders serving on district Farm Credit Boards often had equally difficult decisions to make in setting the policies of the district Banks. The officers of the local associations and the cooperatives borrowing from the Banks for Cooperatives were also faced with tremendous jobs in successfully planning, building, expanding, and operating their organizations. The history of the Farm Credit System has been built by such successful efforts that eventually solved many problems and overcame the mistakes that were frequently made.

Leaders with Vision and Ability

Fortunately for farmers, they have been blessed with many strong, capable, devoted people with broad, forward vision in leadership and subordinate posts in the key management spots in the local Associations, the district Banks, and in the usually sympathetic and understanding supervisory agency—the Farm Credit Administration—as well as the Federal Farm Credit Board and its predecessor, the Federal Farm Loan Board.

To illustrate the type of highly capable people who have been involved in the leadership in Farm Credit, a few will be mentioned as examples to show that the System has been indeed fortunate in attracting highly capable people at all levels—well-trained people with a wealth of important experience, some of whom went on to even larger areas of responsibility in other organizations.

From the opening of the twentieth century onward, farm leaders began insisting that farmers needed a credit system that recognized and understood the needs of farmers. In 1908, President Theodore Roosevelt appointed a Country Life Commission to study the needs of farmers. The Commission was headed by Liberty Hyde Bailey, Dean of Agriculture at Cornell University. The Commission report reflected Bailey's broad range of interest in the problems of rural America[3] and set the stage for a century of unparalleled agricultural development. Among the Commission's key recommendations was to point out farmers' needs for strong cooperatives and an agricultural credit system. Other Commission recommendations that were to become important factors in the development of rural America in the twentieth century included more agricultural research, coupled with an extension system to spread its findings to farmers, and rural free delivery of the mails.

Two of the most celebrated losing candidates for President played important roles in the early development of the Farm Credit System—William Gibbs McAdoo and Charles Evans Hughes. McAdoo, the son-in-law of President Woodrow Wilson, played an important role in the debates on the Federal Farm Loan Act of 1916. He was one of those who favored a privately owned System that resulted in including in the Act a provision to establish the now long-forgotten, dual systems of investor-owned joint stock land banks. McAdoo, as Secretary of the Treasury, was the first Chairman ex-Officio of the Federal Farm Loan Board. In the case to test the constitutionality of that Act in 1921,[4] McAdoo argued the case before the Supreme Court representing both the joint stock land banks and, by appointment from the Attorney General, the public interest. Senator McAdoo battled it out with Alfred E. Smith for the Democratic nomination for President at the long-remembered National Convention in New

---

[3] Bailey was to retire at 50, telling Cornell's president the plan for his life was 25 years to prepare for his career, 25 for his career, and 25 to do what he wanted to do. The last 25 stretched to 43 highly productive years which included authoring more than 65 books, the most important of which was his six volume *Standard Cyclopedia of Horticulture.* His 90th birthday celebration was delayed awaiting his return from a trip up the Amazon in an open boat to collect new specimens of plant life. He was still going strong when he died at 93 following an accident in New York City.

[4] An investor in a Kansas City firm sued to prevent it from investing in bonds of the FLB of Wichita on the basis that the Farm Loan Act was unconstitutional because it made the Bank tax-exempt.

York City in 1924, until a compromise candidate—John W. Davis—won on the 103rd ballot—a record.

Charles Evans Hughes represented the Federal Land Bank of Wichita before the Supreme Court in the same case to test the Federal Farm Loan Act's constitutionality. A former governor of New York, Hughes left the Supreme Court in 1916 to become the Republican candidate. Thinking he had unseated President Woodrow Wilson, Hughes went to bed a winner on election night, only to wake up the next morning as the loser when California shifted to the Democratic column. Reputedly, Hughes lost California because he had slighted the renowned Republican liberal, Senator Hiram Johnson, in his home state on his campaign trip to California. However, Hughes later became Secretary of State and a longtime, moderately liberal Chief Justice of the Supreme Court.

Carter Glass of Virginia was the second Secretary of the Treasury to serve as Chairman of the Federal Farm Loan Board. As Chairman of the House Banking Committee, Glass was known as the Father of the Act which provided for the establishment of the Federal Reserve Banks in 1914. In 1916, his committee had recommended passage of the Federal Farm Loan Act.

A key person in the history of the System was Henry Morgenthau, Jr., first Governor of the Farm Credit Administration. Morgenthau had served Governor Roosevelt as New York State's Conservation Commissioner, and as Chairman of his Agricultural Advisory Committee. As owner-publisher of a Northeast farm paper—the *American Agriculturist*—Morgenthau had come to Washington in 1932 as one of the people the newly elected President had picked to try to determine what should be done to stop a tidal wave of farm foreclosures and build a strong agriculture. As a personal friend of the President, Morgenthau had Roosevelt's ear at any time he felt he needed to talk. Morgenthau brought along with him W. I. Myers, then Professor of Farm Finance at the College of Agriculture at Cornell University.

Myers had done some work for the Federal Farm Board. Its duties included making loans to cooperatives. He also had been financial adviser to the then young and struggling Cooperative Grange League Federation Exchange, then popularly known as GLF and now Agway—on *Fortune's* 1976 list as the 154th largest industrial enterprise. Morgenthau and Myers conferred with agricultural credit, farm organization, and Congressional leaders. Morgenthau depended on Myers to design and work up plans for solving farmers' financial problems. As Myers recalls it, some of the meetings Morgenthau arranged with President Roosevelt were held before the President got out of bed in the morning. Morgenthau and Myers made a good team; Morgenthau would present the overall ideas and Myers would fill in the details. When Morgenthau left the Farm Credit Administration in November of 1933 to become Secretary of the Treasury where he served 11½ years, Myers moved up from Deputy Governor to replace him. Myers pointed out that Morgenthau's drive and administrative ability were important in getting the new Farm Credit program underway.[5]

After serving 5 years as Governor of the Farm Credit Administration, Myers in 1938 returned to Cornell University as head of the Agricultural Economics Department. He later became Dean of Cornell's College of Agriculture. In addition, Myers served in many other capacities, including service as a trustee of the Rockefeller Foundation, Vice Chairman of the Board of the Federal Reserve Bank of New York, and as a member of the boards of directors of many large corporations. He also became chairman of the board of directors of the American Institute of Cooperation when it reorganized in 1945 to operate on a full-time, year-round basis.[6]

The third Governor of the Farm Credit Administration was Forrest F. Hill, popularly known as "Frosty." He was born on a Kansas wheat farm and raised on a wheat farm in Saskatchewan, Canada. For his Ph.D. thesis he had studied the individual loan histories of the Federal Land Bank of Springfield and later had become its Controller. His first assignment at the Farm Credit Administration was to draw up a detailed plan to organize the Production Credit Associations. He then became Myers' Deputy Governor in charge of finance and research. After leaving the Farm Credit Administration in 1940, Hill was the head of the Department of Agricultural Economics at Cornell University and later Provost of the University. From there he went to the Ford Foundation as Vice President for Overseas Operations and continued to serve that organization as a consultant to set up international agricultural research centers long after his official retirement.

The first Land Bank Commissioner in the Farm Credit Administration was Albert S. Goss. Goss was Master of the Washington State Grange and had been active in forming early Federal Land Bank

---

[5] For the program see Chapter 26.
[6] Myers frequently served on committees of national importance, including the commission President Harry Truman sent to Europe after World War II to study conditions there and make recommendations for what should be done to help Europe get back on its feet. The report of the commission laid the groundwork for the famous Marshall Plan to rebuild the wartorn European nations.

Associations in his home state. Goss came to the Farm Credit Administration expecting to be Production Credit Commissioner but was soon made Land Bank Commissioner. He faced the tremendous task of getting the Land Banks in shape to take on the refinancing job that was so necessary to save hundreds of thousands of farmers from foreclosure. When he left the Farm Credit Administration in 1940, he became Master of the National Grange and Chairman of the Credit Committee of the national farm organizations. The committee's chief aim was to have the Farm Credit Administration reestablished as an independent agency after it had been placed in the Department of Agriculture. He kept the committee working toward this goal which was reached after his death.

The first Production Credit Commissioner was S. M. "Steve" Garwood who had set up state agricultural credit corporations in Arkansas to discount farmers' notes with the Intermediate Credit Bank at St. Louis. That operation had proved quite successful. He took on the job of organizing and getting started the newly conceived Production Credit Associations. He was a strong administrator who insisted on building a strong foundation for the Production Credit Associations.

C. R. "Cap" Arnold was Garwood's Deputy and succeeded him in 1938 as Production Credit Commissioner. Arnold had been an Extension economist at Ohio State University. He was widely known and loved throughout the United States as the "daddy" of the Production Credit Associations. An enthusiastic, inspirational leader, he did a tremendous job of nurturing and guarding the PCAs, as well as training them in how to operate. He insisted on sound loans, and a strong financial and membership base, and he campaigned long and hard to drive them toward complete farmer ownership. Arnold firmly believed that farmers—with enough training and information—could own and operate their local PCAs and other cooperatives, and through them the entire system. Farmer members appreciated his faith in them. He insisted on democratic control at all levels. After retiring as Production Credit Commissioner in 1951, he returned to Washington in the summer of 1953 to become Governor of the Farm Credit Administration when Governor Ivy W. Duggan resigned. The Federal Farm Board held its first meeting on December 15, 1953, and asked Arnold, who had done much spade work to help the Board to get off to a fast start, to be the first Board-appointed Governor of the Farm Credit Administration. He refused for health reasons, but agreed to remain in an acting capacity until a permanent

Governor could be chosen to take over. In April 1954, he was succeeded by Governor Robert B. Tootell.

Francis W. Peck was the first Cooperative Bank Commissioner of the Farm Credit Administration. Peck had been an Extension economist at the University of Minnesota. After helping the Banks for Cooperatives get established, he returned to that University as Director of Extension. Later, he became President of the Federal Land Bank of St. Paul and then President of the Farm Foundation. Peck also served as the representative of the Secretary of Agriculture on the first Federal Farm Credit Board from 1953 to 1961.

A. T. Esgate, an Arizona banker, held a wide variety of important positions from 1933 to 1957. He served as Deputy Production Credit Commissioner from 1940 to 1951 under "Cap" Arnold and succeeded him as Commissioner. Esgate was always a strong exponent of sound credit and was highly regarded as a friendly but firm administrator. As one who could be counted on to do a highly conscientious job, he was Deputy Intermediate Credit Commissioner and Deputy Governor on two separate occasions several years apart, under Governors Myers and Tootell. In the latter case he was "First Deputy Governor" in charge of general administration.

I. W. Duggan, who served as Governor of the Farm Credit Administration from 1944 to 1953, became vice president of the Trust Company of Georgia in Atlanta. Before coming to the Farm Credit Administration, he had been a vocational agriculture teacher and an agricultural economist at Clemson and Mississippi State Universities, and had served as chief of the Southern Division of the Agricultural Adjustment Administration. He believed in building a strong system and maximum service to farmers through a team effort.

R. B. Tootell, Governor of the Farm Credit Administration from 1953 to 1968, had been chief reviewing appraiser at the Federal Land Bank of Spokane and on the appraisal staff of the Farm Credit Administration in Washington, D.C. He had then become the head of the Department of Agricultural Economics and later Director of Extension, first at Montana State College, and then at Washington State College.

The Federal Farm Credit Board's two most recent choices as Governor of the Farm Credit Administration demonstrate that Farm Credit is continuing its tradition of choosing a good mix of highly talented people from outside the System and of those who have developed within the System itself.

E. A. Jaenke, Governor from 1969 to 1974, working in tandem

with the Federal Farm Credit Board and district and local directors and officials, spearheaded a successful major effort to broaden the authorities of the System to meet the challenges of the modern and future changing needs of the Nation's food producers and rural residents. Jaenke came to Farm Credit from the U.S. Department of Agriculture where he had been Deputy Administrator of the Agricultural Stabilization and Conservation Service and a Vice President of the Commodity Credit Corporation. Trained in agricultural economics at the Universities of Illinois and Missouri, he had originally come to Washington as an agricultural economist on the staff of Senator Stuart Symington. While with the Agricultural Stabilization and Conservation Service and the Commodity Credit Corporation, Jaenke had received the Arthur Fleming Award as one of the 10 most outstanding young men in government.

On the other hand, the Federal Farm Credit Board, after considering dozens of highly qualified possible successors to continue the implementation of the 1971 Act, when Governor Jaenke left to form an agricultural consulting firm, chose for the first time a Governor who had started within the System as an employee of a local Association. Governor W. Malcolm Harding became manager of a branch office of the Federal Land Bank Association of Winston-Salem, North Carolina, in 1952. Because of his many capabilities, he rose rapidly in the Farm Credit System. By 1972, when Governor Jaenke chose Harding as his Deputy Governor in charge of supervising credit for all parts of the System, Harding had served the Columbia Farm Credit Banks in many capacities. At that time he was Vice President in charge of supervising credit for both the Land Bank and the Intermediate Credit Bank of Columbia.

Another example of outside talent brought into the Farm Credit family is Howard Campbell, FCA General Counsel from December 14, 1969, to June 30, 1972. Campbell, in drafting the Farm Credit Act of 1971, recodifying all the previous Farm Credit legislation back to 1916, did a masterful job of eliminating inconsistencies, broadening the System's powers, and achieving much-needed flexibility in the System's basic charter. His craftsmanship and logic were important factors in winning Congressional approval of that Act. Campbell had come to the Farm Credit Administration from the office of the General Counsel of the U.S. Department of Agriculture, where he had a great deal of experience in preparing legislation and handling other legal matters for the Farmers Home Administration and the Rural Electrification Administration.

Harlan B. Munger, who had served for several years as President

Henry Morgenthau
May–November 1933

Governors of the
Farm Credit Administration

F. F. Hill
1938–1940

W. I. Myers
1933–1938

Governors of the
rm Credit Administration

I. W. Duggan
1944–1953

A. G. Black
1940–1944

C. R. Arnold
1953–1954

**Governors of the
Farm Credit Administration**

R. B. Tootell
1954–1969

E. A. Jaenke
1969–1974

W. M. Harding
1974–

of the Production Credit Corporation of Springfield, became the first president of all four Farm Credit institutions in a Farm Credit district. A few years after he retired, he became the first Chairman of the Federal Farm Credit Board in 1953 in its highly important formative period. Many other Farm Credit-trained men mixed with top farmer cooperative leaders and college educators have contributed much to the successful operations of the Federal Farm Credit Board.

Many outstanding Farm Credit Bank presidents and Farm Credit Administration officials have started their Farm Credit careers in the local Land Bank and Production Credit Associations. Other highly qualified Association managers and Farm Credit Bank officers have been lured away to important positions in other organizations. Farm Credit was reminded of that fact when a Finance Advisory Committee was appointed in 1972 to study the funding of the Farm Credit System. Among the outside financiers chosen for that committee was Darryl Francis, President of the Federal Reserve Bank of St. Louis, who was also serving on the Federal Reserve's Open Market Committee. Francis in his early years had been a highly regarded manager of the St. Joseph and Springfield Production Credit Associations in Missouri. Others who have been involved with Farm Credit and have risen to national prominence include a president of the Ford Foundation, a Commissioner to decontrol prices after World War II, and a Secretary of Agriculture.

An example of the capabilities of the people who were attracted to the Farm Credit Administration and the Farm Credit System is Rowan Gaither, who as a lawyer in the Farm Credit Administration carried on a whirlwind campaign in 1934 and 1935 to get states to amend their laws to remove roadblocks to making operating loans through PCAs. Years later, he became President of the Ford Foundation.

A district Farm Credit official who quickly became nationally known was Roy L. Thompson, who had been a professor of agricultural economics at Louisiana State University before helping to organize Production Credit Associations and then becoming General Agent and President of the Federal Land Bank at New Orleans. President Harry Truman appointed Dr. Thompson, chairman of the three-member special board he created to decontrol prices[7] after World War II.

---

[7] The Price Decontrol Board was charged with removing all price controls in such a manner that it would restore the free market system without upsetting the Nation's economy.

At the beginning of his career, Secretary of Agriculture Earl Butz had served as Assistant Director of Research for the Farm Credit Banks of Louisville where he wrote his Ph.D. thesis on the operations of the Federal Land Bank. He also made a study of Production Credit Associations for the Brookings Institution. He was head of the Agricultural Economics Department and then Dean of Agriculture at Purdue University before becoming Secretary of Agriculture.

Stanley Andrews, former Administrator of the Agency for International Development, not only served as general agent for the Farm Credit Banks of New Orleans in the immediate prewar days, but also had an earlier connection with the Farm Credit System in an indirect way. It was in his office that S. M. Garwood had worked out a plan for setting up the agricultural credit corporations in Arkansas—a testing ground for ideas that were later to be incorporated into the operations of the Production Credit Associations. At that time, Andrews was publisher and editor of the *Arkansas Farmer* and had worked for the old American Cotton Cooperative in the Federal Farm Board era

Robert L. Farrington and John Bagwell both became Solicitors of the U.S. Department of Agriculture. Farrington had served in the loan department of the Federal Farm Board, with the Central Bank for Cooperatives, as FCA Deputy Governor, and as Cooperative Bank Commissioner. Bagwell, who had served as an attorney with the Farm Credit Administration in 1934 and 1935, came back to FCA from the Solicitor's Office in the U.S. Department of Agriculture to serve as General Counsel from 1954 to 1961. He drafted much important legislation including the Farm Credit Acts of 1955 and 1956. As a result both Democrats and Republicans on the Congressional Agricultural Committees recommended him for this top legal post in the U.S. Department of Agriculture.

Roy Greene, an early Deputy Governor in the Farm Credit Administration, became President of Colorado A&M College—now Colorado State University.

Joseph G. Knapp, first Administrator of the Farmer Cooperative Service in the U.S. Department of Agriculture and author of a two-volume history of cooperatives and many other books on cooperatives, started his Government career in charge of the work with farm supply cooperatives in the Farm Credit Administration's Cooperative Research and Service Division.

The Farm Credit Administration and the Farm Credit System have benefited greatly from the broadening experience of some of their officials' moving to and from Washington and the district Banks.

Before becoming a highly respected leader among Land Bank

presidents, Fred Knutsen had served as General Counsel for the Farm Credit Banks of Spokane. In 1954, on leave from Spokane, he served as General Counsel for the Farm Credit Administration at the crucial time when the Federal Farm Credit Board was getting into action and the Farm Credit Administration was again becoming an independent Government agency. Over the years he also made many important contributions in the develoment of Farm Credit legislation, including the Farm Credit Act of 1971.

E. A. Stokdyk, President of the Berkeley Bank for Cooperatives, was one of several important early developers of cooperative and Banks for Cooperatives philosophy, theory, and practical operations. He was loaned to the Farm Credit Administration as a Deputy Governor for a year in the late 1930s to supervise both economic and cooperative research. Previously, what is now the Farmer Cooperative Service in the U.S. Department of Agriculture had been a subdivision of the cooperative division which also supervised the Banks for Cooperatives.

Two others who made particularly important contributions in the early development of guidelines for the operations of the Banks for Cooperatives were S. D. Sanders and J. D. Lawrence. Sanders was Cooperative Commissioner of FCA from 1936 to 1947. He had been general manager of a large poultry marketing and farm supply cooperative in the State of Washington—Washington Cooperative Egg and Poultry Association, now Western Farmers Association. He urged cooperatives to build stronger organizations by getting farmers to increase their investment in the equities of cooperatives. He preached the use of capital revolving plans that retained a portion of the proceeds from farm marketings and the patronage refunds on farm supplies purchased as an automatic way of building up capital.

J. D. Lawrence, who finished his career by serving as President of the Columbia Bank for Cooperatives in South Carolina, learned many things that should be done or avoided in his work with cooperatives in the pre-Banks for Cooperatives days with President Herbert Hoover's old Federal Farm Board. As Deputy Cooperative Commissioner under Peck, Sanders, and Farrington, Lawrence had a strong hand in policy-making. After serving as treasurer of Consumers Cooperative Association in Kansas City—now Farmland Industries—at a time when it was having some financial problems, Lawrence returned to the Farm Credit Administration to become the Director of the Finance and Accounts Division. In the early days of the Federal Farm Credit Board, while on leave from the Columbia Bank for Cooperatives, Lawrence returned to the Farm Credit Administration to serve for a short period as Deputy Governor and Director of the Cooperative Bank Service.

Rufus Clarke, who served at various times as president of each of the Farm Credit organizations in Columbia, spent a year of his earlier career as a Deputy Governor of the Farm Credit Administration.

Homer G. Smith, President of the Central Bank for Cooperatives from 1956 to 1974, started his career with the Farm Credit Administration in 1934 as an Examiner. He transferred to the Production Credit Division in 1936 where he rose to Deputy Commissioner before becoming Deputy Governor and Director of the Cooperative Bank Service in 1954.

Several deans of agriculture and heads of the departments of agricultural economics in Land Grant colleges have served with distinction on the policy-making district Farm Credit boards and the board of directors of the Central Bank for Cooperatives. They usually provided the board a general overview of farmers' problems to the mix of experience on these boards.

The long list of managers and directors of the Nation's most successful marketing and purchasing cooperatives who have served on these boards and on the Federal Farm Credit Board have generally contributed sound business and management experience, a broad interest in farmers' credit problems, and specialized knowledge of the problems of cooperatives. They have been a potent force in producing the successful record of the Farm Credit System.

A brief description of the careers of the above people is given only to illustrate the caliber of the people whom the Farm Credit System has been fortunate enough to have involved in various capacities over the years. Many other equally important people could well be mentioned. The wide range of talents, experience, and points of view gradually helped build a strong cooperative Farm Credit System.

While the overall record of the Farm Credit System and Administration for picking people has been excellent, as might be expected in an organization that has employed thousands of operating officers and employees and has had thousands of local, district, and Federal members of boards of directors, there naturally have been some mistakes in choosing people, and judgmental mistakes by good people. There have even been occasional misdeeds among employees and a few detrimental headlines. However, it is a real tribute to the personnel chosen by the farmer-owned and controlled Farm Credit System that even though it has handled more than $250 billion of loans in its 60-year history, it has never been involved in any major scandal.

Democratic Control Developed

Democratic control—an integral ingredient of the cooperative nature of the Farm Credit System—had its roots in the Federal Farm Loan Act of 1916 that provided for member-borrower control of local National Farm Loan Associations and the election of members of boards of directors of the Federal Land Banks by the representatives of farmers—local boards of directors. The democratic control feature of the System has been expanded and strengthened in much legislation since then, including the Farm Credit Acts of 1933, 1937, 1953, 1955, 1956, and most recently in the Farm Credit Act of 1971.

However, legislation alone does not necessarily achieve democratic control in practice. The original Federal Farm Loan Board, some Farm Credit Bank presidents, some district Farm Credit Boards, and at times officials of the Farm Credit Administration, as the latter day supervisory agency, have distrusted the concept or at least forgotten to honor it in everyday practice. The amendments offered by Senator Henry Bellmon of Oklahoma and accepted in the enactment of the Farm Credit Act of 1971 were generated by his observance of what appeared to him to be breakdowns in the execution of the democratic control concept in some Production Credit Associations. He was trying to make sure that the democratic control idea would be carried out in practice. His amendments to the Act were designed to help make sure that the members had a choice in selecting directors and that they truly represented all parts of the membership.

However, the effort to maintain and strengthen the democratic control in the Farm Credit System has long had many supporters. They would not let the idea die or be forgotten. In fact, those who have done the most to strengthen democratic control of the System have not only used it themselves but have offered opportunities for those at the next level of authority to use it and encouraged them to do so.

Many examples could be cited where democratic control has slowed progress toward generally desired objectives. However, even more examples could be given that have demonstrated that decisions arrived at by democratic action usually are the best decisions. At least, such decisions are more likely to receive popular support and thus achieve the goals sought. The growth and strengthening of the democratic control concept in the cooperative Farm Credit System has served not only to make it increasingly effective but also has helped to attract more and more users, defenders, and supporters.

The reins of democratic control in the Farm Credit System are in the hands of its member-borrowers—farmers and ranchers. They elect their local boards of directors to make policies for their credit and other cooperatives and to choose and guide management and monitor its effectiveness. The local directors that member-borrowers select also act as their representatives in choosing directors for the district Farm Credit Banks and nominees for appointment to the Federal Farm Credit Board.

The job of district boards is to make broad policies and to choose and guide district bank officers. The Federal Farm Credit Board makes policies for the Farm Credit Administration—the supervisory body for the Farm Credit System—and chooses an administrator—the Governor —to carry out those policies. The Federal Board is entrusted by Congress with the responsibility of attaining its objective of maintaining a soundly operated, efficient credit system that is in tune with the changing needs of farmers, ranchers, and other users of the System, now and in the future. In order to achieve this, the Federal Board approves all regulations and needed changes in regulations in order to provide up-to-date guidelines for the System's operations.

This process does not work automatically. If it is to work satisfactorily, member-users of the System must select well-qualified, broad-gauged directors who will represent them well. In order to do this, member-borrowers need to have sufficient information to understand how the System operates and of any problems it may have. Then members need to be urged to evaluate the information and the candidates and to exercise their votes. It is up to the System's user-members to choose carefully and well. They need to be reminded and encouraged to do so at every opportunity.

Chapter 10

BIPARTISAN SUPPORT

The Farm Credit System has generally made strenuous efforts to remain free from the influences of partisan politics, although some exceptions could be cited and the eruption of internal organizational politics has occurred more frequently. However, as a result of endeavoring to avoid partisan politics, the System has long enjoyed support in Congress and in the Executive branch of government, from both Democrats and Republicans.

Remaining even relatively free from politics has not been easy. For example, in 1933, when the Farm Credit Administration was set up and the Farm Credit System expanded to include Production Credit Associations and the Banks for Cooperatives, the Democrats had just regained control of the Government after being out of power for 12 years. The country was in the midst of the greatest depression on record, with many good Democrats and Republicans out of work. Most organizations in the Federal Government were requiring party clearance in order to obtain even low-grade jobs. Usually this was not so in the Farm Credit System.[1]

Myers and Goss both have cited conversations with Postmaster General James Farley, who was then chairman of the Democratic National Committee. Both pointed out that if a credit system was expected to operate successfully, politics could play no part in its operation. Myers particularly points out that Farley's reaction was that if he did a good job in running the Farm Credit System, that would be the best thing he could do for the party.

But, of course, politics never ends with the chairman of a political party. Many lesser lights in both parties from time to time have

---

[1] One FCA employee, for example, who was offered a better job by the top official of the Agricultural Adjustment Administration, was infuriated when his appointment was held up for three months awaiting party clearance. He kept saying, "When I came with the FCA, nobody asked me about my party affiliation!"

tried to use party influence either to obtain appointments or get approval of loans that might not otherwise be made. There were some exceptions in various places at various times, but in general the policy has been to resist such pressures, no matter from whence they came. And a record of resistance is what is important.

Myers in 1975[2] explained, "In important positions we in FCA attempted to get the best qualified men and, if possible, men acceptable to a Democratic Senator from that State. When this was impossible, Forbes Morgan was extremely helpful in getting Democratic political leaders to accept our judgment and approve the best man."[3] Myers in commenting on Morgan also said he was "an able and honorable businessman who served as political advisor and made an important contribution in the selection of highly qualified men for key positions."

However, an oft-told story in the halls of the Farm Credit Administration in those days was that when Myers recruited a new official for Farm Credit, he would say: "Forbes, I've decided we need this man. I do not know his politics. Please see that he is properly cleared." The story may not have been entirely accurate, but the climate that generated the story was a big morale builder for the organization.

This is not to say that there were no exceptions to this general rule. Relatively unimportant positions were found for a few exceptionally worthy Democrats, in order to keep certain members of Congress happy. But these were the exceptions and not the rule. Such people were not put in positions where their duties would have an important effect upon the operations of the organization.

Politics Involved in FCA Transfer to
U.S. Department of Agriculture

All signs point to the fact that the placing of the Farm Credit Administration in the Department of Agriculture in 1939 and the subsequent removal of F. F. Hill as its Governor and the resignation of Albert S. Goss as Land Bank Commissioner were the result of the political ambitions of Secretary of Agriculture Henry A. Wallace, who reputedly hoped to be nominated as the Democratic candidate for President if Franklin D. Roosevelt did not choose to run for a third term in 1940. This, and the subsequent drive to get Congress to

---

[2] Letter to the author, October 13, 1975.
[3] W. Forbes Morgan was an investment banker who had been National Treasurer of the Democratic Party and had close family relations with the White House. He served as Deputy Governor of the Farm Credit Administration.

change the nature of the Farm Credit System, and particularly the Land Banks, from a cooperative credit system to at least a quasi-government system, is discussed in greater detail under "Relationships with the U.S. Department of Agriculture," in Chapter 21, and "Controversy and Politics Rear Their Ugly Heads," in Chapter 27.

Other Political Pressures

Occasionally, there were political overtones in some of the appointments in the various Farm Credit districts. On one particular occasion in the early 1940s, the general agent in the Farm Credit Banks of a particular district went all the way to the White House to try to overturn Governor Black's appointment of a member of the district Farm Credit Board. He was unsuccessful.

A storm of protest arose when stories circulated that a deserving Democratic politician from Kentucky would be appointed Production Credit Commissioner to succeed the incumbent, Cap Arnold, who had had some differences of opinion with Governor Duggan. Duggan has strongly denied that such an appointment was planned. The person involved was made a Deputy Governor and it was observed that Duggan never gave him any really essential duties to perform. This, together with the fact he did not get Arnold's position when it became vacant two years later, would indicate that such had not been Duggan's intention. Arnold was actually succeeded by A. T. (Art) Esgate, an FCA career man who had held important posts for 18 years.

Bipartisan Support in 1953

However, another indication of the bipartisan support for the Farm Credit System came at the time of the passage of the Farm Credit Act of 1953, which again made the Farm Credit Administration an independent agency under the newly created, policy-making Federal Farm Credit Board. The original proposal had been to restrict the President's choices in making his appointments to that Board to the three district nominees made respectively by the Federal Land Bank Associations, the Production Credit Associations, and the cooperative stockholders in the Bank for Cooperatives. The constitutional lawyers had argued that it was unconstitutional to tie the hands of the President to that extent. Harold Cooley, then former Democratic Chairman of the House Agriculture Committee and currently the ranking minority member of the committee, stated that he agreed to change the wording to provide that the President should have to merely "consider" such nominees in making his appointments, only because he knew that the then incumbent of the White House— Dwight D. Eisenhower, a Republican—knew what Congress intended and that he would set a precedent by limiting his appointments to such nominees. Fortunately, President Eisenhower performed as Congressman Cooley had anticipated, and subsequent Presidents have followed that precedent.

Governor R. B. Tootell, who had been appointed head of the Farm Credit Administration in 1954 by the Federal Board appointed by President Eisenhower, reported that when he first met Secretary of Agriculture Orville Freeman, the incoming Democrat in 1961, Freeman asked him, "Is the Farm Credit Administration as untouchable as they tell me it is?" Tootell did not report his reply, but he remained as Governor until he reached retirement age 7 years later. The Farm Credit Act of 1953 had specified the President could ask the Federal Board to remove the Governor of the Farm Credit Administration as long as there was Government capital invested in the System. The implication was, particularly in view of the legislative history, that this provision was only to be used if the Government investment in the capital of the System was being threatened by poor supervision by the Farm Credit Administration.

Federal Board Reaffirmed Nonpartisan Control in 1973

In 1973, when stories circulated that some highly placed Republicans wanted to replace the then Governor E. A. Jaenke, the Federal Board adopted a resolution reaffirming the fact that the Farm Credit Administration and the Farm Credit System should remain untouchable by party politics.

Partly as a result of the Farm Credit System's insistence of remaining above partisan politics, whenever the System—as represented by the Federal Farm Credit Board—has gone to Congress with proposals for amending the law under which the System operates, it has received bipartisan consideration and support. This has been true even in the face of occasional opposition on details from its competitors and from the Budget Bureau (now called the Office of Management and Budget). On the few occasions when such proposals were not accepted by Congress, there usually was a powerful minority group in the System that was strongly opposed to such changes.

Overwhelming Support for 1971 Act

This support from Congress on a bipartisan basis is well illustrated by the passage of the Farm Credit Act of 1971 only a few months after the Federal Farm Credit Board proposed the bill. A few of the original provisions were modified. In most instances the changes resulted from the fact that some people within the System opposed them. Even though the Farm Credit Act of 1971 included rather broad changes in the operations and authorities of the System, and extended the System's services to several new fields, it is variously estimated that the Federal Farm Credit Board was successful in getting 85 percent of what it asked for. The votes in Congress demonstrated sweeping support for the System—331 to 19 in the House and by voice vote in the Senate.

Chapter 11

SYSTEM PERMANENT AND DEPENDABLE

The designers of the various parts of the cooperative Farm Credit System always planned it as a permanent System that would be in operation on an ongoing basis. And that is the way it has endeavored to operate over its 60-year span of life.

System a Yardstick—Not a Fire Department

However, starting in the period following the Great Depression, there have been times when some other lenders, in order to get back into the farm lending field in a bigger way, claimed that after all it was a Government system and as such it should operate only where and when other lenders did not wish to serve farmers. In other words, they would ask it to make loans to farmers and their cooperatives only when they were turned down by other lenders, or in emergency periods when they could not, or preferred not, to make loans.[1]

One point that such critics overlooked was that Congress, when it authorized the establishment of the various parts of the Farm Credit System, expected that they would operate as competitive yardsticks for other lenders at all times, and thus serve the interests of all farmers. It would be impossible for an organization to serve as such a yardstick unless it was in continuous operation. If farmers had to be refused service from the System when other lenders were willing to make their loans, the System could not operate at full efficiency. Thus, the yardstick would be contracted or expanded depending on the availability of credit from other sources. When money was in plentiful supply, the yardstick would be hidden in the closet, only available to borrowers other lenders did not want. Fortunately, Congress has never looked on any part of the Farm Credit System as a fire department to be used only in an emergency.

---

[1] This attitude still persists among some lenders.

A Dependable Source of Credit

The Farm Credit System has convinced most farmers, ranchers, and their cooperatives that it is a dependable source of credit. It is always there with the amount of credit that they need, regardless of general credit conditions throughout the country.[2] Nor is it affected by "tight" local credit conditions. Such dependability is particularly important to farmers and ranchers borrowing from Production Credit Associations, or cooperatives that are borrowing from Banks for Cooperatives, on a recurring year-to-year basis.

The System has long realized that in order to maintain its claim of providing a dependable source of credit at all times, it must have a steady inflow of funds from investors in the Nation's capital markets. To insure such a steady flow of credit from the reservoir of funds in adequate amounts—regardless of any upsurges in the demands of farmers and their cooperatives for sound loans—the System jealously guards its access to investors in the Nation's money markets. It also realizes its responsibility to maintain a strong financial position at all times.

Therefore, the System has placed strong emphasis on the building of adequate provision for possible loss and net worth reserves—usually technically referred to by accountants as surplus. It has also endeavored to make only loans that borrowers will find it possible to repay. The System is well aware that its reservoirs of credit would soon dry up if the back flow of funds fails to arrive on schedule.

It is easy to refer glibly to the dependability of the Farm Credit System, but over the years that dependability has been sorely tested, and it has taken much effort to maintain that reputation. The problems caused by recurring periods of droughts, floods, low prices for farm products, and high production costs have frequently been met and conquered.

The System has a well-earned reputation of staying with farmers, ranchers, and their cooperatives when they have difficulties. Members have come to appreciate that the System doesn't give up easily on a borrower who gets into trouble. The lenders that make up the System have an excellent record of working with their borrowers who are doing their best to repay their loans, when they have difficulty making payments on schedule. Foreclosures on borrowers' assets have been

---

[2] In the early history there were two exceptions. In 1921 the Land Banks had to virtually suspend operations during a court case testing the constitutionality of the Farm Loan Act. In the 1929 to 1933 Depression period, the Land Banks had to restrict new loans.

rare once farmers and their Land Banks recovered from the effects of the Great Depression and the dust bowl years of the 1930s.

Land Banks, Production Credit Associations, and the Banks for Cooperatives have long had policies of not giving up on their member-borrowers as long as they are doing their honest best and have any chance to recover. They want to keep farmers and their coopera-tives in business rather than make money by taking over their prop-erty. When borrowers do have to give up, the System tries to work with them—not only to protect the System—but also to salvage as much as possible for the borrowers.

The then current interpretation of this policy in mid-1975 was best expressed by FCA Governor W. Malcolm Harding in the July–August 1975 issue of *Farm Credits*. He said:

> ### Light at the End of the Tunnel
>
> With the current economic stress in some parts of agri-culture, it is not surprising that FCA, as the Government supervisory body for the FC System, is getting more com-plaints these days from farmers who have been turned down for a loan, or are having trouble repaying one. Doubtless, the well-earned reputation that the System has built up over the years for sticking with farmers through good times and bad is serving the System well during this period.
>
> Increasingly, the question is raised—Has the System changed its lending and loan service philosophy?
>
> Still, our answer is "No."
>
> First, one must understand that, although the System is Federally-chartered and sponsored and, therefore, has an ob-ligation to serve any farmer with a sound basis for credit, its obligation stops there. If there is to be subsidized credit, it necessarily must come from a source other than the Farm Credit System. The System has, on the other hand, an obli-gation not only to protect the investment of its farmer-owners, but to assure them a continuing, dependable source of credit. This not only is sound business, but is the essence of the co-operative basis of the System.
>
> Moreover, there are many occasions when making the loan would be a great disservice. In so doing, it is possible to create greater indebtedness that can result in further erosion or complete loss of the borrower's equity. If there is a change in today's agriculture, it is that a lifetime equity can be wiped out virtually overnight.
>
> Thus, whether it be in today's or yesterday's context, the System's policy of forbearance has remained unchanged. The FC System will stick with a farmer-borrower so long as there remains hope of his being able to work out of financial difficulties—so long as you can see light at the other end of the tunnel.

In the past, some of those lights probably have seemed to some members to be mere flickers at the end of mighty long tunnels, but many of them persevered and eventually burst into the shining sun.

Even with such policies, in the Great Depression years the Land Banks had to take over thousands of farms—because many farmers gave up and left their farms and the others had to be foreclosed because they could not overcome their financial difficulties. However, since 1945 they have had only 840 foreclosures compared to 1,298,000 loans made during those years.[3] During this period, due largely to rising land prices the Land Banks have more than recovered their previous losses. Production Credit Associations have had actual realized losses (net charge offs) of only $90 million or .07 percent of the $140 billion they loaned since their organization in 1933. When valuation reserves of $275 million for estimated future losses are added, the rate goes up to .26 percent of the total loaned. The Banks for Cooperatives' actual realized losses have been $7.8 million or .02 percent of the $50 billion loaned, and reserves of $29 million for estimated future losses on loans now on the books up that rate to .07 percent of the total loaned.

Former Governor Myers' comments regarding the success of the Farm Credit System are the following:

> The FCA was organized at the bottom of the greatest economic depression in history. The land banks had [practically] failed because of inadequate financial strength to withstand bad years.[4] Major factors in the phenomenal growth have been improving economic conditions and the upward general trend of prices, since 1933—combined with sound conservative management of Farm Credit banks. In spite of the mild deflation after World War II and the booms and recessions since that time, the . . . [System] has not been tested by a severe deflation. We are now near the peak of a long period of generally rising prices that began in 1933. . . .
>
> Times of inflation mean high risk and require sound lending policies and maintenance of generous net worth. . . . [The Farm Credit System] has done a great job, due to good luck and good management. . . . [There is] danger of over-optimism because of its record. Low interest rates require no

---

[3] Annual Reports of the Farm Credit Administration, 1946 to 1975, Government Printing Office, Washington, D.C.

[4] Based on other observations by Myers, additional reasons for the Land Banks' financial troubles were that their original capital was too small—$750,000 each—it had to be repaid to the Government too rapidly, earnings were used to pay dividends instead of building adequate reserves, and the emphasis Congress put on small loans resulted in too many loans in marginal farming areas and poor loans in other areas.

doubt of repayment on time of all loans of all Farm Credit units.

He went on to say that directors and officers have a great responsibility in such times.

Chapter 12

ADAPTING LOANS TO FARMERS' NEEDS

One of the basic reasons farmers and ranchers have had for building, owning, and sharing in the control of their own credit cooperatives is to find ways to provide themselves with credit service that can serve their needs most efficiently and effectively.

Sound, Safe, and Constructive Loans

When they were asking Congress to establish the Federal Land Banks in 1916, farm leaders stressed that mortgages on good farms were so safe that they would be excellent collateral for selling bonds to investors. From that start, and with its dependence on the investment market for lending funds, it is not surprising that the cooperative Farm Credit System has always insisted that its rôle is solely in the field of making "sound loans" to farmers, ranchers, their cooperatives, and more recently also to fishermen, farm-related businesses, and nonfarm rural home owners.

A simplified definition of a "sound" loan[1] would be that it is a loan the lender—after careful analysis—expects the borrower can and will repay. It also is constructive credit usually because the loan is expected to be used by the borrower in such a way that it will produce income to repay the loan with interest and enough more to leave the borrower a profit from using the loan. Exceptions to this profit rule might be loans to nonfarm rural home owners. They are chiefly interested in obtaining homes at reasonable cost.

"Soft loans," on the other hand, would be those that such lenders as the Farmers Home Administration, for example, would make to borrowers whose weak or poor financial condition, or other factors, raise serious questions as to their ability to repay. These loans, be-

---

[1] Visitors from other countries who come to study the System ask what a "noise loan" is all about!

cause of the social implications involved, are made to give borrowers a chance to try to improve their operations, their income, and thus their standard of living. Loans of this type usually need to be accompanied by costly technical assistance if they are to accomplish their aim of helping borrowers improve their income. It is generally recognized that the probable rate of loss on such loans plus the cost of supervision will be higher than a business-type organization could afford to absorb. Such loans probably can be justified to help young farmers get started or to reduce the number of farm families who are likely to be displaced and forced to go on welfare in the country or in an urban area unless they get assistance in improving their farming operations. However, because of the risk and cost involved, such loans should be and are made from Government funds.

The cooperative Farm Credit System emphasizes the necessity of making only sound loans for two reasons. First, the System is dependent on investors for its loan funds and has to be sure it can repay them on schedule. Secondly, in its view, only a loan that is sound from the standpoint of the lender can be counted on to be safe from the standpoint of the borrower in normal business circumstances.

The System's credit specialists point out that lending anyone more money than he has a reasonably good chance of being able to repay can do him more harm than good. If a borrower cannot pay the interest on a loan and eventually the principal, the loan may result in increasing his debt load to the point where the creditor has to force the borrower to liquidate his business in order to collect the money. This, of course, jeopardizes the borrower's equity and puts him out of business.

One friend of the System, C. Maurice Wieting, retired Vice President for Information of the Ohio Farm Bureau Federation,[2] reminds us that in the Great Depression of the 1930s the System—especially the Land Banks—made many loans to farmers whose heavy debt loads made them relatively poor credit risks. It should be remembered that most farmers had gotten heavily in debt because of the all-time, disastrously low prices of farm products through the years. In order to try to save as many farmers as possible from foreclosure, the Land Banks were authorized to make second mortgage loans—usually behind Land Bank loans—on behalf of the Government-owned Federal Farm Mortgage Corporation, up to 75 percent of the *normal* value of the farm—then frequently above market prices. Since it was antici-

---

[2]Previously, Wieting also served as Director of Information of the National Council of Farmer Cooperatives.

pated that prices of farm products would return to normal, it was hoped that many farmers could eventually repay their debts.

Farm prices did not fully return to their normal levels until the World War II days—the 1940s. However, a large proportion of those refinanced farmers did pull through. But the continued subnormal prices and two of the worst drought years on record—which created the fabled Dust Bowl on the Great Plains and much of the Corn Belt—took its toll on thousands of farm families who either gave up and abandoned their farms or lost them by foreclosure. Since those days the Land Banks have acquired very few farms—6 in 1974 and 15 in 1975 fiscal years. In contrast, over 97 percent of the farmer-borrowers from the Land Banks have paid their installments on time for several years and in some years have exceeded 98 percent.

An additional point which credit specialists in the System have long and frequently emphasized is that credit is no substitute for income. In other words, if the borrowed money is used for something that does not produce enough income to pay the principal and interest, the cost of borrowing will have to be paid from income from other sources and thus the borrower can be in worse condition than he was before he borrowed if he doesn't have other sources of income.

Constructive, Wise Use of Credit

Because the cooperative Farm Credit System's job is to serve farmers, it is not merely interested in lending money and getting it back. It also is anxious to have its member-borrowers benefit from the use of the credit it extends and has an obligation to help them do so. Therefore, the question arises, what can credit do for its users? That can vary widely, depending on what the member-borrowers want to accomplish with their loans and how wisely or constructively the individual borrower uses his credit.

Frequently, mention is made that credit can be used to increase income by increasing production. But that may not necessarily be why the borrower needs or wants to borrow money. It is but one possible wise or constructive use of credit. There are many other possibilities.

For example, the 60-year-old farmer who has successfully built and developed an efficient-sized business that is producing sufficient income may merely want to use credit to continue to farm at his present level of production. All he needs or wants is a loan big enough to meet his high seasonal operating costs—to buy seed, fertilizer, and chemicals, to replace some worn-out equipment, to pay for hired labor, to meet his tax and insurance bills, plus some money to meet family expenses including his son's or daughter's college expenses. If his net income from his farm production is large enough to repay the loan and the interest, he will be getting the benefit of his normal income and if other credit factors such as his management ability and financial condition are satisfactory, it may well be a sound loan.

Other farmers may invest borrowed capital to increase their net income without necessarily increasing the size of their operation or their production. If their gross income exceeds any added costs, they reap benefits from the use of credit. Such possibilities are many.

The desired results may be attained by using credit to reduce operating costs. Some examples include borrowing to buy or replace machinery or equipment to reduce high labor costs—substituting capital for labor—borrowing in order to take advantage of quantity discounts or lower prices by placing advance orders for such items as fertilizer.

Credit also may be used to increase income by paying the cost of shifting from low return enterprises to those that are more profitable when there are long-term changes in the supply and demand relationships. Such uses of credit may not necessarily increase total production.

When farmers use their loans to buy more land from neighboring farmers to make greater and more efficient use of their heavy equipment or an underutilized labor supply and management skills, they may be increasing the production of their family units. However, they may not be increasing total production.

In addition, farmers and ranchers may use some of their borrowing capacity to increase their production and thus their incomes in a variety of ways. These include such things as buying better but more expensive seed, more fertilizer, larger quantities of more costly chemicals, higher producing livestock, and better livestock feed.

The constructive uses to which cooperatives can put credit are somewhat similar to those used by their farmer and rancher members and vary almost as widely. They include using credit to continue their normal operations, to improve the efficiency of current operations, to buy better or more effective equipment or to replace some that is worn out or obsolete, to add new services to present members, and to expand or merge to serve more members.

No matter how the credit is used, an important test of how wisely it is used is whether it achieves the aims of the borrower and produces enough income to repay the loan with interest—and still leave some extra margin to cover the risks involved.

PCAs Depart from Collateral Lending

Until the Production Credit Associations began operating, most short-term lenders decided on how much money they would loan depending chiefly on how much money they thought they could recover if they had to sell the personal property the farmers gave as collateral. Such collateral was in the form of mortgages on such things as equipment and livestock and liens on growing crops. However, Production Credit Associations developed a different method of making credit decisions. They decided that the man, his financial condition, his management ability, how he was going to use his loan, and his repayment capacity were more important than the collateral he might be able to give.

Production Credit Associations realized that they would be doing a farmer no favor if they had to take possession of his crops, livestock, or equipment in order to get their money back. If that became necessary, it would mean the farmer would either be put out of business, or his farming operations would have to be seriously curtailed as a result of the Association's collecting its loan.

When it came to the man factor in analyzing an application for a loan, the Association wanted to be sure of his honesty and integrity. For example, they would check on his reputation for paying his bills.

When it came to judging a man's management capability, his past production records were important. His performance record in getting ahead financially could be determined by comparing his financial condition with earlier statements, if available, to see if his net worth was growing. This philosophy is even more valid today.

In order to determine a man's financial condition, Production Credit Associations began asking for a financial statement which would show what he owned and what he owed. If this resulted in a reasonable cushion of net worth, the loan should be relatively safe for both the farmer-borrower and his Association.

As far as the purposes for borrowing were concerned, Production Credit Associations began asking for a list of expected income and expenses and divided the expenses into three categories—necessities, needs, and wants. Necessities are items that have to be financed in order for the farmer to carry on his farming operation. These include such things as seed, feed, fertilizer, spray materials, repairs, the cost of hired labor, taxes, fire insurance on buildings, and family living expenses.

Production Credit Associations classified needs as those things that the farmer-borrower could well use in his farming operation, but at the same time could do without, or at least delay, without curtailing his farming operation.

Wants are classified as things that would be nice to have if the money was available, such as extra cars, radios, TVs, and new furniture.

Naturally, necessities are the first things that have to be included in any financing package. The Associations lend the farmer money to buy or invest in items in the need category if he is in a sufficiently strong financial condition that there is no question that he will be able to repay that additional portion of the loan without difficulty. They also lend for items in the want category when the borrower is in very strong financial condition.

In the early days, the Production Credit Associations sent out a representative, usually then called an inspector, to look over each farmer's operation to get a better idea of how the farmer was carrying on his operation and whether he actually had all the assets that he showed on his financial statement. Such a representative would then make a report which would be submitted with other information to the Association's loan committee. Each loan committee consisted of two farmer-directors and the secretary-treasurer, now called the manager or president. This loan committee would decide whether a loan should be made and for how much. As time passed, and the Production Credit Associations developed highly trained credit personnel and had a great deal of experience with a large proportion of their member-borrowers, they modified these procedures in various ways. In the case of relatively small loans, the board of directors may give the manager or credit specialist the right to approve loan applications up to some specified figure. Another variation is for the loan committee, before the season starts, to approve a line of credit for the larger borrowers who have a relatively good record with the Association and who remain in strong financial condition. The Associations still make periodic farm visits.

Banks for Cooperatives Chart New Courses

When the Banks for Cooperatives started operation in 1933, they entered troubled waters. In most areas of the country there were plenty of farmer cooperatives. The Cooperative Research, Education, and Service Subdivision of the Farm Credit Administration, which was a line descendant of the Cooperative Marketing Division of the U.S. Department of Agriculture that had been established in 1926 by the Cooperative Marketing Act of that year, estimated there were 10,800. By 1974 there were only 7,768, as estimated by that same organization, now called the Farmer Cooperative Service of the U.S. Department of Agriculture.[3] But today's cooperatives are much larger, stronger, and more effective than those of 40 years earlier. In areas such as the South where cooperatives had left many blank spaces 40 years ago, farmers now are well served by cooperatives.

The newly established Banks for Cooperatives' domain in 1932 was inhabited by many long-established, successful local marketing and farm supply cooperatives. There were also a few well- and favorably known regional and federated cooperative organizations such as the California Fruit Growers Exchange, now Sunkist Growers; California Walnut Growers Exchange, now Diamond Walnut Growers, Inc.; California Fruit Exchange, Challenge Creameries, Inc., at Los Angeles; and a group of West Coast egg marketing cooperatives that maintained a highly successful East Coast federated marketing organization known as Pacific Egg Producers that sold top quality, carefully graded eggs in East Coast markets for premium prices. Spreading out from the East Coast were a group of farm supply regionals which included Eastern States Farmers and Cooperative Grange League Federation Exchange (GLF) which merged in the 1960s to form Agway, Inc.; Missouri Farmers Association and the Midwest Farm Bureau farm supply cooperatives, including what are now Landmark in Ohio, Farm Bureau Services in Michigan, FS Services, then only in Illinois; the Indiana Farm Bureau Cooperative Association; and the pioneer in promoting sweet cream butter—Land O' Lakes Creameries.[4]

There were also a few struggling nationwide cooperatives organized from the top down by the Federal Farm Board—rather than by local cooperatives. These included the National Livestock Producers, National Wool Marketing Corporation, Farmers National Grain Corporation, and the American Cotton Cooperative Association. But there were thousands of small, weak cooperatives throughout the country. Hundreds of zealously organized and operated cooperatives had come and gone. They left behind a reputation of cooperative failures. It was a legacy that had to be lived down.

Under the leadership of Frank Peck and later Samuel Sanders

---

[3] For more details on Farmer Cooperative Service, see "Farmer Cooperative Service" in Chapter 21 and "Farmer Cooperative Service on FCA Team" in Chapter 26.

[4] Consumers Cooperative Association, Kansas City, now Farmland Industries, the Nation's largest farm supply cooperative, was just getting started.

from the Washington Egg and Poultry Cooperative—successive Co-operative Bank Commissioners in the Farm Credit Administration—the Banks for Cooperatives' presidents and their boards of directors soon recognized that beyond the effects of the Great Depression, the causes of longer term weakness and failures of many cooperatives included poor management, lack of member understanding and support, and inadequate financing.

It was easy to see why many cooperatives had failed and why local commercial bankers had been wary of lending much money to cooperatives. It did not take long or require much persuasion for the Banks for Cooperatives to realize they needed to look at such factors as membership support and management capability, as well as the current financial condition in analyzing loan applications.

Peck and Sanders soon realized the need to organize, or help organize in collaboration with other organizations, many educational and training meetings, conferences, and workshops for cooperative directors, managers, and staff specialists as a means of strengthening the credit base for their loans. Such activities still continue because the need for educational programs never ends. As Owen Hallberg, President of the American Institute of Cooperation, puts it, "We are addressing a passing parade."

In order to help farmers increase equities in their cooperatives and give them a stronger financial base, Sanders urged farm coopera-tives to pay patronage refunds in equity securities that could be paid off—revolved—when the cooperative accumulated enough capital to do so. In the case of marketing cooperatives, he urged the accomplish-ment of the same objective by having them make capital retains for each unit marketed. This program became an important factor in many cooperatives strengthening their capital base which enabled them to expand their services.

Credit at Reasonable Cost

One of the cooperative Farm Credit System's original and con-tinuing objectives is to make credit available to farmers, ranchers, and their cooperatives at reasonable cost—the lowest cost possible that is consistent with building and maintaining a strong financial structure. One of the ways the System uses to try to reach this objective is by reflecting the wholesale cost of money in the Nation's financial markets and adding thereto only the actual cost of operating the banks and associations of the System plus the amounts needed to build adequate valuation and net worth reserves. The latter reserves the accountants usually refer to as "surplus." The bylaws of the individual local credit associations and their district Farm Credit Banks all provide for returning net margins above the operating costs and the amounts needed for building adequate net worth reserves to the users of the System either in the form of dividends or as patronage refunds.

Savings Returned to Member-Borrowers

Since 1945, the Farm Credit System has returned a total of $516 million of savings to its users in the form of dividends and patronage refunds, either in cash or in evidences of equity that will be revolved out and paid in cash at a later date. This total includes $147.7 million to members of Land Bank Associations; $75.1 million to members of Production Credit Associations; and $15.3 million to other financing institutions using the services of the Intermediate Credit Banks since 1957. In addition, the Banks for Cooperatives have returned $277.9 million to cooperatives obtaining loans from them which, of course, have accrued to the benefit of their farmer-members. These returns of net margins to the users of the Farm Credit System, of course, have resulted in reducing further the actual cost of credit.

Limits on Interest Rates Removed

Originally, Congress provided that the Land Banks could not charge more than 1 percent above what they had to pay investors for their loan funds and in no case more than 6 percent, which was about the going rate on commercial loans at the time and thus considered reasonable.

However, prior to the establishment of the Land Banks, farmers in many areas were paying considerably higher rates. In Texas the *average* rate on farm mortgages in 1915 was reported to be 10 percent—the highest average for any state. According to the first annual report of the Federal Farm Loan Board in 1917, the Land Bank interest rate was 5 percent. The Board also thought it was incumbent on the Land Banks to pay dividends to farmer-borrowers through their National Farm Loan Associations as soon as possible. Its attention undoubtedly should have been focused on building reserves so badly needed by the new organizations.

The 6 percent maximum limitation on Land Bank loans remained in effect until the mid-1960s when the general level of interest rates in the financial markets where the Land Banks sell their bonds approached 6 percent. At that point Congress removed that limitation.

As the average-sized loan has increased over the years and the total dollar volume of loans has risen, the Land Banks and Associations have had no difficulty in operating within the limited margin Congress has prescribed.

In the case of the Federal Intermediate Credit Banks, Congress specified they should not pay more than 6 percent interest on their debentures—now bonds. This limit also had to be removed as the general level of interest rates rose in 1966.

Availability of Credit Even More Important Than Cost

As interest rates generally continued to reach successive record high levels in the 1965 to 1975 period, most farmers, ranchers, and co-operatives, while they did not like paying high interest rates, found that having an adequate supply of credit when it was needed was even more important than the cost of money.

Member-borrowers from the Farm Credit System at least have the assurance that interest rates will be no higher than necessary because their variable rate loans will go down if the cost of money to the System declines. In addition, they know that any margins beyond those that are actually necessary will be returned to them in the form of dividends and patronage refunds.

Income Needed to Build Reserves

That part of the interest income which is used to build adequate net worth reserves is important to both present and future members. Reserves benefit members in many ways. First, the reserves by strengthening the financial structure of the Banks tend to keep the interest rates that the Farm Credit Banks have to pay to investors for lending funds as low as possible. Secondly, reserves help to insure the continued capacity of the Banks to operate and serve present and future members. Third, reserves help to hold down members' interest rates, by lowering the average cost of money to the Banks and by providing them with interest-free capital with which to make loans.

The last point is well illustrated by an incident that occurred during the tight money period of 1966. At that time the Land Banks had not begun to charge interest on their loans on a variable rate basis. Some of the competitors of the Land Banks were spreading the word that the Banks were in deep trouble because they had so many long-term loans outstanding at interest rates below the then current cost of money. This happened at the same time Fred Gilmore, Deputy Governor and Director of the Land Bank Service of the Farm

Credit Administration,[5] began to publicly call attention to the fact that the Land Banks had had the foresight to build large reserves that were keeping their average cost of money within manageable limits. The adverse stories soon stopped being circulated.

Loan Fees Related to Costs

As part of the whole idea of keeping the cost of credit to farmers and ranchers as low as possible, the Land Banks and Production Credit Associations have tried to keep any loan fees at a minimum that is closely related to the actual cost of the services provided.

The Production Credit Associations help to reduce credit costs to their members by only charging interest on each dollar for the actual number of days that it is outstanding. Thus, the budgeted loans and lines of credit provided by the Production Credit Associations make it possible for farmers to arrange for credit for the whole season without having to pay interest on the full amount for the entire period. Money is advanced to borrower-members as they need it and is repaid as they receive income from the sale of their products.

Another factor which reduces the cost of credit to member-borrowers of the Production Credit Associations and Banks for Cooperatives is that they have the use of all the money they borrow rather than having to use some of it to maintain minimum balances. Some might counter that on the other hand Production Credit Associations' and Banks for Cooperatives' members do have to own stock in proportion to the size of their loans. However, this stock entitles them to their share in the savings from their lending organizations that are returned to them in the form of dividends on their stock or patronage refunds. Increasingly over the years, the cooperative Farm Credit System has tended to reduce or hold down the credit costs to farmers, ranchers, and their cooperatives who borrow from other lenders, because their rates are strongly influenced by the rates charged by the cooperative Farm Credit System.

Conditions Dictated Separate Organizations

In the early days of the Federal Land Banks, an appraiser hired by the Farm Loan Board, and later the Farm Credit Administration,

---

[5] Gilmore had long service in the Federal Land Bank of Omaha, including some as Vice President, before assuming this position in the Farm Credit Administration in 1958. From 1961 to 1968 he was President of the Omaha Stockyards Company, then he resumed his position of Land Bank Commissioner in the Farm Credit Administration from which he retired in 1972.

would visit each farm and make an appraisal of its value as a basis for determining how much money the Land Bank would lend on the property. Up until 1933, such appraisals tended to be based on the market value of the property as judged by such a trained appraiser. In 1933, market values were extremely low; in fact, many farms could not have been sold at any price. At that time, it was decided the loans would be based on appraised *normal* agricultural values.

In general, normal values were those which could be justified on the basis of the production capacity of the farm under normal farm product prices and normal costs of production, supplies, and operating expenses. Actually, during the Depression such normal values were frequently sufficiently above the existing market values that the resulting loan was equal to or greater than the current market value. Such appraisal policies helped enable the Land Banks to lend enough money to individual farmers to refinance their scaled down, existing debts.[6] To help accomplish this, the Federal Land Banks were handling what were then known as Land Bank Commissioner loans and were empowered to make either first or second mortgage loans on behalf of first the Land Bank Commissioner and then the Federal Farm Mortgage Corporation, which together with other debts could not exceed 75 percent of the appraised normal value of the property. At that time Land Bank loans were limited to 50 percent of the value of the land plus 20 percent of the insured value of the buildings.

Land Bank Commissioner loans originally could not exceed $5,000. The amount was later increased to $7,500. In practice, the Land Banks in many cases took first mortgages on the property in combination with a second mortgage Land Bank Commissioner loan made on behalf of the newly created Federal Farm Mortgage Corporation.

When the Federal Farm Mortgage Corporation stopped making new loans in 1947 and was placed in liquidation because it was no longer needed, Congress authorized the Federal Land Banks to make first mortgage loans up to 65 percent of the appraised normal value of the farm property, including the buildings. Later, Congress authorized the Land Banks to lend an additional amount to cover the cost of buying the 5 percent stock required from each borrower to invest in his local National Farm Loan Association (now Federal Land Bank Association).

---

[6] County debt adjustment committees helped get creditors to agree to scale downs of farmers' debts. For details see "Farmers' Debts Scaled Down" in Chapter 26.

Appraisals Lagged Behind Market Values

After the prices of farm products rose during and following World War II and during the Korean War, and as it became increasingly unlikely that farm prices would decline to their former levels, it was necessary from time to time to change the level of normal values of farms, based on higher and higher average prices received for farm products. Such adjustments were made by the Farm Credit Administration rather reluctantly and lagged far behind the need for them. As a result, the maximum the Land Banks could lend on farms frequently was less than 50 percent of the market value of the property.

For many years, the Farm Credit Administration's Research Division, in cooperation with the Appraisal staff in Washington, made studies of the long-term trends in prices farmers received for their farm products as an aid to estimating the value of farms in terms of the amount of farm income they would produce and how much of that income would be available to repay debts. In addition, the Appraisal Subdivision of the Land Bank Division of the Farm Credit Administration made many field studies to keep track of the productivity of farms and their market prices. About 1950, the Appraisal Subdivision, in cooperation with the Federal Land Banks, began setting up benchmark farms on which they obtained detailed data on a continuing basis as an aid to arriving at normal agricultural values in various areas of the country.

Over a long period of continuing rising prices it became more and more evident that the normal value concept for appraising farms would always lag behind the actual conditions on the farm, because they were based on price levels over a past period of time. With few interruptions, farm land values were continually rising. Finally, in the Farm Credit Act of 1971, on the recommendation of the Federal Farm Credit Board, the *normal* value requirement was dropped, and appraisals began to be much more influenced by current market prices of farm land.

The 1971 Act also raised the top limit on the size of Land Bank loans from 65 percent of the appraised value to 85 percent. The previous limitations of 65 percent of the appraised *normal* value almost automatically kept loans low enough so that there was little danger that the Land Banks would loan too heavily. Under the new limitations, the margin for error has been greatly increased. Now, the Land Banks and Associations have to weigh much more carefully such factors as the borrower's management ability, his financial position, the nature of his farming operation, and individual farming industry trends.

The Land Banks do not intend, nor are they expected, to loan every farmer the full 85 percent limit on the value of his property. Rather, there is considerable room for credit judgment to be made. The Banks endeavor to make loans up to the full 85 percent of the appraised value of the property only in cases where the farmer has demonstrated a high degree of management ability, and other factors are favorable.

In 1974, 50 percent of loans were made for less than 70 percent of the appraised value. Another 38 percent fell in the range between 70 and 79 percent.

The normal value concept for making long-term farm mortgage loans served its purpose well during the Depression years, when the prices of farm land and the products produced were at abnormally low levels. However, that concept gradually outlived its usefulness. In fact, looking back, the Farm Credit System under the strong influence of the supervisory agency—the Farm Credit Administration— took much too long in abandoning that concept. Thus, FCA's adherence to the normal value concept for many years prevented the Land Banks and Land Bank Associations from being anywhere near as much service to farmers as they should have been and, in most cases, wanted to be.

Credit Specialists Tailor Loans to Individual Farmer's Needs

One of the highly important factors in the success of the Farm Credit System has been that it has specialized in making loans to farmers and adapting its operations and loan terms to the needs of individual farmers. Since all its credit specialists are engaged only in making loans to farmers, ranchers, and their cooperatives—and since 1971 also to commercial fishermen and rural home owners— they become specialists in adapting loan terms to the individual needs of the System's borrowers. This is particularly important in modern times when conditions are changing so rapidly and the nature of the farming business is in a continual state of change. The terms and conditions for loans that might have particularly fitted the needs of farmers 10 years ago do not necessarily meet those farmers' needs today. And tomorrow's needs also will be different from today's.

Since the cooperative Farm Credit System is owned and controlled by farmers, its operating officers, as well as the boards of directors who make the policies for it, are particularly aware of the changes that are occurring in farming and sensitive thereto. They are continually looking for better ways to serve farmers' needs. However, even with this objective, one of the best informed credit specialists in the country feels that while the Farm Credit System is still the leader and pacesetter in the field, it hasn't had enough imagination and innovativeness to keep up with rapidly changing needs of farmers and ranchers in the last 10 to 15 years. In his judgment, the System's credit specialists have not been able to develop the skills of sophisticated loan analysis rapidly enough to keep up with changing needs. He believes their lack of skills development results in their having to be overly conservative in order to protect the System. In the process, they are missing the opportunity to do more constructive lending.

Fortunately, this same observer feels some of the Farm Credit Banks are recognizing the need to upgrade the skills of their staffs. He says they are willing to spend the kind of money that is needed to provide top quality training. They are also carrying on dynamic recruiting programs that aim at hiring university graduates from the very top of their classes, no matter what it takes to get them. In planning for the future, these Banks are determined to have the best available talent. He believes that many of the Intermediate Credit Banks have progressed further in these directions than all but one or two Land Banks because they have given more consistent attention and emphasis to their recruiting and training programs for a longer period of years.

Chapter 13

DELEGATING RESPONSIBILITY AS CLOSE
TO THE GRASS ROOTS AS POSSIBLE

Today, it is a generally accepted principle that the Farm Credit System should be run by farmers, and that the policy and operating decisions should be made as close to home—on the firing line—as feasible. Over the last 60 years, most of the discussions on this policy of the Farm Credit System's operations have not been whether the principle is sound, but on where to draw the line between district or local policy and operation and supervision.

Congress, in passing the original Federal Farm Loan Act in 1916, made it quite clear that it expected the Federal Land Banks and the Federal Land Bank Associations to become a cooperative credit system in which farmers would have the responsibility of organizing and operating their local associations, and in owning and having a voice in running their district Federal Land Banks. However, the Act itself contained many restrictions and limitations on the Banks' operations. That isn't surprising since Congress was embarking on uncharted waters and it wanted to ensure the success of the System. With no experience to draw from, it provided too much restriction in some areas and not enough in others. For example, it limited mortgage loans to $5,000 but let any 10 borrowers form a local association.

Farm Loan Board Had Reservations

The original Federal Farm Loan Board reacted very similarly. For example, in its first annual report, the Board said,[1] "This Board recognizes and appreciates the cooperative features of the Farm Loan Act and the intention of Congress that these banks should ulti-

---

[1] First Annual Report of the Federal Farm Loan Board, Government Printing Office, Washington, D.C., 1918, p. 12.

115

mately become links in a great cooperative chain. For these reasons, it is entirely proper that the Farm Loan Associations should ultimately name two-thirds of the directors." However, the Federal Farm Loan Board rightfully was conscious of its responsibilities of protecting the Government's investment in the 12 Federal Land Banks, and for seeing that the new credit system was successful in accomplishing the aims that Congress had set for it. It went on to recommend an amendment to the Act that would provide that the Government should name a majority of each Bank's board of directors as long as the Government owned a majority of its stock. It also was careful to see that plenty of guidelines, policy matters, and regulations were decided upon in Washington.

Myers Believed in System's Cooperative Destiny

There probably was no one who believed more in the destiny of the Farm Credit System as a cooperatively owned and operated system than Bill Myers. And he was careful to see that strong cooperative features were written into the Act setting up the Production Credit Associations and the Banks for Cooperatives.[2] He was sure that such a System would serve farmers well and would have great potential for improving the health of the general economy.

Myers preached the idea of a cooperative credit system on every occasion. He did so well at it that his concept became thoroughly ingrained in the System, even though there have been occasional instances of officials who have forgotten this basic principle. For example, in the fall of 1935, in his speech to the American Farm Bureau Federation's annual meeting, Myers made a strong effort to get the Federation *not* to ask for a continuation of the then emergency subsidized interest rate being provided by Congress on the Federal Land Bank loans. Even the Farm Bureau leadership of Ed O'Neil, its longtime President, was strongly advocating a continuance of this temporary emergency subsidy for Land Bank borrowers. The main thrust of Myers' argument for abandoning this policy was that the Farm Credit System had been designed to be a *cooperative* credit system. As such, it should no longer have subsidies from the Government but should stand on its own feet.

---

[2] One example is that the Farm Credit Act of 1933, to assure that control remained in the hands of active members, provided that a PCA member who did not have a loan for 2 years would have his Class B voting stock converted to Class A non-voting stock.

Myers was completely committed to the philosophy and concept that the System should be controlled by farmers and their representatives at the local Association and district Bank levels, and that they should have the authority and responsibility necessary to carry out such duties. However, he was still conscious of the fact that it was up to the Farm Credit Administration to protect the Government's investments in the System, particularly those in the Production Credit Associations and Banks for Cooperatives, which were new and untried organizations with officers and directors who had not yet been tested. He also was determined that the System would justify the Government's temporary investment in its capital by successfully carrying out the assignments Congress had given it.

Myers continually endeavored to gain acceptance for the concept that the System was to be owned and run by farmers and ranchers for their benefit. However, when he felt it necessary to protect the Government's or the farmers' interests, he did not hesitate to do so. In most instances, he found it possible to do so by providing strong leadership and by counseling and advising with district directors and Bank officials.

Training for Authority Begins

In this period, much of the relatively close supervision was in itself a form of training, and was looked upon in that vein. Even in this emergency period, Myers provided leadership to develop a training program that looked to the future. In 1934, when night work, not just a few hours' overtime, was common practice, Myers set up a whole group of evening courses for employees of the Farm Credit Administration in Washington, to be taken on a voluntary basis. But at the same time, he was thinking in terms of training the whole organization including the actual farmer-borrowers.

Meaningful Annual Meetings Part of Program

For example, before the first year's annual Production Credit Association meetings were scheduled, he borrowed Ted Clauson, a membership relations specialist for the Cooperative GLF Exchange—now Agway, Inc.—to come to Washington to help make the overall plans for that series of annual meetings. He wanted to be sure that the farmers understood that the Associations belonged to them and they had an important part to play in their operation. As part of that program, Clauson, working with "Cap" Arnold and the Production Credit Division membership relations specialist, Cameron Garman, devised a set of charts to explain the organization of the System and report on the year's financial results. These charts, which included condensed financial statements, were made large enough so they could be read by audiences of several hundred people.

By 1935, the Land Bank Division of the Farm Credit Administration also was working with the Federal Land Banks to develop meaningful annual meetings and other member relations programs for the National Farm Loan Associations—now Federal Land Bank Associations. It recruited W. A. Cleveland from the Federal Land Bank of St. Paul and former Professor of Agricultural Economics at North Dakota A&M College—now North Dakota State University—to work with the Land Banks to develop such programs.

First Training Courses Developed

The following year, Arnold and Garman, under Commissioner Garwood's leadership, prepared a kit of four courses for the Production Credit portion of the System, to be given over a 2-day period. These courses covered subject matters such as the history of the Farm Credit System, operation, credit, and membership and public relations. The courses were tested first on members of the Production Credit Division staff in Washington. Then, in a team effort with the secretaries of the district Production Credit Corporations, the courses were given to the staffs of the Production Credit Corporations and the directors and managers of the local Production Credit Associations.

But this program did not stop there. For several years these training courses, or shortened versions, were given for new personnel in the districts and Associations. As the districts learned from experience, they developed and carried on their own continuing training programs.

Frequent Conferences Part of Training

Beyond course work, the Farm Credit Administration held frequent conferences for officers of the districts' organizations, which to a large extent were training as well as planning sessions. They in turn held at least annual conferences of boards of directors and managers of the local Associations. From these beginnings, the Farm Credit System developed a variety of training programs for district and Association personnel. As they became more affluent and experienced, these programs became more sophisticated and used more and more outside talent to inspire and upgrade the knowledge and ability of the people involved.

Such programs from the first were aimed at training people to be able to accept more and more responsibility and authority. As these objectives were accomplished, with a few interruptions, such authority and responsibility was delegated first to the districts and then by most of them to their local Associations. In the policy-making field, it was the boards of directors who assumed these additional authorities and responsibilities; in the operating field, it was the chief executives.

Were Training Programs Successful?

Has this combination of training and delegation of authority and responsibility worked in actual operation? In 1940, which was past the peak, the Farm Credit Administration had over 1,400 employees. By 1975, when the volume of business was many times as large, the number of employees on the FCA payroll was down to 221. The story in the Farm Credit districts is very similar. The number of employees in the district banks followed the same trend. By 1975, even though business had continued to multiply both in the amount of money loaned and the number of farmers and cooperatives having loans, they had an average of only 212 employees.

The Land Banks made the largest reductions in their personnel as they built stronger, more capable local associations and gave them more authority and responsibility. The increased authority given to Production Credit Associations and the accompanying reductions in personnel of the Production Credit Corporations and Intermediate Credit Banks were considerable, but not as striking, because the local Production Credit Associations had had much more responsibility from the beginning and the Production Credit Corporations and the Federal Intermediate Credit Banks had never had staffs as large as those of the Land Banks.

Did Overemphasis on Economy Mar Effectiveness?

The continued drive for economy—during three decades—that went along with these programs in the Farm Credit Administration and the System went too far and lasted too long, in the opinion of many observers. These observers feel that the devotion to economy at all levels prevented many associations, district banks, and the Farm

Credit Administration from developing improved and expanded recruiting, training, and fringe benefit programs needed to attract and
hold highly capable staffs and to raise their expertise, skills, imagination, and innovativeness to the levels necessary to serve fully and
properly the rapidly changing and complicated needs of modern
agriculture.

Training and Authority Increased Incentives

Starting in the 1960s, with the encouragement and counsel of
H. T. "Bill" Mason, Deputy Governor of the Farm Credit Administration,[3] many Farm Credit Banks began to increase the emphasis
and upgrade the level of their management training and development
programs. Mason's successor, Jon F. Greeneisen, has continued to
encourage and work closely with the Banks in their efforts to keep
abreast of the modern management training and development programs and to utilize them to increase the effectivenss of their junior
and senior officers.

Many more milestones marking the progress of training programs
in the Farm Credit System could well be mentioned. One of the
factors that made such programs successful was the desire of people,
whether policy-makers or operators, at both the district and local
association levels, to have more of a say about their own business.
The opportunity to do so made participating in training programs
more meaningful. It increased the incentive to do a top-quality job
when additional responsibilities and authorities were delegated to
them.

More Farmer-Elected District Directors

One of the details along the way that should not be overlooked
is the Farm Credit Act of 1937. It was a signpost along the road to
indicate the direction the Farm Credit System was taking. That
Act, among other things, provided that in addition to the National

---

[3] Mason had a good mix of an early career of 16 years with the Federal Farm
Loan Board and the Farm Credit Administration, supplemented by a span of 11
years' experience as an official of the Reconstruction Finance Corporation and
Chief Budget Officer and Executive Assistant to the Assistant Secretary of the
Treasury, before returning to the Farm Credit Administration as Deputy Governor in charge of administrative functions from 1957 to 1972. He also became
Secretary of the Federal Farm Credit Board, following the retirement in 1964
of J. Mahlon Selby who had also served as Executive Assistant to the Governor
of the Farm Credit Administration since 1941.

Farm Loan Associations (Federal Land Bank Associations), Production Credit Associations, and stockholders of the Banks for Cooperatives electing one member each to the district Farm Credit Boards, the National Farm Loan Associations would nominate candidates for the Governor of the Farm Credit Administration to appoint as their second member on the Board. This was important because users of the Farm Credit System received a voice in selecting a majority of those on the district Boards—four of the seven members on each board were still appointed by the Governor of the Farm Credit Administration.

Act of 1953 Gave Further Impetus

But the Farm Credit Act of 1953 went even further. It gave farmers and their cooperatives additional incentives to keep moving forward. It also gave the Federal Land Bank Associations, Production Credit Associations, and the borrowers from the Banks for Cooperatives the right to elect two members each to the district boards when the user-stockholders owned two-thirds of the stock of the Banks. They were also given the right to nominate their separate nominees for membership from their districts on the Federal Farm Credit Board.

But Congress did not stop there. It also instructed the new policy-making Federal Farm Credit Board to devise plans to enable farmers to become complete owners of their cooperative Farm Credit System and also to delegate more and more authority to the district Farm Credit Boards and Banks, and the local Associations.

Some Associations got the mistaken idea that when the farmers became complete owners of the Farm Credit System, they would be almost completely independent of Government regulation. They overlooked several facts. First of all, Congress did not say that. Secondly, Congress mentioned *delegating* authority rather than abolishing it.

When authority is delegated from one person or organization to another, that does not mean that the delegating authority loses the responsibility for seeing that such authority is correctly used. Therefore, it becomes incumbent upon any person or organization that delegates authority and responsibility to lay down guidelines as to how they expect that authority to be used. The delegation of authority also implies that if it is not used correctly, that delegation can be rescinded.[4]

---

[4] This subject is also discussed in "Incentives for System Becoming Completely Member-Owned," Chapter 5.

Also sometimes overlooked is the fact that all kinds of financial institutions are supervised by either the Federal or state government that charters them. Commercial banks are supervised by the Federal Reserve System, the Federal Deposit Insurance Corporation, and the Controller of the Currency. Savings and loan associations and credit unions are supervised either by state or Federal organizations charged with those duties. Insurance companies, being chartered by the states, are under the supervision of state insurance regulatory bodies.

Farm Credit System Unique in Supervision

The Farm Credit System is unique in that the user-owners of the System, through their elected representatives, have a voice in selecting all but one of the members of the Federal Farm Credit Board which is the governing body of their supervisory agency—the Farm Credit Administration. That assures the System of an understanding and sympathetic supervisory organization. System officials, in the Banks and Associations, may not always agree on what should be done at the local, district, and national levels, but at least they always get an understanding hearing.

Naturally, organizations that are being supervised want to be allowed to do the things they decide should be done. Usually, those in the Farm Credit System agree that some supervision is necessary. But frequently uppermost in their minds are the things they believe should be required of *other* organizations for the best interests of the System as a whole. The Farm Credit Administration is responsible to Congress to see that the System is operated in such a way that it carries out Congress' objective of giving the best possible service to its borrowers at the lowest possible cost. Congress has also made it responsible for protecting the interests of investors in the System's securities. And in all matters it must keep in mind the protection of the public interest.

It is generally recognized that many human beings are inclined to seek and cherish large amounts of power. Most people fail to recognize even small amounts of such tendencies as motivating their own actions. Too often supervisory organizations like the Farm Credit Administration—as well as those being supervised, like the Farm Credit Banks—do not recognize that the desire for power for themselves is one of the important motivations for the positions they take. At that point each tries to rationalize its actions. Thus, the supervisory agency—in this case the Farm Credit Administration—may sometimes have been too slow to act or agree to changes in response to the needs of member-borrowers and the Banks they are supervising. At other times the Banks' requests for changes in the rules may have been partially sparked by the subconscious desire to acquire more power for themselves. The Associations, the Banks, and the Farm Credit Administration have had to be pushed at times into doing what seemed to be obvious.

There also have been people on the district Farm Credit Boards who wanted more authority and responsibility delegated to them, but they in turn were not willing to delegate such powers to the paid officials of their Banks or to the local Associations which they in turn supervised. The problem is to strike the proper balance between supervision and delegation. It is a "give-and-take" proposition that will probably always leave room for disagreement, discussion, and improvement. Fortunately, the democratic control and "checks and balances" built into the Farm Credit System enable such problems to be worked out eventually.

Differential Supervision of Credit

A recent development, made possible by the flexibility provided by the Farm Credit Act of 1971, was instituted by Governor Harding when he was Deputy Governor for Credit. With the encouragement of Governor Jaenke and the approval of the Federal Farm Credit Board, he devised a program that was named "differential supervision." Under that policy, greater authority and responsibility are delegated to those Banks and district boards that are doing the best job in carrying out their responsibilities. On the other hand, those that do not come up to the operating standards and goals of service approved by the Federal Farm Credit Board receive closer supervision. This program has been further developed and fine tuned under the leadership of C. K. Cardwell, Harding's successor as Deputy Governor.

For example, the Farm Credit Administration, first by direction of the Congress and later by regulation, required that loans above a certain size be approved in Washington. These loan limits grew larger and larger as the farm business increased in size and the Banks developed greater financial strength and acquired the ability to handle large and complicated loans.

For many years, the limits were applied uniformly within the various systems of Banks in terms of either specified dollar amounts or in terms of the percentage the loan was of the net worth of the organization making the loan. Under the differential supervision program, Banks that have demonstrated their ability to handle large and complicated loans have greater authority in terms of how large their loans can be without prior review and approval by the Farm Credit Administration. Those who have not demonstrated an equal amount of expertise in controlling their credit operations receive more supervision.

Such supervision is provided because the larger the loan the more devastating the effects of the losses would be to the financial strength of the local Association and the Bank. A large loss or losses could impair their future ability to serve their members. The Farm Credit Administration's supervision is designed to protect not just the individual association or bank but also the interest of other organizations in the System and their member-borrowers. For example, if one Bank's loans were allowed to get out of hand or deteriorate to the point where its ability to meet its obligations to investors was impaired, the other Banks in that group would be affected, and through them, farmers all over the country.

General Role of the Farm Credit Administration

The role of the Farm Credit Administration as interpreted and proscribed by the Federal Farm Credit Board[5] is in part as follows:

> The essential responsibility of the Farm Credit System is to improve the economic well-being of farmers, ranchers and their cooperatives by providing to them the best possible credit service at the lowest possible cost consistent with sound operations. As the supervisory agency, the role of the Farm Credit Administration is to assure that Farm Credit Banks and Associations fulfill this responsibility in accord with the Farm Credit Act of 1971.
>
> In addition to policies established by regulations, the Federal Farm Credit Board has established policies to direct the functions of the Farm Credit Administration. A primary objective of this policy is to place decision-making authority as close to the borrower as is consistent with demonstrated capacity for performance. The application of this policy is directly dependent on the acceptance and effective discharge of responsibility by the Banks and Associations. The basic functions of the Farm Credit Administration are to be conducted in accord with the following guidelines. . . .

[5] Forty-first Annual Report of the Farm Credit Administration and the Cooperative Farm Credit System—1973–74, Farm Credit Administration, Government Printing Office, Washington, D.C., 1975, p. 12.

As a general rule, the banks and associations shall have opportunity and latitude to manage their operations in carrying out their responsibilities. The performance of individual Farm Credit institutions in meeting the objectives of the law, regulations and System policies will, in large measure, determine the degree to which supervisory authority will be exercised by the Farm Credit Administration. However, supervisory actions shall be taken in the measure and manner necessary in specific circumstances, particularly when the welfare of present and future borrowers, individual institutions, a banking system, the Farm Credit System as a whole or the Nation is involved. . . .

The Farm Credit Administration will continue to represent the System at the national level to Congress, government agencies, investors and the general public in the dissemination of information and making reports. . . .

. . . The public interest in the effective operation of the System is protected by regulation, supervision and examination of Farm Credit institutions and their activities. The Farm Credit Administration is responsible for providing leadership to assure that the System maintains the highest standards of good corporate citizenship and responsive service to present and future borrowers.

Examinations Important

Any organized business should be independently audited periodically in order to make sure its financial statements properly reflect the true condition of the enterprise. In addition, auditors often point out ways in which business controls and accounting procedures can be improved.

Financial institutions wherever they are chartered—state or Federal—are examined by some government authority. The FCA's examinations are made under the direction of the chief examiner who reports directly to its Governor. Examinations of the Banks and Associations in the Farm Credit System test the accuracy of their financial statements and records. FCA examiners also check to see that these organizations are following the laws and regulations administered by the Farm Credit Administration. All Banks in the Farm Credit System and the Production Credit Associations are examined at least once a year and all Federal Land Bank Associations at least once every 18 months. All functions and operations performed in the Farm Credit System are subject to review, appraisal, and evaluation by the Office of Examination. These include, in addition to their financial condition and that of their entities, their financial statements and records, programs and activities initiated and conducted by directors and employees; lending policies, practices, and procedures; servicing of loans; service to all eligible borrowers; adequacy of internal controls and management operations.

Examinations include the identification and clarification of problem situations; the effect or potential effect of each problem; the methods bank management uses in dealing with the problem situation, the causes of the problem, and possible solutions or corrective action. Examiners' reports on such matters are limited to intra FCA offices and serve as a basis for supervisory plans and, activities. These examinations "provide specific assurance as to the financial soundness and integrity of Farm Credit institutions."[6] Such examinations enable the Farm Credit Administration to "identify and evaluate System activities and trends, analyze the relative performance of Banks and Associations, and initiate appropriate corrective action."[7]

Examiners are directed to report fully to management and boards of directors their findings on problems and their effects; however, evaluative data and recommendations are to be reported only to FCA supervisory officials.

As volume of business and size of loans have rapidly increased in the past 10 years, the importance and difficulty of performing the examination function has increased tremendously. Under the leadership of Kenneth J. Auberger, Chief Examiner, who also now serves as Deputy Governor, more sophisticated methods of analysis and examination, including the use of computers, have been developed to meet the challenge.

---

[6] *Ibid.*, p. 124.
[7] *Ibid.*

Chapter 14

ORGANIZING TO GIVE FARMERS
THE BEST POSSIBLE SERVICE

In 1963 the three groups of banks that made up the cooperative Farm Credit System agreed to jointly employ the nationally recognized marketing consulting firm of Lippincott and Margolies to develop a coordinated corporate identification program. In its study of the System, this firm was struck particularly by two features of the System—the complexity of its organizational pattern and what the consultants considered its unique unifying goal of service to farmers and ranchers.

There has long been agreement within the System that its job is to give farmers the best possible credit service at the lowest possible cost consistent with building and maintaining a strong, soundly operated System that can continue to serve them in the future. But there has been continuing disagreement regarding how to organize the System to deliver the best service.

Two Farm Mortgage Bank Systems

However, one of the most noticeable mistakes that Congress made in the original Federal Farm Loan Act was to provide two systems of farm mortgage banks—one the cooperatively oriented system of the Federal Land Banks, and secondly the private investor-owned joint stock land banks.[1] This in itself was a compromise.

Some people in Congress thought the way to solve the farmers' needs for additional credit was for the Government to help organize a cooperatively owned system. Another group thought that if private investors could have the opportunity to set up Federally chartered farm mortgage banks, without any Government capital, but with

---

[1] See "Joint Stock Land Bank Competition" in Chapter 23.

authority to sell tax-exempt bonds to investors, they could solve farmers' credit problems and make a profit. As a result, of course, there were immediately two types of farm mortgage lenders. A total of 88 joint stock land banks were chartered from 1917 to 1933, when Congress placed them in liquidation. Some of the banks never got into operation. Some had already merged or voluntarily liquidated, and five were placed in receivership. By the end of 1932, only 46 were operating. Many had overlapping territories. Most were undercapitalized. Poor management was common. All suffered from the low prices for farm commodities and the resulting low farm income which made it extremely difficult for most farmers to pay their debts.

Overlapping Local Associations

In addition to this built-in competition between the two systems of Land Banks, Congress also authorized any 10 farmers to organize a National Farm Loan Association (now Federal Land Bank Association) to get loans from their district Federal Land Bank. There was no provision in the law, nor did the Federal Farm Loan Board that supervised the Banks and Associations until 1933 prevent competing groups of farmers from going into business in the same territories. By November of 1917, 1,839 National Farm Loan Associations had been chartered. That number grew steadily until it reached almost 5,000 at the end of 1932, of which 4,649 were still operating.

FICBs Organized

When Congress established the 12 Federal Intermediate Credit Banks in 1923, by way of the Agricultural Credits Act, there was again a compromise. There were several proposals for filling farmers' needs for short-term credit. Rather than decide between some of these proposals, Congress put two bills together and authorized competing types of institutions. However, Congress did provide that the Federal Intermediate Credit Banks should come under the supervision of the Federal Farm Loan Board at the national level and should come under the policy-making Federal Land Bank boards of directors at the district level. The Federal Land Bank presidents also became presidents of the Federal Intermediate Credit Banks, although in some districts managers were appointed to run the operations of the Intermediate Credit Banks under the general direction of the presidents. In fact, for the first 17 years of their operation, the Intermediate Credit Banks were practically operated as departments of the Land

Banks. Thus, cooperation between the two sets of organizations was assured.

System Rounded Out—FCA Created

The Farm Credit Act of 1933 rounded out the Cooperative Farm Credit System. No new agricultural lending institutions have been added to the Farm Credit System since that time. A few months earlier, the Farm Credit Administration had been established by Executive Order of the President, which brought together all then existing credit organizations serving farmers. In addition to the Federal Land Banks, the Federal Land Bank Associations, the Joint Stock Land Banks, and the Federal Intermediate Credit Banks also transferred to the Farm Credit Administration were the 12 Regional Agricultural Credit Corporations from the Reconstruction Finance Corporation, the Crop and Seed Loans from the U.S. Department of Agriculture, and the funds for the Secretary of Agriculture to invest in Agricultural Credit Corporations and Livestock Loan Companies, which Congress had hoped farmers would use to capitalize organizations that could discount notes with the Federal Intermediate Credit Banks.

Except for the Federal Land Banks, the Federal Land Bank Associations, and the Federal Intermediate Credit Banks, the other organizations brought under the supervision of the Farm Credit Administration were either gradually or eventually phased out or transferred to the Farmers Home Administration, as not being part of the permanent cooperative Farm Credit System.

The Farm Credit Act of 1933 set up 12 Production Credit Corporations, one in each Federal Land Bank District, to organize, capitalize, and supervise the authorized local Production Credit Associations. The Act also provided for the setting up of 12 district Banks for Cooperatives, located in each of the 12 Federal Land Bank Districts, plus a 13th Bank for Cooperatives known as the Central Bank for Cooperatives, in Washington, D.C.

Why So Many Separate Organizations?

Since the end of World War II, hundreds of people from other countries have come to the United States to study the Farm Credit System. They have come from the well-developed countries, as well as from those that are in the early stages of development, to get ideas on how to best serve the credit needs of farmers. As Jack Gabbedy, the agricultural representative of a commercial bank in Perth, Western Australia, expressed it: "I've kept telling our people that the United States had the best farm credit system in the world. They finally insisted that I come over to the United States and study your system."

Many of these representatives from other countries have raised the question, "Why does the Farm Credit System have three sets of banks and two sets of local associations?" The answer of many Farm Credit people over the years has been "If we were doing it over again, we probably wouldn't."

Conditions Dictated Separate Organizations

Former Farm Credit Administration Governors W. I. Myers and F. F. Hill—both of whom were on the scene when the Farm Credit Act of 1933 was being drafted—have explained that the conditions at that time determined why the new organizations were set up under separate management. The Land Bank presidents had a tremendous crisis facing them in 1933. Most of their affiliated National Farm Loan Associations, of which there were nearly 5,000 with overlapping territories and part-time secretary-treasurers, were in sad financial condition. A large portion of the farmers who had loans from the Land Banks could not make their scheduled payments, because of the extremely low prices farmers were receiving for their products. Hundreds of thousands of other farmers across the country were faced with the possibility of foreclosure on their farms, and Congress had given the Land Banks the job of refinancing their debts.

Myers and Hill also reported that most of the Land Bank presidents felt they would not be able to take on the additional duties of providing operating or production credit to farmers. Hill remembers that Myers received a message from E. H. Thomson, a long-time, highly respected President of the Federal Land Bank of Springfield, urging him not to set up the production credit system, because there was already an almost impossible job to be done. Both have said they felt that if the Land Banks were given the job, they would not have been able to get the Production Credit Associations off the ground. Early in the 1960s Hill went on to say, "But we never expected the two systems would remain separate this long."

Joint Management Not Feasible Pattern at Start

C. R. "Cap" Arnold, long-time Deputy Production Credit Commissioner, Production Credit Commissioner, and for an interim period, Governor of the Farm Credit Administration, in his history of the

Production Credit Associations, recalls that when he went out to the St. Louis Farm Credit District to help organize the first Production Credit Associations, word came from Governor Morgenthau ordering the new Production Credit Association boards of directors to hire as a secretary-treasurer someone who had a similar position with a National Farm Loan Association. This would have created joint management.

However, Arnold reported that he objected on the grounds that they were telling these new Production Credit Association boards of directors that farmers were going to run the Associations. "So how could we tell them who to hire as their secretary-treasurer to manage the Association?" Of course, there was an average of about four NFLA secretaries per Production Credit Association to choose from. But Arnold points out that most of these secretary-treasurers were part-time people who often had conflicts of interest because they were also in the real estate or insurance business, or some other endeavor. Most of them were not qualified to organize and operate a Production Credit Association.

While Morgenthau withdrew his order, there were several joint secretary-treasurers of National Farm Loan Associations and Production Credit Associations scattered around the country in the early years, particularly in the St. Louis, Columbia, Springfield, and Berkeley Farm Credit districts. Some of these arrangements continued into contemporary times. Others were discontinued for various reasons, but usually at the time of changes in personnel.

Expansion of FICBs Considered

Myers reports that consideration was given to expanding the authorities of the Federal Intermediate Credit Banks so that they could make a wider variety of loans to other cooperatives. After all, they had been making loans to cooperatives on the security of commodities stored in bonded warehouses. They also had a successful record of operation and a good reputation in the financial markets where their debentures were being sold. However, it was decided that the cooperatives needed their own source of credit in the form of the Banks for Cooperatives, since the Federal Intermediate Credit Banks would be busy handling the business of the newly organized Production Credit Associations.

Efforts to Coordinate to Better Serve
Farmers Began Early

During the 1934–35 period, Governor Myers, Land Bank Commissioner Albert Goss and Production Credit Commissioner S. M. "Steve" Garwood sent memoranda to the presidents of the Federal Land Banks and the Production Credit Corporations in each of the districts requesting them to do everything possible to get the Production Credit Associations and National Farm Loan Associations working together as a team to serve farmers' credit needs. The Farm Credit Administration provided a large quantity of a two-color folder explaining the kind of credit available, for the Associations to send out jointly to farmers.

In many cases, the secretary-treasurers of the two types of Associations did work closely together and farmers benefited from their cooperation. There have been and are many examples of coordinated efforts to serve the total credit needs of farmers. But rivalries did grow up and misunderstandings did occur. Too many of such examples still persist.

Conflicts Over Who Gets Paid First

During the early post-Depression years, when farmers' incomes were still low and they were carrying extremely heavy loads of debt, there were frequent disagreements as to who should be paid first, the Federal Land Bank that had the first mortgage on the land, or the Production Credit Association that was providing the operating credit. Actually, the individual member-borrower could not get along without either of them. If the Land Bank insisted on the farmer using all his income to meet the installments on his loan, and the Production Credit Association refused to finance him for another year, that would leave the Land Bank with a loan that could not be paid. Or, if the Production Credit Association insisted on being paid off first, and the Land Bank as a result decided to foreclose, the Production Credit Association also stood a good chance of losing its money. Eventually, many of these problems were resolved by reaching agreements to share in the money farmers had available to meet their debt payments.

District Banks' Efforts to Work Together

Most of the district Farm Credit Boards have generally recognized the need to have their Farm Credit Banks—particularly the Land Banks and Intermediate Credit Banks—and their affiliated Associations work together in order to provide farmers and ranchers the best possible service. Results have varied by districts and from year to year.

Some district Boards have given more attention to the subject than others and, therefore, the results have differed. Some have encountered difficulties in getting cooperation between the Banks because of personality clashes between top Bank officials and traditions of rivalry between their Banks or overzealous efforts to build large, independent organizations.

General Agents Forerunners of Chairmen of Presidents' Committees

In 1933 when the Production Credit Corporations and the Banks for Cooperatives were added to each district's organization, Governor Morgenthau appointed, with the concurrence of each district Board, a General Agent to serve as coordinator of the services of the four organizations and as the focal point for his communications with the districts. Gradually, the General Agent was picked from among the four presidents of the organizations for that district. His major duty as a General Agent was to see that the Farm Credit Banks worked together in every way possible for the benefit of farmers.

The Farm Credit Administration eventually allowed the districts to abolish the job of General Agent and in its place have the Farm Credit District Board elect a chairman of a presidents' committee to act as the coordinator and supervise any joint personnel employed by the Banks. In many districts, this responsibility is rotated.

Springfield Has Joint Officers

Early in the 1940s the Farm Credit Board of Springfield broke new ground. It appointed one man, Harlan B. Munger, as President of all four organizations—Federal Land Bank, Federal Intermediate Credit Bank, Production Credit Corporation, and Bank for Cooperatives.[2] At the same time, it developed a pattern of joint secretary-treasurers (managers) for all its Federal Land Bank Associations and Production Credit Associations. It has maintained that pattern ever since. Up until 1975 it had separate officers under the President for the Bank for Cooperatives, but the other officers of the Federal Land Bank and the Federal Intermediate Credit Bank were joint officers of both organizations. By 1975, all officers of the three Banks became joint officers.

―――――――

[2] After retirement, Munger became the first Chairman of the Federal Farm Credit Board in 1953.

When the Springfield organization plan was adopted, FCA Governor Ivy W. Duggan urged other district Farm Credit Boards to take similar actions. However, the only other district Farm Credit Board to take somewhat similar action in this period was Baltimore. In fact, his strong advocacy of such coordination programs became one of the root causes of his strained relations with Land Bank Commissioner James Isleib and Production Credit Commissioner Arnold, as well as with many Bank presidents and district boards.

Baltimore Plan—Some Joint Officers

The Farm Credit Board of Baltimore approached the problem somewhat differently. Soon after Springfield developed its coordinated pattern, it persuaded most of its National Farm Loan Associations (now Federal Land Bank Associations) and Production Credit Associations to employ joint managers. However, at that time Baltimore did not adopt joint management for any of the district Banks. One comment on how that arrangement worked was made by William H. Johnson, then Secretary of the Production Credit Corporation. He said, "It doesn't make sense. I visit the joint Production Credit and National Farm Loan Association office to discuss public and membership relations and advertising programs, only to find that last week a membership relations man from the Land Bank visited the same Association, and a specialist on advertising will be there next week." He went on to say that he had offered to give up this officer's position and become the first joint field man for both the Land Bank and the Production Credit Corporation, as he soon did.[3] Later, the Farm Credit Board of Baltimore appointed a joint president of the Federal Land Bank and the Production Credit Corporation. For about 20 years it has had a joint president of the Land Bank and Intermediate Credit Bank.

Drive for Farm Ownership Spurs Action

In 1955, the Federal Farm Credit Board presented plans to Congress to speed up the repayment of Government capital in the Banks for Cooperatives and to have the Production Credit Associations gradually become the owners of their district Production Credit Corporations. A few Production Credit Associations joined in opposing the

---

[3] Later, Johnson served as the joint Director of Information for all the Farm Credit Banks of Baltimore where he was long in great demand for talks to service clubs and farm and cooperative audiences to tell the story of the Farm Credit System.

plan for having the Production Credit Associations invest in and become the owners of the Production Credit Corporations in their districts. As a result, Congress adopted the proposal dealing with the Banks for Cooperatives as the Farm Credit Act of 1955. But Congress indicated to the Federal Farm Credit Board that before it passed a plan for the Production Credit Associations to become the owners of the Production Credit Corporations, it wanted more agreement from the people in the System as to what they wanted.

At that point, the Federal Farm Credit Board held a series of meetings with PCA directors and managers throughout the country to discuss various plans for attaining that objective. In several places, the question was raised as to why a plan should not be worked out for the Production Credit Associations to become the owners of the Federal Intermediate Credit Banks, since this would be necessary before the System could completely pay off the Government capital in the System.

FICBs and PCCs Merged

Then the Federal Board had the Farm Credit Administration staff design a new plan by which Production Credit Corporations would be merged into the Federal Intermediate Credit Banks, and then have the Production Credit Associations gradually invest in the capital stock of the merged institutions. This was again taken to the country in a series of meetings at which the plan was discussed. The plan received general approval. The proposal was then presented to Congress by the Federal Farm Credit Board and passed as the Farm Credit Act of 1956. The mergers were effective January 1, 1957.

In view of the wide diversity of strongly held views on this subject, a year earlier it would have been difficult to find anyone who thought the merger could be accomplished in the foreseeable future, not to mention within a year. Much of the credit for this accomplishment is due to Federal Board member Frank W. Peck's diplomatic and tactful handling of both the 1955 and 1956 series of meetings which he chaired.[4]

The plan for the Production Credit Associations to acquire ownership of the Federal Intermediate Credit Banks required them to invest

---

[4] Peck, the Secretary of Agriculture's appointee to the Federal Board, 1953 to 1961, had been the first Cooperative Bank Commissioner of the Farm Credit Administration, Director of Extension at the University of Minnesota, President of the Federal Land Bank of St. Paul, and President of the Farm Foundation.

$15 million in capital stock of the Banks over a 3-year period. In order to gradually increase that investment, the Intermediate Credit Banks were to charge interest at high enough rates so that they could declare patronage refunds in the form of capital stock to the Production Credit Associations and in the form of participation certificates to other financing institutions using the services of the Banks. By 1968 these accumulated investments enabled the Federal Intermediate Credit Banks to repay the last of their Government capital.

Other District Work-Together Efforts

While the Farm Credit Board of Omaha has not come forward with any elaborate programs to achieve good teamwork among their Banks, over the years, some observers feel that under the Board's leadership that district has had better results than most districts that do not have a joint president of two or more organizations. However, for several years the Omaha Board required periodic reports from each Bank on its contacts with the other Banks' associations and co-operatives while they were on field trips.

The St. Paul Board long has been concerned about this problem of getting its organizations to work together. As far back as the 1940s, it assigned the duty of getting the two types of organizations to work together—especially on housing—to an officer on the staff of what is now known as the Office of Joint Services. However, as late as the early 1970s the St. Paul Board was still having to insist that the presidents of the Land Bank and the Intermediate Credit Bank develop better teamwork.

About 1963, a member of the St. Louis Farm Credit Board, in an informal discussion with representatives from other districts and the Farm Credit Administration, said that his board had found it almost impossible to develop proper coordination and cooperation between the Land Bank and the Intermediate Credit Bank. He pointed out that the board was in St. Louis only two or three days a month and much could happen between meetings. The ensuing discussion revealed that Donald Bushnell, Director of the Land Bank Service, who also served as Deputy Governor, thought that this was not important. Deputy Governor H. T. "Bill" Mason took issue with him.

Shortly after this discussion, the St. Louis Farm Credit Board, at the time of the retirement of two of its presidents, considered the possibility of appointing one president for all three Banks. At about the same time, the Columbia District Board was considering a similar step. Governor Tootell was reported to have discouraged both boards from taking such action. When the matter came to the attention of the Federal Farm Credit Board, it informed Tootell that while it was not encouraging such actions, it would prefer that he not discourage such proposals in the future.

In 1965, the President of the Federal Land Bank of Columbia retired and that Board appointed Robert A. Darr, the president of the Federal Intermediate Credit Bank, to be a joint president.[5] A revolt of the managers of the Federal Land Bank Associations, predicted by some, did not materialize. Darr had quickly discussed the subject with a large proportion of the managers of the Federal Land Bank Associations in his district. Subsequently, several Land Bank and Production Credit Association boards of directors have chosen joint managers and decided to operate under the title of "Farm Credit Service."[6]

---

[5] Darr had been elected President of the Production Credit Corporation in 1951 and President of the Federal Intermediate Credit Bank in 1954.

[6] The merits of this approach are still debated in the System today. For example, in commenting on an early draft of this portion of the manuscript, W. N. Stokes, Jr., author of "Credit to Farmers" and retired President of the Federal Intermediate Credit Bank of Houston who also had served as President of the Houston Bank for Cooperatives and early in his career had served in the Legal Division of the Farm Credit Administration and with the Federal Land Bank of Houston, said in part:

> You have several discussions of cooperative working relationships between Land Bank and Production Credit Associations—and among the banks at the district level. These are objective and well handled, but they appear to me to assume as an unquestionable premise that all of such things are good *per se*. . . . All sides of the issue at least should be mentioned. The basic issue, of course, is "joint management" of banks and associations. . . .
> . . . The ever-present potential for conflict of interest on the part of a person wearing two hats, or three hats. Each of the institutional groups within the System has functions, goals and responsibilities differing materially from those of the others; each has equity ownership residing in groups and institutions differing widely from that in the others. Anyone who maintains that difficult and sometimes grievous conflicts of interest may not arise simply has not been there. Simplistic but illustrative examples: do you make an advance on a PCA loan in serious difficulty in order to pay a maturing land bank installment? Do you withhold foreclosure action on a land bank loan because of heavy involvement (and need for delay) by a Production Credit Association? . . .
> I just cannot conceive one group getting a fair shake when it is subject to the decisions of a man who also has heavy responsibilities to an entirely different institution. In these times when conflicts of interest are so prominent, when their exposure creates such volatile reactions, I am surprised that everyone continues to ignore its potential for damage."

(*Footnote 6 continues on next page*)

The Farm Credit Board of Berkeley also has long emphasized one-stop service for the two types of Associations. The accompanying table on page 141 indicates this policy had produced more results than in other districts. It also has some joint managers' arrangements that date back to the early 1930s.

In order to get true cooperation between people in different organizations, it is necessary to have people who believe in and are committed to an increase in teamwork and cooperative endeavor. As one observer of the cooperative Farm Credit System has frequently remarked, "If I was a Farm Credit Bank official or local Association manager and wanted to be sure to maintain the status quo, I would do everything possible to cooperate with my counterpart in the other organization, to see that between us we gave the best possible service to farmers. If I didn't do that I would be afraid that some day the member-owners would rise up and make some changes."

There are examples that indicate this is not such a "far-fetched" idea. Development of a districtwide plan to achieve one-stop service for Land Bank and Production Credit Association members was triggered by the report of a Users Committee appointed by the Farm Credit Board of Louisville. Another example was cited in a report on One-Stop Service.[7] It said:

> The Douglas (Georgia) Production Credit Association and Federal Land Bank Association of Douglas became jointly housed in 1971, and in 1972 they elected to operate under joint management. The PCA and FLBA members requested these developments and the association boards of

---

In commenting on this subject, Gordon Cameron, long President of all three Farm Credit Banks of Springfield, said:

> In Springfield we take the position our banks and associations are working for the good of farmers generally—building institutions to serve them. Our first question was "What is best for farmers?" Our second question: "Can the goal be accomplished without compromising the financial integrity of the individual bank or association?" If it could not be then we would try for a solution that would serve the farmer's interest and be fair to the corporation. This we were able to do. In areas of possible conflict of interest, the boards agreed on policy guidelines before issues arose so that when one did it could be decided on principles rather than on emotions or personalities.

[7] Unpublished report of Research Division of the Farm Credit Administration made to the Federal Farm Credit Board, October 1974.

directors actively sought to provide one-stop credit service. It was believed that the associations could provide better credit service by (1) reducing the time required to provide financing because of improved borrower information and "education" of the borrower; (2) making lending more flexible by better balance and scheduling of long and short term debt; (3) enabling the association to better compete with commercial banks for unexpected short term financing and (4) establishing a system of record keeping which automatically became more efficient as a result of records being retained in branch offices, thus reducing travel. Initially, association cost of operation increased, mainly as a result of personnel training, but costs have now fallen below the previous levels of the two associations.

There are many examples of Farm Credit Bank officials and Association managers who do a good to excellent job of cooperating to give farmers the best possible service. However, the exceptions always stand out and point up the lingering basic problems which have not changed materially over the years, even though progress has been made in many areas.

In 1939 Vernon Vine, then Director of Information for the Farm Credit Banks of Spokane,[8] arranged a tour throughout the Spokane district to get material to use in his various publications. He said that he wrote the secretary-treasurers of both types of associations at the various stops he planned and asked them to get together and decide which farmers they should visit. He reported that, in most instances, it was evident that those managers had not discussed their mutual problems for a long time. In fact, he said that as they drove down the road together, one of them would frequently mention, "Oh, there is one of our members' farms," only to discover that his counterpart was not aware of the fact.

A member of the staff of the Farm Credit Administration recalls an incident in Illinois in the early 1960s. The Land Bank Association and a branch office of the Production Credit Association had adjoining upstairs offices. The FLBA manager reported the Production Credit Association had moved out without giving him advance notice. When the Farm Credit Administration representative and the Federal Land Bank Association manager visited the PCA office, the PCA representative remarked, "Oh, we expect a doctor here will move out soon and

---

[8] Vine was later a member of the Information Division of the Farm Credit Administration and subsequently Associate Editor and later Public Relations Director of the *Farm Journal.*

we figured you could move in then." The question came to mind, "Wouldn't he have gotten a better reception for his idea and improved his chances for its acceptance if he had talked it over in advance?"

About 1967, the same FCA staffer recalls that he visited adjacent offices of a Land Bank Association and a Production Credit Association in California. When he finished discussing the next day's plan in one office, he said he was going next door for the same purpose. He was told the office was closed, but the staff was still at work. He then suggested knocking at the inside door between the two offices, only to be told, "Oh, we never use that door. We keep it locked." This illustrates the fact that physical proximity does not guarantee cooperation in the farmer's interest.

Current examples of the same poor relationships could be cited, but the examples given are merely to illustrate the attitudes that can develop rather than point to any particular person, association, or district.

Joint or Adjacent Housing

From 1934 on, the Farm Credit Administration and several district Farm Credit Boards have made efforts to get the Land Bank Associations and the Production Credit Associations to at least locate in the same town, so that farmers who used both types of associations could take care of their credit problems without traveling many miles between two sets of offices. There also have been continuing efforts to get the two types of associations to maintain joint or adjacent offices. Several times over the more than 20-year history of the Federal Farm Credit Board, it has informed the district Farm Credit Boards of its policy that joint or adjacent housing—"One-Stop Service"—should be encouraged in the best interests of the System's farmer-members. The Federal Farm Credit Board reemphasized that policy as recently as 1974. The report on its June 1974 meeting said:[9]

> *One-Stop Service*—The Board reviewed its long-standing policy (December 7, 1960) encouraging one-stop credit service and noted with disappointment the lack of progress as indicated by current statistics on joint and adjacent FLBA and PCA housing. The Board reaffirmed and emphasized its 1960 policy on the desirability of one-stop credit service and

[9] Federal Farm Credit Board Summary Report of Meeting, Farm Credit Administration, Washington, D.C., June, 1974.

requests district boards to review, analyze, and strengthen policies to expedite joint and adjacent housing of association offices at every opportunity, such as territory adjustments, consolidations and mergers, site acquisitions, and construction or modification of office buildings. Furthermore, the Board solicits recommendations from district boards on how the System can make greater progress in this area and asks that they be forwarded to FCA by October 1, 1974. Also, the Board directed staff to study and develop information on results of joint and adjacent housing to serve as a basis for improving services to borrowers.

The latest report on the number of joint and adjacent offices shows the following:

Federal Land Bank Association Officers That Were Joint or Adjacent with a Production Credit Association Office, September 24, 1974

	Total Offices [1]		FLBA Offices Joint or Adjacent with a PCA Office	Percent Joint or Adjacent Offices
	FLBAs	PCAs		
Springfield	65	65	65	100
Baltimore	129	129	129	100
Berkeley	55	78	44	80
Spokane	67	96	52	78
Columbia	121	203	78	64
St. Louis	236	267	146	62
St. Paul	143	265	88	62
Louisville	242	304	138	57
Omaha	172	183	78	45
New Orleans	125	121	44	35
Wichita	143	97	25	17
Houston	132	115	7	5
United States	1,630	1,923	894	55

[1] All offices including headquarters, branches, and contact points.

Territorial Differences Cause Problems

Unquestionably the differences in the territories served by Land Bank and Production Credit Associations have been a deterrent to the development of more joint and adjacent offices and, to an even greater extent, the increase in the number of joint management arrangements. These differences stem from the fact that the original

National Farm Loan Associations (FLBAs) could be formed by any 10 farmers who wished to form an association. Overlapping territories were common. Production Credit Associations, with the exception of a few overlaps caused by chartering specialized statewide associations, were granted exclusive territorial rights. Traditional differences are difficult to break down.

However, the Land Banks working with their Associations were able to overcome such difficulties within their own system in the process of merging Associations from a total of 5,000 down to 550. Gradual mergers have also reduced Production Credit Associations from 600 to 430. Unfortunately, in most districts, little attention has been given by either the Federal Land Banks or the Federal Intermediate Credit Banks to align the territories of the two types of Associations. Many Associations that have wanted to work together, however, have found ways to overcome such difficulties and mesh their services to farmers. They have accomplished this in a variety of ways. One of the most common is to locate branch offices at the headquarters of one or more of the other Associations. In some cases they even find it possible to establish a greater number of branch offices and thus bring service closer to their members by employing joint personnel to handle the business of both Associations.

Only Those Who Want to Cooperate Will Work Together

Some observers point out that experience has shown that cooperation does not come easily where vested interests are involved. They suggest that if closer operational teamwork to give farmers the best possible service is to be achieved, the best approach is for local Association and district Farm Credit Boards—as the policy-making representatives of farmers—to insist on cooperation and closely monitor the results of their edicts.

One suggestion has been made that local Association boards meet jointly before any consideration is given to making any changes in office space arrangements by either Association and between such times they hold two or more joint meetings a year to receive reports on what has been done to achieve full cooperation in serving farmers, as well as plan future joint endeavors or activities of mutual interest.

The Berkeley and Spokane Farm Credit Boards report[10] they

---

[10] "One-Stop Credit," report of Research Division, Farm Credit Administration, to the Federal Farm Credit Board, October 1974.

do not approve, except under unusual circumstances, new FLBA or PCA office facilities that do not provide for joint housing. The St. Paul Board approves all changes in housing arrangements. In concluding its report on "One-Stop Service," to the Federal Farm Credit Board in October 1974, the Research Division of the Farm Credit Administration stated:

> New and dynamic approaches to the task of encouraging one-stop service in the FLBA/PCA system do not spontaneously occur when relying on the natural course of events. One-stop service requires director leadership. A strong point can be made that the district boards and bank management are in the best position to set the stage, atmosphere and example for encouraging the development of one-stop credit service among the associations. The natural course of events will require a long term period for the System to complete the development of one-stop credit service because of the overriding influence of personal opinions and self interests of association directors and management. However, since the associations that moved to joint/adjacent offices in recent years are unanimous in their belief that borrowers' interests are better served under the one-stop credit service concept, continued attention should be given to this issue.

Cooperation Within FCA

In the opinion of many observers, frequently the earlier difficulties in getting the district Banks and local Associations to work together actually started in Washington. From 1933 to 1953, the Farm Credit Administration had five Presidential appointees. In addition to the Governor of the Farm Credit Administration, the President also appointed a Land Bank Commissioner, an Intermediate Credit Bank Commissioner, a Production Credit Commissioner, and a Cooperative Bank Commissioner. Under the leadership of Morgenthau, Myers, and Hill, the Commissioners worked together relatively well. At times after that period, some of the Commissioners were quite conscious that they were Presidential appointees and thus not wholly responsible to the Governor of the Farm Credit Administration, even though many of their powers—especially in the case of the Production Credit Commissioner—were those that the Governor had delegated to them.

Abolition of Presidentially Appointed
Commissioners Helped

The Farm Credit Act of 1953 which again made the Farm Credit

Administration an independent agency outside the U.S. Department of Agriculture and established the Federal Farm Credit Board as its policy-making body, also abolished the Presidentially appointed Commissioners. The power to appoint all subordinates was given to the Governor of the Farm Credit Administration. Governor R. B. Tootell appointed four Deputy Governors. The chief Deputy was in charge of administration. The others were Directors of the Land Bank Service, Short-Term Credit Service (later renamed the Production Credit Service), and the Cooperative Bank Service.

Under this arrangement, the "line officers" were responsible only to the Governor. Traditional rivalries between the three parts of the System were difficult to overcome, but much more cooperation was achieved under the Deputy Governor-Service Director arrangement than existed under the Presidentially appointed Commissioners.

Farm Credit Act of 1971 Aids Teamwork

After the Farm Credit Act of 1971 eliminated most of the technical inconsistencies that had grown up in the law between the three groups of Farm Credit Banks, Governor Jaenke, with Federal Board approval, published one Manual of Regulations to cover the entire Farm Credit System. This replaced a set of several previous manuals. But more importantly, the new Act set the stage for better understanding on the part of all connected with the System, and a better working relationship among the Banks in the districts. The reorganization of the Farm Credit Administration by Governors Jaenke[11] and Harding, which followed functional lines rather than Bank Systems lines, also made possible more consistent supervisory efforts with the three Banks in each district. The responsibilities of all Deputy Governors now involve all branches of the System instead of three each being responsible for only one.

Cooperation in Information, Public Relations, and Advertising

In the field of information, public relations, and advertising, the record of inter-Bank and inter-Association cooperation has been relatively good. Much progress has been made particularly in more recent years, even though in 1933 all Farm Credit districts had joint informa-

---

[11] On announcement of the change, Deputy Governor and Director of Land Bank Service Gilmore commented, "It is an idea whose time has come."

tion and public relations personnel and in the mid-1970s only nine districts had such people.

In the immediate years before the advent of the Farm Credit Administration, the Land Banks and Intermediate Credit Banks jointly employed Edwy B. Reid—later to serve 18 years as the FCA's Director of Information and Extension—to handle their public relations in Washington. Reid had been USDA's first Director of Information—1916 to 1920—and then a representative of the American Farm Bureau Federation in Washington. In the latter position he had been one of the incorporators of the American Institute of Cooperation. During this period the Intermediate Credit Banks did some national advertising of their debentures.

Farm Credit Banks Jointly Employed Information Men

In 1933, FCA's Land Bank Commissioner Goss appointed an information agent in each district, on the Farm Credit Administration payroll, to inform farmers about the availability of Land Bank Commissioner loans. These loans were being handled by the Land Banks. Within a few months, these people were transferred to district payrolls to tell the story of the entire cooperative Farm Credit System. However, the title "Information Agent" survived for nearly 20 years—long after anyone remembered its origin. Gradually, titles changed to Director of Information or Director of Public Relations. More recently, one or two have become Director of Communications—following the modern concept and trend in industry.

Banks Employed Extension Specialists

These information people's efforts were soon supplemented in most districts by a specialist who developed programs to encourage the teaching of the wise use of credit by vocational agricultural teachers in high schools, the Land Grant colleges, and the Extension Service. In addition, the Banks in two or three districts employed home economists to work with the high school teachers and the specialists in the Extension Service to teach farm wives why farm family expenses needed to be geared into farm debt management and how that could be done.

The personnel in these fields were jointly employed by the Farm Credit Banks in each district. They worked in close cooperation with the Information and Extension Division staff of the Farm Credit Administration.

Houston

Louisville

Columbia

Wichita

Baltimore

St. Louis

St. Paul

Springfield

Omaha

New Orleans

Spokane

Sacramento

District Information Staffs Cut, Then Expanded

In the 1940s the drive to cut costs, combined with the inclination of each Bank to handle everything within its own separate control, resulted in the number of districts with a jointly employed information-public relations or information-extension person declining to four. In addition, one district used one person half-time. All the full-time extension people departed or were assigned to other duties.

By the mid-1970s, nine districts had directors of information or public relations jointly employed by all three Banks. Several also had assistants. In addition, most of the individual Banks had one or more senior or junior officers working on some phases of public and membership relations and advertising programs. A total of 55 representatives of the district Banks—either jointly or individually employed—participated in the 1975 Information Conference in Washington under the capable leadership of FCA's Director of Information, Carroll Arnold.

All 37 Banks Cooperate on Movies

Cooperation for a coordinated effort in the communications field has been considerably broader than that. In 1963 the 37 Farm Credit Banks for the first time joined in sponsoring a motion picture film explaining the entire Cooperative Farm Credit System under the guidance of a committee headed by Gordon Cameron, President of the Farm Credit Banks of Springfield, who represented the Land Banks. Other members of the committee were Robert Darr, then President of the Intermediate Credit Bank of Columbia, and John Eidam, President of the Omaha Bank for Cooperatives. This film was preceded—starting in the late 1940s—and soon followed by productions explaining the services of each of the three banking groups. Such joint productions have continued in later years. These films have long been widely used at farm meetings, in schools and universities, and on television.

Systemwide Corporate Identification

Also in 1963, the three banking groups cooperated in employing a nationally recognized New York firm[12] specializing in corporate iden-

---

[12] Lippincott and Margolies had developed new corporate identifications for some of the largest national corporations including major oil companies and the Chase Manhattan Bank and the Royal Bank of Canada. With the Farm Credit System as a reference, the firm was engaged by the Internal Revenue Service to modernize its image, including simplifying and redesigning its tax forms.

tification to develop a coordinated, System-wide identification program. The consulting firm would have preferred to see the System adopt a single emblem for the entire System, but a set of related symbols was a big step forward when compared to the countless unrelated varieties previously used.

First 37 Bank Ad Series

On recommendation of the annual System-wide Information Conference, all 37 Banks agree to a united three-ad nationwide advertising campaign to introduce the new corporate identification program, with the prior understanding there would be no attempt to develop additional System-wide advertising beyond the three-ad campaign. These three advertisements were carried in *Farm Journal, Progressive Farmer,* and the *Cooperative Digest.*

Most of the Farm Credit districts supplemented and reinforced this national advertising campaign by using the nationally produced advertisements in their state farm papers, at considerable savings on production costs. As a result of this united campaign on the System's new series of related emblems, the agricultural community quickly became aware of the System's new identity.

Joint 37 Bank Public Relations Fund

Going further, in the 1960s the 37 Banks of the System first established a System-wide public relations fund to use in developing better understanding with the various agricultural and cooperative communications groups. This program was initiated at the request of the System's Information and Public Relations Conference and under the coordinating leadership of Jon Greeneisen—then FCA's Director of Research and Information and since Secretary to the Federal Farm Credit Board and FCA Deputy Governor.

Banks Cooperating on Advertising

In the early 1960s the Springfield Land Bank and Intermediate Credit Bank and their affiliated Federal Land Bank Associations and Production Credit Associations began a coordinated advertising program in their state and regional farm papers. A few years later they began placing ads in the regional edition of the *Farm Journal.*

Another pioneer was the Columbia district. It went even further than Springfield by developing a broad district-wide, coordinated advertising program using a variety of media in 1964. This district-wide program includes the Columbia Bank for Cooperatives, as well as the other two banks and the local Associations.

Also beginning in the mid-1960s, the Intermediate Credit Banks on the one hand, and the Land Banks on the other, began getting groups of banks together to engage in regional advertising in regional and national farm publications. Gradually, these two advertising programs developed into national programs. The three groups of banks embarked on a System-wide advertising program in 1976—the Bicentennial Year.

Banks Coordinate Computer Services

The Farm Credit System has a long history of pioneering in the use of electronic data processing. In the early 1970s, a Farm Credit Administration staff member received a call from the U.S. Department of Agriculture. He was asked if he knew the answer to a question asked by International Business Machines, Inc. The company wanted to know whether the Department of Agriculture had used Hollorieth tabulating cards before 1940. He suggested there must be better sources of such information within the U.S. Department of Agriculture, such as Harry Trelogan—an FCA alumnus—Administrator of USDA's Statistical Reporting Service and as such coordinator of the department's huge computer system. Learning that Trelogan was out of town, the FCA'er, getting over the shock of being asked such a question, said, "Why, yes. The Farm Credit Administration came into the Department in 1939 and FCA was using IBM tabulating equipment as early as 1934 to prepare statistical reports."

Although not part of the answer, he also recalled that the Federal Land Banks started using such equipment about the same time to speed up the handling of the backlog of loan applications by keeping track of their progress through the Land Banks, and to pinpoint the bottlenecks, and for loan experience studies. One of the important qualifications for district statisticians—later called directors of research—in those years was that they know how to use such equipment. The New Orleans statistician, Elmer H. "Red" Mereness was credited with having pushed IBM into some of its early improvements. He would call in the IBM representative and explain to him some new operation they wished to perform and ask him to go back and see what IBM could work out.

Soon some of the Land Banks also began using such equipment to prepare their individual loan statements, and this equipment was transferred to the Land Bank accounting departments.

Early Modern Computer Applications

Relatively early in the development of modern computer systems, several Land Banks and Intermediate Credit Banks started studying how they could be effectively used in their operations. The Springfield and Columbia Federal Land Banks and Federal Intermediate Credit Banks, plus the St. Paul Federal Intermediate Credit Bank, conducted some of the earliest studies. Gradually, most of the Federal Land Banks and Federal Intermediate Credit Banks became interested.

On their own initiative and with the encouragement of the Farm Credit Administration, the Farm Credit Banks have developed a series of cooperative arrangements.

System Has Five Computer Centers

By 1976 the Farm Credit Banks maintained computer centers at Columbia, Louisville, St. Paul, Omaha, and Wichita. Springfield was planning eventually to transfer its Federal Intermediate Credit Bank processing to St. Paul and its Federal Land Bank processing to Omaha. Most of the Banks and Production Credit Associations had terminals linked to a computer center by telephone. Each of the computer centers processed accounting work for their group of Banks and Associations as a basic activity.

In various combinations, the Federal Land Banks, Federal Intermediate Credit Banks, and Production Credit Associations in the 12 Farm Credit districts and 10 of the 13 Banks for Cooperatives were processing their accounting by computer. The computer centers also were providing farm record accounting for members of Production Credit Associations in 10 Farm Credit districts. In some districts this was called Agrifax—a term originated in St. Paul. In addition, the Omaha computer center was providing, through Farmbank Research and Information Service, management information to all the Land Banks and Intermediate Credit Banks—a service started by the Land Banks in Columbia and then transferred to the Omaha center in 1970. In 1974 the Intermediate Credit Banks decided to develop a similar service in cooperation with the Land Banks.

To the extent the various Farm Credit Banks have worked together on the use of computer centers, they have undoubtedly reduced the overall costs, even though at times they found it difficult to work out mutually satisfactory plans that insure service and distribute the costs on an equitable basis. But the willingness to carry on sometimes tedious negotiations in a spirit of cooperation and compromise should provide members more and better services plus long-term savings in the years ahead.

Chapter 15

GUARDING AGAINST THE RISKS
OF LARGE LOSSES

Any lending organization has to consider the possibility of a large borrower, or a series of large borrowers, defaulting and leaving the lender with losses too big for it to absorb. Prolonged adverse economic conditions, or several years of bad weather—such as droughts— in the case of farm loans, resulting in a large accumulation of losses on loans, can very quickly erode previously sizable reserves. The Federal Reserve Board and the Comptroller of the Currency give close attention to commercial banks' reserves and check to see that they do not exceed the legal limit on a risk exposure they can assume in relation to their size. The Federal Deposit Insurance Corporation is actually a share-the-risk program brought on by the flood of bank failures in the Depression of the 1930s.

The Need for Adequate Reserves Recognized

Congress, the supervisory agency—the Farm Credit Administration—and the Banks and Associations making up the cooperative Farm Credit System have always been concerned about the possibilities of large losses. They have developed a variety of safeguards against such possibilities. Following the high rate of losses by the Land Banks and Associations sustained in the Depression years,[1] the Association and district Farm Credit Boards and the Farm Credit Administration have emphasized the need for building adequate reserves.

---

[1] Colonel Frank W. ImMasche, a member of the Research Division of the Farm Credit Administration until he joined the Air Force in World War II, states that some of the lending organizations in the West that were obtaining loan funds from the Federal Intermediate Credit Banks were also insolvent and the Regional Agricultural Credit Corporations organized in that emergency had to fill the gap until the Production Credit Associations were organized.

However, the question always remains: "Are the reserves big enough to absorb the shock of big losses on one or more large loans or a large number of losses resulting from generally poor economic conditions or disastrous weather, or long periods of extremely low prices for the farm products produced in the area?"

Land Bank Solutions to the Problem

When Congress passed the Federal Farm Loan Act establishing the Federal Land Banks in 1916, it set the minimum loan at $100 and the maximum at $10,000. In its First Annual Report, the Federal Farm Loan Board informed Congress that the average size of the 64,000 loans farmers obtained from the Banks was $2,291.[2] In this same report, the Board asked Congress to increase the maximum to $25,000 because in many areas if a farmer needed a loan at all, $10,000 was not enough. In 1923, Congress, in enacting the Agricultural Credits Act authorizing the establishment of the Federal Intermediate Credit Banks, which was an amendment to the Federal Farm Loan Act of 1916, increased the maximum size of Land Bank loans to $25,000. However, it specified that preference should be given to loans of $10,000 or less. Myers points out that the early limitations enacted by Congress and the Federal Farm Loan Board's regulations which overly encouraged small loans was self-defeating. It resulted in a large share of the Land Bank loans being made on poor farms or to farmers who lacked management ability. Such loans, in Myers' opinion, were a major factor in producing the Land Banks' high rate of delinquencies and foreclosures in the 1930s.

Congress gradually raised the limitation on the maximum size of mortgage loans as the size and value of farms increased. In the Farm Credit Act of 1971 the Congress eliminated the maximum limitation which at that time was $400,000. Supplementing these maximums the Farm Credit Administration by regulation required its prior approval of loans over a continually rising amount. As explained in "Differential Supervision of Credit," Chapter 13, starting in 1974, the Farm Credit Administration required prior approval of large loans only on a selective basis.

Under their agreements with Land Bank Associations, the Land Banks agree to share in their losses. As provided for in the Farm Credit Act of 1971, the Land Banks can now participate with each other in

---

[2] First Annual Report of the Federal Farm Loan Board, Government Printing Office, Washington, D.C., 1918, p. 19.

large loans. These provisions furnish a means for local associations to share their risks through the Land Banks and for the Land Banks to share the risks with one another.

Land Banks Shared Risk Early

The collapse of wheat and livestock prices following World War I, combined with severe drought years in Montana, produced a severe shock in the 1920s for the fledgling Land Bank System. As mentioned earlier in connection with the joint liability on Land Bank bonds,[3] the Spokane Land Bank had so many loans in default and foreclosured farms on its hands that it could not meet its obligations to bond buyers. The other 11 Land Banks had to come to the rescue.

Building Viable NFLAs a Problem

One of the toughest sets of problems the Land Bank portion of the Farm Credit System ever had to solve—other than its gearing up to handle the tremendous refinancing job of the 1933–35 period—was how to develop strong local cooperatives from weak National Farm Loan Associations,[4] a large share of which were insolvent. The unfortunate combination of misguided policies and the results of national financial collapse in the 1929–33 period, in which farmers were particularly hard hit, had created an almost impossible situation.

Associations Small, Overlapping Territories

The Farm Loan Act of 1916 had provided that 10 farmers who could qualify for a total of $20,000 in Land Bank loans could apply for a National Farm Loan Association charter. For the most part, the Federal Farm Loan Board granted charters to any group that could qualify. No attempt was made to prevent overlapping territories. This resulted in competition between National Farm Loan Associations, even where the lending territory was not large enough to support the operating needs of one Association. As a result, a large share of the Associations were run by part-time secretary-treasurers, such as real estate and insurance agents, bankers, county agents, and farmers.

---

[3] See "Joint Liability Tested Early" in Chapter 6.
[4] The National Farm Loan Associations are now called Federal Land Bank Associations.

Lacked Reserves

The business of the Associations was largely making new loans. Secretary-treasurers were not paid a salary. They received a fee for each new loan. Most Land Banks paid dividends to the National Farm Loan Associations instead of building strong reserves. The National Farm Loan Associations in turn paid out most of these dividends to farmer-members rather than for strengthening either their operations or reserves.

To make matters worse, as Myers points out, the Land Banks had used the loan endorsements of the National Farm Loan Associations to push the losses back on the Associations, and they did not have adequate reserves to cover the losses. They were in no position to absorb the shock of the avalanche of defaults and foreclosures of the 1930s.

During the 1933–35 refinancing period, the Land Banks were too busy with the flood of applications for loans to give any attention to this problem. In some areas new Associations were formed because hopelessly insolvent Associations could not make new loans. Many loans had to be made directly to the borrower rather than through the National Farm Loan Associations. In many Associations that could make loans the secretary-treasurers got relatively rich from the new loan fees they collected.

Rebuilding Started

Starting in 1936, the Land Banks and the Farm Credit Administration began to try to devise ways of correcting these situations. The drive to get groups of two or more National Farm Loan Associations began, but went slowly partly because secretary-treasurers did not want to lose their potential source of income from new loan fees. Some boards of farmer-directors did not want to give up their own local Associations.

Compartments of new borrowers were established in some insolvent Associations where the amount of stock impairment was not too great, in order to enable such Associations to make new loans. This involved separating the equities of old and new borrowers. Some Banks began to decentralize additional functions to the Associations and reimbursed them for doing so. This began to give the National Farm Loan Associations a source of income. But these were only half measures that patched up the patients.

Reorganization and Rehabilitation of NFLAs

In the period 1943 to 1947, all the Land Banks—starting with Houston—adopted plans that solved most of these problems. The Land Banks, by this time in relatively good financial condition, decided that if they were going to build a strong, healthy Land Bank System they needed to restore the reputation of the National Farm Loan Associations and build them into efficient, financially strong local organizations.

The reorganization and rehabilitation plans adopted varied between districts. However, the plans generally provided for:[5]

1. Paying off in full farmer-members whose stock had been retired when they repaid their loans at less than par value because the value of Associations' stock was impaired. This cost the Land Banks $16.5 million.
2. Releasing the National Farm Loan Associations from their matured indebtedness owed the Banks under their endorsement liability.
3. Establishing credits to Associations to create reserves for estimated losses on their outstanding loans.

The adoption of these plans had highly important effects on building the future strength of the Land Bank System. All National Farm Loan Associations became solvent. When the program began in 1943, the value of the stock of 55 percent of Associations was impaired. It was much easier to merge Associations and realign territories. By 1950 the number of Associations had been reduced from 3,687 to 1,216 and by 1975 to 553. The program resulted in reducing the costs of operating the Associations and the Land Banks. Subsequent reimbursement plans for performing a continued growing number of services for the Land Banks, plus bank dividends, at last provided income to the National Farm Loan Associations. They had money to pay adequate staff salaries and office expenses, build adequate reserves, and pay dividends to member-borrowers. In addition, the Banks adopted plans to share in future losses.

The foundation had been laid for building the strong local credit cooperatives—now Federal Land Bank Associations—that exist today.

---

[5] Sixteenth Annual Report of the Farm Credit Administration, 1949-50 fiscal year, Government Printing Office, Washington, D.C. 1950, pp. 94-97.

By 1975 the Associations were able to operate as full partners with the Land Banks in serving their members' long-term mortgage needs.

PCA Safeguards

In the case of the Production Credit Associations, loans over 15 percent of an Association's net worth required approval of their supervisory Production Credit Corporations up until their merger with the Federal Intermediate Credit Banks in 1957, when the Federal Intermediate Credit Banks assumed that responsibility. Loans over 35 percent of a PCA's net worth had to be approved by the Farm Credit Administration. Under the Farm Credit Act of 1971 these fixed requirements were eliminated.

In the years following World War II, Governor Duggan became concerned about the ever-growing size of large PCA loans. In several speeches he mentioned his concern and pointed to a study of farms in Tompkins County, New York, made by Stanley Warren at Cornell, which showed that in 1907 it would have taken a farmer 10 years of losing his production costs to completely use up the equity in his or her farm. By 1947 it would have taken only 2½ years. The opportunities for farmers to make money had increased, but the lenders' possible losses were much greater too.[6]

Duggan also appointed a committee of high-level economists to study the problem of Production Credit Associations sharing the risks of loss on large loans. This committee was chaired by Former Governor Hill, then head of the Department of Agricultural Economics at Cornell University; other members were William G. Murray of Iowa State University, who in the 1930s had been Director of Research for the Farm Credit Administration and was the author or co-author of several editions of a text on agricultural finance; R. J. Saulnier of Barnard College, who later served on the President's Committee of Economic Advisors; Earl Butz of Purdue University, who was years later to become Secretary of Agriculture; George Aull of Clemson University; and A. R. Gans, Director of Research for the Federal Land Bank of Springfield. This Committee came up with four possible methods of sharing the risks on large loans.

However, at that time few Production Credit Associations or district Production Credit Corporations were concerned about the problem. FCA Production Credit Commissioner Arnold and the PCA

---

[6]"Changes in the Dollar Side of Farming," AE 759, Department of Agricultural Economics, Cornell University, Ithaca, N.Y., 1950.

leadership in general feared that any risk-sharing plan would weaken the individual PCA's board of directors' sense of responsibility for keeping its own house in order. They also shunned the idea of members of one Production Credit Association having to share the cost of the mistakes of another Association.

However, as loans grew larger and larger, the Federal Farm Credit Board in 1966 approved risk-sharing plans in eight Farm Credit districts.

Since the passage of the 1971 Act, Production Credit Associations also have been permitted to sell participations in their loans to the intermediate credit banks.

BCs Share the Risk Through Participations

Even in 1933 when the Banks for Cooperatives were established, it seemed obvious that the loans of some cooperatives were going to be relatively large. There was not enough money available to give each district Bank enough capital to enable it to handle large loans. Therefore, it was decided to highly capitalize a 13th or Central Bank for Cooperatives to handle large loans and loans made to cooperatives operating in more than one Farm Credit district. In the 1933–55 period, some of the officials of the Cooperative Bank Division of the Farm Credit Administration served on its board of directors. They also served as operating management for the Central Bank. As Homer G. Smith—President of the Central Bank for Cooperatives, 1956 to 1974—points out in his history of the Central Bank, under this arrangement the Farm Credit Administration automatically was in charge of approving large loans to cooperatives.[7]

Toward the end of this period, the Central Bank began to shift its direct loans to the district Banks for Cooperatives and became a bank that participated in loans that were larger than the loan limits of the district Banks that were based on the size of the district Banks' net worths. Thus, the Bank for Cooperatives' System had a built-in loss-sharing plan.

According to Smith, following the passage of the Farm Credit Act of 1955, which provided a plan for cooperatives gradually but systematically replacing the Government-owned capital in the 13 Banks for Cooperatives, some of the district Banks or members of their boards

---

[7] Homer G. Smith, "The 13th Bank," Central Bank for Cooperatives, Denver, Colorado, 1976. Before becoming President of this Bank, Smith had been Deputy Governor and Director of the Cooperative Bank Service, Farm Credit Administration, and Assistant Deputy Production Credit Commissioner.

of directors questioned the need for the Central Bank. They wanted to share the Central Bank's Government-owned capital and the earnings thereon.

The earnings of the Central Bank at that time amounted to about 60 percent of interest payments and were allocated to the district Banks in proportion to the interest paid on participation loans from that district. Those Banks with few participation loans received smaller shares of the Central Bank's earnings. Those who wanted to share in part or all the Central Bank's capital believed that large loans could be handled by several district Banks participating in them.

Some of the district Banks for Cooperatives have participated in some of the larger loans—particularly in cases where a loan involved a merged cooperative which had previously borrowed from another Bank for Cooperatives. However, in Smith's opinion, such arrangements got too many people and organizations involved in cases where three or more district Banks were needed as participants because of the size of the loan.

The issue of capitalization was at least partially resolved by the Central Bank making a total of $24 million in direct loans to the district Banks in 1958 at low interest rates.[8]

Under 1975 regulations, the largest combination of loans the System could provide to any one cooperative was just under $196 million. Any cooperative whose total credit needs were above that amount would have to involve outside lenders either as participants or as separate loans. For many years some cooperatives have supplemented their BC loans with loans from commercial banks, even in cases where they had not reached the BC loan limit. Some credit people look with favor on such arrangements under certain circumstances, but others would much prefer a single financing package, which can include commercial bank participation, as a means of keeping all concerned working together and providing proper credit controls.

Risk-Sharing Plans Grow in Importance

In summary, the various parts of the cooperative Farm Credit System go about it differently, but they are all using some method of reducing or sharing the risk on larger loans. In general, these plans fall into two categories—risk-sharing agreements and participation of

---

[8] A legal opinion held that if the Governor of the Farm Credit Administration reduced the Central Bank's capital the money would have to be returned to the Agricultural Marketing Act Revolving Fund rather than transferring it directly to the district Banks for Cooperatives.

more than one lending organization in loans that are too large for one lender to take all the risks. As the size of loans from all parts of the Farm Credit System continues to grow so rapidly, these risk-sharing programs become more and more important factors in protecting the financial strength of the individual lending entities within the System and thus its future ability to serve farmers, ranchers, their cooperatives, and other borrowers.

Chapter 16

ADEQUATE CAPITALIZATION HIGHLY IMPORTANT

The cooperative Farm Credit System, having learned from its own past, has long appreciated the advantages of having a strong capital base—capital stock investments from its members plus net worth reserves built up from accumulated earnings. The "reserves" are usually labeled surplus by accountants to distinguish them from valuation reserves which are a deduction from the loan assets which provide for possible future losses on existing loans. These valuation reserves, although not part of the Banks' capital structure, protect that capital base from being eroded when losses occur.

During recent years of rapid growth in loan volume, committees of presidents of the three banking groups making up the Farm Credit System have given careful consideration to projecting the future capital needs of the System and the best ways to meet them. On occasion, the Bank presidents as a group have exerted internal discipline by requiring some Banks to increase their capital base.

Forward planning for capital needs is highly important because the rapidly expanding volume of loans in modern times requires a continually larger capital base to support it. What is adequate capitalization today can soon become too small for tomorrow's loan volume. If any Bank in the System fails to build capital currently for future loan needs, it could be faced with a situation where loan demands from its members grow so fast that it does not have sufficient capital to borrow the needed loan funds.

An extreme example of the possible increase in demand for loan funds came in the winter months of 1973 when the need for loans from grain cooperatives arising from the big American sale of grain to the Soviet Union shot up the loans of some midwestern Banks for Cooperatives from 50 to 100 percent in the span of one or two months.

Early FLB Capitalization Problems

The Farm Credit System can look back on its own demonstration of the results of undercapitalization from the history of the Land Banks in the period 1917 to 1933. Congress authorized the Treasury to invest only $750,000 in the startup capital for each bank—a total of $9 million. The National Farm Loan Associations started operations with practically no capital stock. It came only as borrowers acquired stock in connection with their loans. And when farmers invested in stock equal to 5 percent of their loans, the National Farm Loan Associations were—and still are—required to invest a like amount in the Land Banks. Any earnings on the NFLAs' capital were dependent on the payment of dividends by the Land Banks. However, the NFLAs used most of such amounts received from Land Banks to pay dividends to borrower-members. Thus, they were not building a capital base and had practically no reserves to cover their losses from loan endorsements. This situation was not fiscally improved until the mid-1940s when the Land Banks rehabilitated the National Farm Loan Associations, provided them income, and helped them develop financial plans as explained in "Rebuilding Started," Chapter 15.

The Land Banks were required to start retiring their Government-owned stock as soon as the NFLA-owned stock equaled that owned by the Government—$750,000 per Bank. Then the law specified that they were to use one-quarter of any additional amounts of stock purchased by the National Farm Loan Associations to retire Government stock. This prevented any rapid build-up of capital stock investments.

The law also provided that 20 percent of any net earnings were to be retained as reserves until the reserve account equaled 20 percent of the outstanding capital stock. After that, only 5 percent of net earnings were to be transferred to reserves. The Banks paid out most of the remaining earnings in dividends, thus capital accumulated relatively slowly from this source. Thus, the capital acquired by the System was far from sufficient to absorb the losses of the Depression years and, as a result, the Government had to invest large amounts of capital in the form of stock and paid-in surplus during that period.

Since the Depression experience, the Land Banks and Associations have been particularly conscious of the need for adequate capital. They are careful to build up adequate net worth by accumulating savings.

PCAs Had Capital from Start

Having seen the disastrous results of having insufficient capital in the National Farm Loan Associations, Myers' plan for the organization of the Production Credit Associations included Government investments in capital stock at the local Association level. He was anxious to see that they did not have to immediately start making loans regardless of their quality in order to get income to run the Associations. They had income from the interest on their investments of their capital in Government bonds to tide them over until they could build a sufficient quantity of good loans.

Under the leadership of Cap Arnold and the Production Credit Corporations, the Production Credit Associations were continually urged to build adequate reserves as well as build additional capital by convincing farmers they should voluntarily invest in more PCA stock than the 5 percent the law required.

In the years since then, under the leadership of the Federal Intermediate Credit Banks, the Production Credit Associations have continued to enlarge their capital. They have done so largely by charging enough interest and loan fees to provide sufficient income to add adequate amounts to their net worth reserves as well as to provide adequate provision for losses on loans outstanding.

BCs Started with Large Capital Base

Fortunately for the 13 Banks for Cooperatives, the $178.5 million balance remaining from the Federal Farm Board's revolving fund[1] that Congress made available for their original capital was sufficient to produce interest income. It also provided income to build reserves during the years their volume of sound loans was gradually growing.

The passage of the Farm Credit Act of 1956 provided a means by which cooperatives could replace the Government capital over a period of years. That Act specified that the cooperatives should build up their investments in the Bank by buying stock in proportion to their interest payments on their loans and by having the Banks for Cooperatives pay patronage refunds in the form of capital stock and allocated surplus.

Adequate Capital Affects Cost of Loan Funds

One of the factors that has made it possible for the Banks in the Farm Credit System to borrow at rates that are only a small fraction

---

[1] Technically known as the Agricultural Marketing Act Revolving Fund, that Act, passed in 1929, established the Federal Farm Board.

above those paid by the Government is their strong capital base—
by the mid-1970s nearing the $5 billion mark. Thus, adequate capital
tends to hold down the interest rates the System has to charge on its
loans.

Chapter 17

LEARNING FROM EXPERIENCE—
OWN AND OTHERS'

"Experience is a great teacher"—*if* we are willing to pay heed. Forward-moving individuals and organizations learn from the mistakes and successes of others as well as from their own.

The various parts of the Farm Credit System have learned a great deal from each other as well as from their own experience and from that of other organizations.

Impatient or objective observers might well question whether sometimes the various parts of the System have been too slow in learning from their own experience and from that of the other Banks and Associations. What is important is that they have learned. Here are some examples:

The Federal Land Bank portion of the System learned the importance and viability of the cooperative idea from the German Landschafts and other European credit systems. The amortized loan idea also came from Europe.

Some observers believe that the Landschafts had learned some lessons from the successes and failures of the colonial Land Banks in the America of that period.

The Production Credit Associations and the Banks for Cooperatives learned much from the earlier experience of the Land Banks. In some cases Congress learned it before they started and put it in the law which authorized them.

Both the Production Credit Associations and the Banks for Cooperatives used the Land Bank principle of having borrowers invest in their capital stock.

The Intermediate Credit Banks and the Banks for Cooperatives learned how to sell securities to investors from the Land Banks and used a joint Fiscal Agent.

The problems the National Farm Loan Associations had because of overlapping territories led to exclusive territories for most Production Credit Associations. Also, efforts were made to assign PCA territories that were large enough to produce sufficient loan volume to pay Association costs.

The Banks for Cooperatives learned many things from the experience of the Federal Farm Board, including the fact that it is better to build cooperatives up from the local level than down from the national level.

The Production Credit Associations learned from the early NFLA experience the need for building adequate reserves.

The Banks for Cooperatives and Intermediate Credit Banks in the 1950s adopted the idea of paying patronage refunds in capital stock and other forms of equity from other types of American cooperatives that had used it for many years as a method to accumulate sufficient capital. Like other cooperatives, the Banks for Cooperatives also revolve out—pay off—the oldest equities when accumulations are more than needed.

The Banks for Cooperatives started using variable interest rates in their loan agreements in 1953. The idea spread to the Production Credit Associations in 1957 and to the Federal Land Banks in 1963. However, the Federal Land Banks had for many previous years reduced their billing rates on old loans when interest rates on their bonds went down.

The Production Credit Associations began offering group credit life insurance to their members in 1952. The Federal Land Bank Associations did the same a few years later.

In the mid-1970s the Federal Intermediate Credit Banks decided to establish a computerized management information service in cooperation with the Federal Land Banks which had originated that management tool in 1970.

Research Important to System [1]

An important factor in learning as much as possible from experience is conducting organized research to analyze past operations and determine what factors produce satisfactory or unsatisfactory results. The cooperative Farm Credit System and its supervisory organizations—first the Federal Farm Loan Board and then the Farm Credit Administration—have long recognized that the study of past experi-

---

[1] Dr. Gene Swackhamer, Deputy Governor, Office of Finance and Research is responsible for much of the analysis of the research program in the Farm Credit System.

ence could provide guidelines that would produce a greater degree of success in future lending operations.

Early agricultural finance research was undertaken primarily at Land Grant colleges. It was not until 1922 that the Bureau of Agricultural Economics was formed within the U.S. Department of Agriculture to undertake land and commodity price analysis. The Cooperative Marketing Act of 1926 also created a Cooperative Division in the Department of Agriculture to assist farmer cooperatives.

The Federal Farm Loan Bureau, in the Treasury Department, under the auspices of the Federal Farm Loan Board, undertook studies to minimize the effect of loan losses caused by agricultural distress on the financial condition of the banks in an effort to maintain the marketability of FLB, FICB, and Joint Stock Land Bank securities. However, until the creation of the Farm Credit Administration in 1933, the Federal Land Banks and Federal Intermediate Credit Banks were largely dependent upon their own research initiatives, the work of agricultural colleges, and commodity price information from the Department of Agriculture.

Cornell University pioneered in farm management, farm records, and land appraisal research. Forrest F. Hill (who became Governor of the Farm Credit Administration 10 years later) completed a Ph.D. at Cornell University in 1928 which analyzed Federal Land Bank loans using Springfield district data and "punched cards"—the first known use of this technique in the System.

The Farm Credit Administration and the Farm Credit Banks have conducted many research projects independently and jointly and also in cooperation with the Department of Agriculture, the agricultural colleges, and the state experiment stations to study the factors affecting their lending practices. Many of the research studies prior to World War II involved searching for the reasons for losses on farm mortgage loans in order to avoid high rates of loss on future loans.

These research projects ranged from studies to classify the land in order to relate the quality of farm land to the debt-carrying capacity to the problems associated with particular types of farms such as fruit, vegetable, and poultry farms to studies of production, income, and expense of livestock ranches to determine their debt-carrying and repayment capacities. The latter study, made in the late 1930s, led the Land Banks and Production Credit Associations to pay more attention to the total debt rather than relying too heavily on the value of the ranch for real estate mortgage loans or the value of personal property such as livestock for operating loans.

After establishment of the Farm Credit Administration in 1933, many of the research functions of the Federal Farm Loan Board and Bureau were consolidated into a Division of Finance and Research. This unit according to early annual reports (a) assisted banks in the formulation and execution of financial policies, (b) compiled and analyzed financial and statistical data on operations, (c) handled fiscal operations, (d) conducted agricultural credit studies in cooperation with state colleges, and (e) cooperated in the research carried on by the district directors of research or statisticians.

The economic experience of the 1930s caused an expansion of the research efforts of the district banks—particularly the Land Banks— to explain what had gone wrong and to provide future early warnings to management. The research effort within the institutions of the Farm Credit System reached a peak about 1942. Many of the economists were livestock and commodity specialists who focused on price forecasting. Some of the district directors of research concentrated on analysis of price trends in specialty crops and other high risk loan areas.

By 1945, the enthusiasm for research within the Farm Credit System had waned. There was much pressure to reduce personnel in continuous economy waves. After all, the farm economy had recovered beyond expectations and continued preparation for an agricultural depression seemed less important. Further, many of the directors and officers of the System were concerned that research effort was duplicating the work of the Land Grant agricultural universities also being supported by farmers. Others saw research as a nonproductive overhead expense which increased the cost of credit rather than as an investment in problem solving. In one or two districts the research effort consisted largely of speech writing, public relations, or the interest specialty of the bank director of research or statistician.

In 1938 research in the Farm Credit Administration was split off from the Finance and Research Division and was made a separate Economic and Credit Research Division. This unit continued the prior research efforts to provide assistance in policy development, to establish normal commodity prices in connection with Land Bank appraisals, and to analyze agricultural credit conditions.

In 1955 the research and information divisions in the Farm Credit Administration were combined and both functions were restricted by limited budgets. Research had to be restricted largely to data gathering, tabulation, and analysis functions. National surveys of Production Credit Associations and Land Bank loan characteristics were made together with commodity and industry studies. Surveys of farm real estate mortgage recordings, and economic counsel to the Governor and staff consumed most of the time of the limited research staff. Little attention could be given to or was desired in the field of financial markets.

In 1962 the Banks for Cooperatives commissioned Russell C. Engberg, who had just retired as the Director of Research and Information, to make an in-depth study of their experience in financing cooperatives to determine which factors were involved in the growth or deterioration of cooperatives as a guide to future financing and counselling activities. In order to help cooperatives analyze their own situation, they published the study in book form.[2]

The credit crunch and inflation of 1966, which resulted in President Lyndon Johnson interceding on one occasion in the Farm Credit Banks' bond marketing, caused shock in the Farm Credit System. The System was unprepared for this contingency and the resulting allocation of credit. Research had not been asked to study financial markets, but the impact on research was every bit as great as the Depression of the 1930s. For perhaps the first time since the 1930s both the Farm Credit System and the Banks realized that they had a role of a financial intermediary which included obtaining funds as well as lending and collecting loans. The stability of financial markets prior to 1966 had lulled the Farm Credit System into a false security. The credit crunch struck at the most vital attribute the System can offer farmers—assured availability of funds.

Subsequent to the 1966 experience, a 1969–70 liquidity crisis and a 1974–75 international banking crisis, research in the Farm Credit System has been strengthened. In 1968, Dr. John Brake, on leave from Michigan State University, projected loan demands of the System to 1980. Dr. L. L. Boger, also of Michigan State University, made then and has since updated projections of the future needs for loan funds for the Central Bank for Cooperatives in his report, "Furrows on the Street." The Land Banks created an imaginative loan data base called Management Information Service (MIS), to provide information and analysis on Land Bank loans and borrowers and were later joined in this effort by the Intermediate Credit Banks.

The Farm Credit Administration increased the manpower of its research effort and broadened the research functions to include money and capital market analysis as well as increased effort toward analysis of rural credit markets. A visiting scholar program was commenced in

---

[2] Russell C. Engberg, "Financing Farmer Cooperatives," Bank for Cooperatives, Washington, D.C., 1965, p. 167.

1971 to provide short-term technical support and long-term educational support within agricultural and business schools. The Fiscal Agency added a research component and employed a financial economist. More effort has been expanded to automate data handling and analysis in operations, supervision, and examination through the creation of a network of regional computer centers. Several studies such as "Financing the Needs of the Farm Credit System," the Wharton School, University of Pennsylvania, 1973; "Financing Young Farmers," the Farm Credit Administration, 1974; "Toward a New Funding Strategy," McKinsey & Company, Inc., 1975, and the Task Force on Cooperative Finance, the Farm Credit Administration, 1975, provide technical counsel and recommendations to the System.

Will the efforts of the 1970s better serve the farmer and his cooperative in their quest for reasonably priced loans and services? It appears that the important questions are being addressed both in the areas of funding and credit. Research is being asked to address these issues and the support has greater clarity of direction and expectation. There is a deeper appreciation in the cooperative Farm Credit System that with autonomy, independence, and delegated authority also go responsibilities to maintain and develop assured funds for rural communities. Research is expected to assist in this task.

In addition to the economic and credit research carried on by the Finance and Research Division of the Farm Credit Administration in the Finance and Research Division from 1933 to 1937 and by the Economic and Credit Research Division, from 1938 to 1953 the Cooperative Research and Service Division of the Farm Credit Administration and its predecessors were carrying on a continual flow of studies of the problems of marketing, farm supply, and business service cooperatives which were of particular importance to the Banks for Cooperatives, as reported in "Farmer Cooperative Service on FCA Team," Chapter 26 and in "Financing Food for Freedom," Chapter 28.

Chapter 18

ADVICE, COUNSEL, AND FINANCIALLY RELATED SERVICES

The idea of lenders providing advice and counsel to their borrowers is far from new and cannot be claimed as an innovation by the Farm Credit System.

Lenders for centuries have been giving advice and counsel to their borrowers without realizing it. The very terms they imposed on their borrowers provided not only the advice and counsel but also required that it had to be followed. The difference in the advice and counsel provided by the Farm Credit System is that it is provided by people who know farming and farmers' problems. They specialize in extending credit to farmers and their cooperatives.[1] Thus, they usually have the knowledge and experience to provide relatively wise counsel. In addition, the counsel is being provided by people who are actually employed by farmers or cooperatives through their ownership of the organization handling the loan. Therefore, to a major extent, the motivation is to serve the borrowers—whether farmers or cooperatives.

Providing related services along with financing developed gradually over the years, but more rapidly in recent times—in response to the increased need arising from larger, more complex farming and cooperative enterprises. It received an added stimulus from the Farm Credit Act of 1971, which specifically provided the authority for such services within certain limitations.

Providing Advice and Counsel—Often Informally

Much of the advice and counsel, other than that contained in the terms of the loan and, in the case of the Banks for Cooperatives the

---

[1] Since the Farm Credit Act of 1971, the System also finances nonfarm rural home owners, farm-related business, and commercial fishermen.

loan agreement, is given on an informal basis. Managers or presidents of Land Bank Associations and Production Credit Associations are so conscious of the fact that they should not be supervising the farmer's operations that they give this advice and counsel almost without recognizing that they are doing so.

For example, a PCA manager in California some years ago emphasized that he did not tell farmers how to operate their businesses. He overlooked the fact that the owner of a 60,000 hen poultry operation about an hour before had remarked, in his presence, that he never made any changes in his operation without first discussing them with his PCA manager. He also had forgotten that he had just remarked, as he passed a farm down the road. "I told him that he'd better either decide to expand his 5,000 hen operation and really do a job, or go out of the poultry business."

The very way in which the PCA loan process is structured not only contributes to making sure a loan is sound from the standpoint of the lender and safe from the standpoint of the borrower but also counsels, educates, and advises the borrower. For example, the Associations require estimates of income and expense, and financial statements, and they want to know how the farmer intends to use the loan. They also want to know how and when he expects to repay his loan. Providing such information makes it necessary for the farmer to look at the facts and do some analysis on his own behalf. If the Production Credit Association, in analyzing a loan, finds weaknesses in a member's operations, they are pointed out or discussed with him.

When a Federal Land Bank Association appraises a farm that a member or prospective member is intending to buy, it is giving the applicant advice and counsel by providing him with a gauge as to what it is worth. Farmers also frequently discuss with the Land Bank Association whether they should buy more land. In cases where applicants are purchasing their first farms, they may well come to the Land Bank Association to find out what farms may be available and get some general idea as to their value.

Another form of advice and counsel comes when farmers are having difficulty in meeting their loan payments because of reduced income or other problems. The Federal Land Bank Associations and Production Credit Associations usually help them work out plans for meeting their obligations.

With BCs, Law Makes Counseling a Duty

The law under which they are chartered makes it a responsibility of the Banks for Cooperatives to provide advice and counsel to co-operatives. The advice and counsel provided by the Banks for Co-operatives has been a highly important ingredient in starting young, successful new cooperatives, avoiding the formation of cooperatives that have little chance of success, and in building strong, efficient, ex-panding cooperatives. The Banks for Cooperatives have helped many long-established cooperatives that have gotten into financial difficul-ties develop plans that got them back on their feet. Many of today's largest and most successful cooperatives have used the counsel and advice of the Banks for Cooperatives in building their present enter-prises and organizations.

The Banks for Cooperatives have long carried on education and training programs with cooperatives through meetings, workshops, and conferences. They are designed to find solutions to common prob-lems and train various specialized personnel. Many of these have been jointly sponsored by such organizations as the Farmer Coopera-tive Service, the Extension Service, the American Institute of Co-operation, the National Council of Farmer Cooperatives, the National Milk Producers Federation, the Cooperative League of the USA, the state Cooperative Councils, and other organizations.

Financially Related Services Offered

The seeds for providing financially related services were planted in the earliest years of the Federal Land Banks. In its second and third annual reports, the Federal Farm Loan Board alluded to the re-sponsibilities of the Federal Land Banks in this regard.

In its 1919 Annual Report the Board mentioned that the Land Bank presidents believed that it was the intention of Congress that the "Federal Farm Loan System" should be of help to farmers in more ways than simply lending money at a reasonable rate of interest.[2]

Early Self-Insurance Ideas—1918

Even earlier, in its second annual report, for the year 1918, the Board suggested to Congress that the Land Banks be given the au-thority to provide title insurance to their borrowers.[3] It came to this conclusion after citing the fact that the records in some areas were

---

[2] Third Annual Report, Federal Farm Loan Board, Government Printing Of-fice, Washington, D.C., 1920, p. 16.
[3] Second Annual Report, Federal Farm Loan Board, Government Printing Office, Washington, D.C., 1919, pp. 11-12.

practically nonexistent because of neglect or destruction. It also pointed out that in some areas, title records could not be traced back to the sovereign grants, nor even to the point beyond all possibility of contest. The Land Banks required that as a minimum.

The Board reported that the leading surety companies of the country had united in writing bonds to guarantee the interested banks from loss by reason of failure of title. This guarantee was based on a search of the record for the period necessary to vest title by possession, which it said varied from 8 to 21 years. The bonding companies were charging one-quarter of 1 percent of the amount of the loan for this service. The Board believed that the Federal Land Banks could do this at a smaller cost to the farmer by charging a smaller title guarantee fee and at the same time build up a title guarantee fund to cover possible future losses brought about by title failure.

The Board also asked that rather than have the Land Banks require fire insurance be purchased from insurance companies, the Land Banks collect a fire insurance fee from each borrower with which to pay any losses which might be incurred.

The Board pointed out that this plan had the advantage of providing the Banks with uniform insurance contracts and avoiding the expense of checking on borrowers' insurance policies and their payments.

Congress took no action on any of these suggestions. Such ideas were again being discussed in the mid-1970s.

Group Credit Life Insurance Offered

In the early 1950s, two insurance companies began to discuss with the Production Credit Associations the possibility of providing their members with group credit life insurance. They suggested that such insurance would not only give the members the protection necessary to pay off their loans in case of death, but it also would make the loans safer from the standpoint of the Production Credit Association. After the insurance companies had gotten a number of Production Credit Associations interested, they took up the subject with the Production Credit Corporations of those districts. They were interested and asked for clearance for such a new service from the Farm Credit Administration. After careful consideration and discussion with the Production Credit Corporations, the Farm Credit Administration agreed to allow the Production Credit Associations that were interested to provide such a service to their members.

However, the Farm Credit Administration and the Production

Credit Corporations insisted that such a program be designed to properly safeguard against any possible abuses. These safeguards included the provision that group credit life insurance be offered to members only on a purely voluntary basis—no member would be required to buy the insurance being offered by the Production Credit Associations.

No employee of a Production Credit Association was to receive remuneration from the insurance company involved. At the start of the program, the same was true of the Production Credit Association itself. In 1958, this was amended to allow remuneration from an insurance company but not beyond the actual costs involved. In the 1966 credit crunch, this restriction was removed in order to help Production Credit Associations hold down interest costs.

Soon after the Production Credit Associations began this program, several Federal Land Banks authorized their Associations to provide a similar service to their member-borrowers.

By the mid-1970s, all Production Credit Associations and Federal Land Bank Associations were offering this service to their members under contracts with 1 of 11 insurance companies. An estimated[4] 75 percent of PCA members and a somewhat smaller percentage of Land Bank Association members had a total of about $10 billion of group credit life insurance coverage.

Group Hail Insurance Added

In 1968 the Federal Farm Credit Board authorized the Production Credit Associations to offer group hail insurance to members under similar arrangements as those for group credit life insurance. By the mid-1970s, other insurance proposals were being studied for the possibilities they have for Production Credit Associations providing additional services to their members.

Electronic Farm Record Service

In the mid-1960s, several Federal Intermediate Credit Banks began exploring the possibilities of providing their members with electronic farm records services, by making use of the computers they had set up to use for keeping their accounting records. This service is made available to PCA members in 10 districts on a volun-

---

[4] Estimates provided by R. Bland Lee, Vice President, Old Republic Life Insurance Company.

tary basis in order to make it possible for them to have the advantages of professional accountants compiling their farm records on a modern computer. Such a service not only provides member-borrowers with up-to-date information regarding their farm operations on a regular basis, but it also provides data they can use in analyzing their farm businesses. This becomes particularly important as farms continue to grow larger and more complex. Each farmer can arrange to make pertinent data available to the person who prepares his income tax return.

PART FOUR

Working Relationships with

Other Organizations

and Groups

The cooperative Farm Credit System grew out of the needs of farmers as expressed to Congress by individual farmers, their farm leaders, and the farm press. Over the ensuing years, the cooperative Farm Credit System has been fortunate in having had continued wide support and understanding from the entire agricultural community. This has been particularly important to the System in times of stress when things were not going too well. These relationships also have been an extremely important factor in increasing the use of the System by farmers and their cooperatives, and in building a large, successful System with strong bipartisan support from passing generations of legislators.

Chapter 19

FARM AND COOPERATIVE ORGANIZATIONS LEND SUPPORT

The national farm and cooperative organizations, as well as their state and local member units, have almost uniformly maintained a keen interest in building and operating a strong cooperative Farm Credit System. They have rushed to its support when crucial issues threatened its future existence. They have been effective in enlisting legislative support when new laws or amendments were needed to improve the ability of the System to serve farmers. These organizations include the National Grange, the National Council of Farmer Cooperatives, the American Farm Bureau Federation, the National Milk Producers Federation, the National Farmers Union, the Cooperative League of the USA, and, in more recent years, the National Farmers Organization. The efforts of these organizations have been supplemented by those of local and regional farmer cooperatives and state cooperative councils.

The importance of working together in obtaining useful agricultural legislation was particularly demonstrated at the time of the passage of the Farm Credit Act of 1971. Most of the proposals for new authorities contained in that Act had grown out of the Report of the Commission on Agricultural Credit on which representatives of these organizations had served, along with representatives of the Farm Credit System.

Building a Cooperative System

In its early reports, the Federal Farm Loan Board—the first supervisory agency for the Federal Land Banks—made frequent reference to Congress's desire to build a great cooperative credit system and to its belief in that concept. However, the stress on the cooperative nature of the System varies by Farm Credit district and over time, depending upon the leadership in those districts.

Some of the Federal Land Bank officials for a period of time got away from the idea that they were a cooperative, even though they continued to stress that they were owned by farmers.

By the mid-1970s, several Land Bank presidents, as well as other Farm Credit Bank presidents, had become active in general cooperative affairs. However, as late as 1974, one Land Bank president claimed that the Federal Land Banks were not cooperatives. One cooperative purist[1] comments that this FLB president is correct because even though the Land Banks are owned and controlled by farmers and operate for their benefit, they do not pass their savings back to farmers in direct proportion to the amount of interest paid. Federal Land Banks and Federal Land Bank Associations return their savings to farmers as dividends on the stock which they buy in direct proportion to the loans they obtain. As they make their loan payments, they reduce the principal amount of their loans, and the amount needed to pay interest declines while the amount of their stock ownership remains the same. However, the Federal Land Banks and Federal Land Bank Associations pass the test of farmer-ownership and control.

When W. A. Hoag referred to Production Credit Associations as cooperatives in their formative days, his superior warned him against doing so because he felt that would be giving them the kiss of death. He cited farmers' many bitter experiences with failures of cooperatives. However, his attitude changed considerably as Myers more and more stressed the cooperative nature of the System in his public speeches.

Becoming Part of the Cooperative Family

The idea of the Farm Credit System being part of the larger cooperative family took a considerable time to be generally recognized, not only within the Farm Credit System but also by other types of cooperatives. Many of them looked upon the Farm Credit System as a Government program rather than as a cooperative. Some Farm Credit Bank presidents seemed to prefer a banker image to a cooperative image.

In the late 1930s, the Cooperative Research and Service Division of the Farm Credit Administration—now the Farmer Cooperative Service in the Department of Agriculture—was preparing a series of

---

[1] W. N. Stokes, Jr., retired President of the Federal Intermediate Credit Bank of Houston, who previously served as President of the Houston Bank for Cooperatives.

educational circulars for use in the vocational agricultural courses in high schools. Part of this series was designed to tell how farmers could use the services of various types of cooperatives. When the suggestion was made that two of the circulars in this series be devoted to how to use National Farm Loan Associations and how to use Production Credit Associations, the idea was turned down by both the Production Credit Commissioner, Steve Garwood, and the Chief of the Cooperative Research and Service Division, Tom Stitts.

When this came up in staff meeting, Myers insisted that both publications be included in the series. It was reported that Garwood was so upset over the decision that from then on he sent his deputy, C. R. "Cap" Arnold, to staff meetings. He was more sympathetic to the cooperative idea and became a strong advocate of it as time went on.

FLBAs and PCAs Start Working
with Other Cooperatives

Gradually, the Banks for Cooperatives laid more stress on the fact that they themselves were cooperatives. National Farm Loan Associations and Production Credit Associations began to join and participate in cooperative organizations such as the state councils of cooperatives and the American Institute of Cooperation. As a result, farmers' marketing and farm supply cooperatives began accepting them as cooperatives.

Articles about the Land Banks and Associations, Production Credit Associations, and Banks for Cooperatives in the *News for Farmer Cooperatives*, published by the Cooperative Research and Service Division of the Farm Credit Administration and now the Farmer Cooperative Service of the U.S. Department of Agriculture, helped achieve this goal. News about these organizations in the publications of other cooperatives also helped them to be recognized as cooperatives. Having all parts of the Farm Credit System receive the *News* kept them informed about other cooperatives. It helped them to gradually recognize themselves as part of the wider cooperative family.

The Banks for Cooperatives were early participants in and frequently cosponsors of the programs of the American Institute of Cooperation. As years went by, more and more local Associations and district Land Banks and Intermediate Credit Banks joined, participated in, and assumed leadership roles in the American Institute of Cooperation. Many have served on its Board of Trustees and as its officers. Some Farm Credit Banks have not only contributed to the financial support of the National Council of Farmer Cooperatives but have also formally joined it. Much the same is true with the work of the state councils of cooperatives. FCA Governors Tootell, Jaenke, and Harding have also served on the AIC Board of Trustees and have actively encouraged its support by the Cooperative Farm Credit System. The Farm Credit sessions and luncheons at AIC summer meetings long have drawn large audiences.

Aubrey Johnson, when he was Vice President of the Federal Intermediate Credit Bank of St. Paul, was one of the organizers, a strong supporter and a board member of Cooperative Management Development, Inc., which started under the auspices of the Cooperative League of the USA. Several of the Farm Credit Banks have participated in its program.

Governor Jaenke of the Farm Credit Administration served on the planning committee of the Graduate School of Cooperative Leadership at the University of Missouri for several years.

Chapter 20

WORKING WITH EDUCATIONAL
ORGANIZATIONS

Educational organizations such as the Land Grant colleges, the Extension Service, and the vocational agriculture teachers and their state departments of vocational agriculture have all helped build a strong and useful Farm Credit System.

These organizations have taught farmers how to use the best farming methods and how to manage successful farming operations, including the wise use of credit. They have pointed out the advantages of getting credit from the cooperative Farm Credit System and have explained how it operates.

The Extension Service has played many key roles in the organization and building of the System from its very beginning. For example, Fred Merrifield, retired President of the Wichita Bank for Cooperatives and General Agent of the Farm Credit Banks of Wichita and currently Executive Secretary of the Oklahoma Wheat Growers Association, remembers his own early involvements with the Farm Credit System. As County Agent he organized and served as secretary-treasurer for his local National Farm Loan Association in Oklahoma. In 1933, as a state extension official, he was a member of the team that toured the state helping to organize Production Credit Associations. Later in his Extension capacity, he cooperated with the Bank for Cooperatives in its various educational and training programs. Many similar experiences could be cited throughout the country.

Particularly in the early years, local Associations and district Farm Credit Banks recruited many county agents, vocational agricultural teachers, and state extension personnel for their staffs. However, this practice is now less frequent than in the earlier days, because the System "grows" or develops more of its own staffs. The Banks and Associations hire agricultural college and business school graduates, put them through well-organized orientation and training programs, and then promote them as their abilities expand.

Educators Helped Organize Local Associations

County agents, vocational agriculture teachers, and specialists on the staffs of the state extension services and agricultural colleges helped organize the National Farm Loan Associations, Production Credit Associations, and new farmers' marketing, farm supply, and business service cooperatives—in the latter case frequently in collaboration with the Banks for Cooperatives. Jointly with the Banks for Cooperatives, the state cooperative councils, the Farmer Cooperative Service, the Extension Service, or the American Institute of Cooperation have frequently organized cooperative educational and training programs for cooperative directors, officials, and staffs. Often such plans have resulted from the efforts of two or more of such organizations.

The Land Grant colleges have independently or under Farm Credit Bank or Farm Credit Administration sponsorship conducted many credit and cooperative research projects. They have also conducted many conferences, workshops, and schools for the Farm Credit System officers and staffs.

Joint Extension–FCA Program

From 1933 to 1953, the Farm Credit Administration had an arrangement with the Extension Service in Washington by which the Farm Credit Administration paid the salaries of one or two Extension specialists in credit and cooperatives, and the Extension Service paid the travel expenses.

The duties of these people, who included James L. Robinson, the last of such employees and the one who served the longest, included the preparation of materials for use by the Extension Service and vocational teachers in their educational programs. They also, in cooperation with Farm Credit district representatives, maintained relations with Federal and State Extension, vocational agriculture departments, and the Land Grant college teaching staffs, to help them work out plans for including the subject of credit and the Farm Credit System in their teaching programs. In 1953, the Extension Service, over Governor Arnold's objections, insisted that Robinson and his duties be transferred to it.

In addition, from 1935 to the mid-1940s, the Farm Credit Administration hired three home economists to work with the home economics teachers in the high schools and the home economists in the Extension Service to include the subject of agricultural credit in their programs. The Farm Credit Administration, for a period of about 30 years starting in 1933, had on its staff one or two specialists who worked with the Negro vocational agricultural teachers and those on Negro Extension staffs.[1]

Most of the Farm Credit Banks either jointly or individually have continued close relationships with state vocational agriculture departments and Extension services and some have prepared teaching materials for their programs. One example of such materials is the frequently brought up-to-date text on the use of credit now jointly published by the Omaha and Louisville Farm Credit Banks. It is entitled "Credit in Agriculture."

Since the 1950s Paul Mohn, business management economist in the Federal Extension Service, has worked closely with the Banks for Cooperatives in developing joint training projects with cooperatives.

---

[1] With the integration of educational organizations this became a function that was no longer needed.

Chapter 21

FCA RELATIONS WITH OTHER BRANCHES OF GOVERNMENT

The excellent bipartisan support that the Farm Credit System has received from Congress over the years already has been discussed in "Bipartisan Support," Chapter 10. The support from the White House has also usually been good.

Starting with President Woodrow Wilson's signing of the Federal Farm Loan Act in 1916, most Presidents have approved legislation affecting the cooperative Farm Credit System, either directly or indirectly.

President Warren G. Harding, after calling on Congress to take such action, signed the Capper-Volstead Act in 1922 and thus set the stage for a greater development of farmer cooperatives that has been financed by the Banks for Cooperatives since 1933.

President Calvin Coolidge signed the Cooperative Marketing Act of 1926 that established the Cooperative Marketing Division in the U.S. Department of Agriculture to carry on research, service, and educational work with cooperatives. This Division was transferred to the Federal Farm Board in 1929 and thus became part of the Farm Credit Administration in 1933.

In 1929, President Herbert Hoover asked Congress to establish the Federal Farm Board to promote the development of cooperatives and to provide financing for them—a major part of Hoover's answer to the farm problem. In 1933, the Cooperative Marketing Division and the money salvaged from the revolving fund were merged into the Farm Credit Administration. The money was used to capitalize Banks for Cooperatives.

On his inauguration day, March 4, 1933, President Franklin D. Roosevelt took over the leadership of the Nation. He was faced with more serious emergency situations than any incoming President since Abraham Lincoln. Runs on commercial banks, for example, were of panic proportions. In order to forestall a complete breakdown of the

Nation's banking system, he closed all banks that very day until further notice. Business bankruptcies were a daily occurrence. Crowds of farmers threatened sheriffs at tax sales. Bread lines of unemployed were a daily sight all across the country.

Although faced with this myriad of problems, President Roosevelt almost immediately began to reorganize the Government's scattered attempts to provide agricultural credit assistance. Before the end of the month of March, he issued an Executive Order bringing all existing Government agricultural credit agencies together into the Farm Credit Administration. By May 12, 1933, he signed the Emergency Farm Mortgage Act, thus giving the Land Banks the responsibility of refinancing farmers' debts. The Act also gave the Land Banks the resources and authorities needed to do the job.

By June 16, 1933, President Roosevelt had signed the Farm Credit Act of 1933, rounding out the permanent group of banks and associations that make up much the same cooperative Farm Credit System of today. Roosevelt had given advance blessing to these plans, including the establishment of the permanent Banks for Cooperatives and Production Credit Associations.

President Dwight D. Eisenhower played a crucial role in the development of the Farm Credit Act of 1953, which again made the Farm Credit Administration an independent agency in the Executive branch of the Government. He had promised such action in a campaign speech at Omaha, Nebraska, September 18, 1952.

There he said, in part, "The Federal Farm Credit Board, elected by farmer-members, should be established to form policies, select executive officers and to see that sound credit operations will not be endangered by partisan political influence."

Presidents Kennedy and Johnson did not remove the Governor of the Farm Credit Administration appointed by the Federal Farm Credit Board during a Republican Administration.

President Richard M. Nixon signed the Farm Credit Act of 1971, although he declined holding any ceremony to mark the event. This Act modernized the basic legislation for the entire cooperative Farm Credit System. It also greatly expanded its scope of service and improved its ability to provide that service.

President Gerald Ford in 1976 approved legislation making it possible for more cooperatives operating as a public utility—such as rural electric cooperatives—to qualify for loans from the Banks for Cooperatives.

Federal Farm Credit Board
1953

Governor C. R. "Cap" Arnold
1954

Commission on Agricultural Credit
Whose Study Paved the Way
for the Farm Credit Act of 1971

President Woodrow Wilson
Signing Federal Farm Loan Act
July 17, 1916

President Warren G. Harding
Signing Capper-Volstead Act in 1922

President Harry S. Truman Smiles
as Million Dollar Check Brings Dividends
of Federal Farm Mortgage Corporation
to $100 Million in 1951

President Dwight D. Eisenhower Signs
Farm Credit Act of 1953

Relationships with Treasury Department

The cooperative Farm Credit System has had relatively close relations with the Treasury Department over the years, although under varying circumstances. In the beginning the *ex officio* Chairman of the Federal Farm Loan Board was the Secretary of the Treasury. The administrative work of the Federal Farm Loan Board was carried out through the Federal Farm Loan Bureau of the Treasury Department. The supervision of the Federal Land Banks, the National Farm Loan Associations (now the Federal Land Bank Associations), and the Federal Intermediate Credit Banks was one of the functions transferred to the Farm Credit Administration in 1933. However, Myers reported that after Morgenthau left the Farm Credit Administration to become Secretary of the Treasury, he continued to give sympathetic support to it and to the System at critical points in the emergency period.

While Government capital was invested in the cooperative Farm Credit System—up until 1968—the various revolving funds such as those of the capitalization of the Federal Intermediate Credit Banks, the Production Credit Corporations, and the Banks for Cooperatives were held on deposit at the Treasury Department, subject to call by the Governor of the Farm Credit Administration. Although inactive since 1968, the revolving funds for the Governor to make emergency investment in Banks for Cooperatives and the Federal Intermediate Credit Banks or Production Credit Associations are still held by the Treasury Department.

Until 1974, when such functions were transferred to the Federal Reserve Bank of New York, the transfer of funds from bond sales and repayments was handled through a "symbol account" in the Treasury Department.

The Treasury Department is by far the largest issuer of securities in the Nation. Its securities are sold to much the same types of investors as the bonds of the Banks in the cooperative Farm Credit System, along with those of other organizations using the Agency Market to raise their funds; hence, the Treasury has always maintained a close interest in the Farm Credit System security operations. Before approving issues of the bonds of the Land Banks, Intermediate Credit Banks, and Banks for Cooperatives, the Governor of the Farm Credit Administration discusses, at great length, such proposed issues with representatives of the Treasury Department. These discussions involve the amount of money being raised by each issue and the maturity dates of the issues.

From the time of the passage of the Corporation Control Act in 1946, until the Federal Intermediate Credit Banks started paying off their Government capital and thus became mixed ownership corporations, the Governor of the Farm Credit Administration was required to get approval from the Secretary of the Treasury before he could issue new bonds.

At times, these discussions—"consultations"—except in the case of the bonds of the Federal Intermediate Credit Banks when the Government still owned all their capital, have sometimes resulted in changes in the length and maturity of the bonds to be issued to terms that were not exactly what the particular group of Banks preferred to issue. However, such coordination with the financing efforts of the Treasury Department, and the other financial organizations selling their securities in the Agency Market, probably has worked out in the long run to the advantage of the cooperative Farm Credit System and its members.

In 1973, Congress authorized the establishment of a Federal Financing Bank to handle the money-raising activities of most of the organizations using the Agency Market for the sale of their securities. However, the Farm Credit System, the Home Loan Bank System, and the Federal National Mortgage Corporation (Fannie Mae) were exempted from having to use the facilities of the Federal Financing Bank.

If these exemptions had not been included in the Act establishing the Federal Financing Bank, it would have eliminated the cooperative Farm Credit System's direct access to the Nation's financial markets. The cooperative Farm Credit System has long insisted that it needed this direct access to investors in order to insure its ability to meet the needs of farmers and their cooperatives for funds to carry on their farming operations.

The System and the Farm Credit Administration have made it clear to the Treasury and to key Congressional leaders that the type of financing provided by the cooperative Farm Credit System cannot wait any length of time to have the funds that farmers and their cooperatives need, because of the seasonal and biological nature of farming and the perishability of its food products. The System's record of responsibility and cooperation also probably stood it in good stead in obtaining this exemption.

The Treasury undoubtedly would have preferred a neater package with no exemptions. However, the Farm Credit System and the Farm Credit Administration had long ago made the Treasury knowledgeable about the importance of the needs of agriculture to the entire economy. In addition, the Treasury knew that the System had performed well and cooperated wherever possible over the years. It also knew from past experience that Congress would take a dim view of cutting off the cooperative Farm Credit System's direct access to the money markets and thus run the chance of endangering the Nation's food supply in some future administration.

Relationships with the U.S. Department of Agriculture

The Farm Credit System has had a wide variety of separate relationships with different parts of the Department of Agriculture. These relationships have also varied in different periods of its history.

Before the U.S. Department of Agriculture Years

For a period of 14 years—1939 to 1953—the cooperative Farm Credit System's supervisory agency—the Farm Credit Administration—was part of the U.S. Department of Agriculture. Before that, from 1933 to 1939, the Farm Credit Administration had been an independent agency.

During the 1933–40 period, Henry A. Wallace was Secretary of Agriculture. A major part of his solution for raising the prices farmers received for their products, and thus their income, from the disastrous levels of the Great Depression was to curtail production by getting farmers to sign agreements to plant no more than their allotted share of various basic crops. These included wheat, corn, cotton, tobacco, and peanuts. Those who signed such agreements were then eligible for loans to store these products. If the price went below the loan value, the Government would take the stored crop in full payment for farmers' loans.

The Agricultural Adjustment Administration wanted the Farm Credit Administration to require farmers to sign up for this program so that they would be eligible to obtain operating loans from the Production Credit Associations. The Farm Credit Administration pointed out that Congress had not seen fit to specify such arrangements and the whole philosophy of the Farm Credit System was to let farmers make their own business decisions. In addition, if the Production Credit Association required its members to sign such agreements in order to get loans and then had difficulty in repaying them, they would have an alibi for not repaying their loans.

Finally, the Farm Credit Administration agreed to ask the Production Credit Associations to encourage their members to sign up where such an agreement would enhance the probability of the farmer having enough income to repay his loan, but not to require it. Secretary Wallace reportedly was upset because the Farm Credit Administration would not cooperate in requiring compliance with the farm program. By Executive Order of President Roosevelt, the Farm Credit Administration became a part of the U.S. Department of Agriculture, effective July 1, 1939.

The controversy over that action and its political and philosophical overtones began a stormy period of Farm Credit System relations with Secretary of Agriculture Wallace. Some of the storm subsided, however, when his efforts to alter the basic nature of the cooperative Farm Credit System failed, and he became Vice President. (See "Controversy and Politics Rear Their Ugly Heads," Chapter 27, for more details.)

However, the suspicion of political influences on the System remained and was a major factor in the build-up that resulted in the passage of the Farm Credit Act of 1953 which again made the Farm Credit Administration an independent agency.

In the first year or two of A. G. Black's service as Governor of the Farm Credit Administration (1940 to 1944), there were some indications that he looked to some of the Secretary of Agriculture's immediate staff for guidance on basic Farm Credit decisions, but there was less evidence of that being the case after Claude Wickard became Secretary of Agriculture in 1941, at the time Wallace became Vice President.

Governor Duggan says there was no interference in policy matters—1943 to 1953. He remembered, once in Secretary Clinton Anderson's tenure, when there was an attempt to influence action on a loan to a cooperative. Then, Duggan said the making of loans was not his job, but if it came to him for approval he would have to turn it down. When he explained his reasons, he received no further pressure.

Perhaps part of the image the Farm Credit System had of the U.S. Department of Agriculture was due to the way certain FCA administrators communicated with the Farm Credit Banks. If general government-wide regulations on such matters as personnel and budgets were passed on to the Farm Credit Administration by the Department of Agriculture, these officials gave them the strictest possible interpretations and sent them on to the Farm Credit Banks as the USDA's rulings. For example, on one occasion the FCA Director of Personnel gave the following as his reason for not taking a desired action: "I do not *think* the Department would *like* us to do that." The FCA division chief replied, "We do not do it that way in our Division. We do what we think is right and if they do not agree they will have to tell us. So far we have had no problems."

Relations with the Secretary's Staff

Another example of this type of interpretation of USDA messages is cited by a former FCA division chief. He remembers that early in 1953, shortly after President Eisenhower had taken office, he received a call from the Deputy Governor for Administration telling him to devise a plan to cut his budget by 15 percent, in line with a Government-wide edict from the U.S. Department of Agriculture, by the next morning. Instead, the division chief prepared a memorandum explaining why he was already seriously understaffed. In the discussion of his memorandum, he mentioned that a friend in the USDA Office of Budget and Finance had told him, "Oh, that isn't supposed to apply to FCA—you have already cut down too much." At that point the division chief's proposal for lowering by three grades one highly overrated position, rather than resulting in a reduction in staff, was accepted at the comptroller's suggestion.

When the Farm Credit Administration first became part of the Department of Agriculture, the FCA Information Division was informed that all future publications would have to be cleared by the Department's Office of Information for coordination and transmittal to the Government Printing Office. When it was pointed out that FCA publications came out of the FCA budget rather than the Department-wide printing budget, the Director of Information for the Department settled for a carbon copy of manuscripts being sent to the printer. There was occasional kidding about when the Farm Credit Administration was going to learn it was part of the U.S. Department of Agriculture, when FCA's Information Division had good reason not to be part of some overall USDA programs. However, the relationships with the Director of Information remained excellent. The Farm Credit Administration gladly cooperated on any Department-wide information projects that seemed to be in the best interest of the farmer-members of the Farm Credit System. The relationships between the Office of Information of the Department of Agriculture and the Farm Credit Administration continued to be excellent after the Farm Credit Administration again became an independent agency.

Federal Extension Service

The discussion of these relationships is covered under the heading, "Joint Extension-FCA Program" in Chapter 20.

Farmer Cooperative Service

For several reasons, the Farmer Cooperative Service has always had close working relationships with the Farm Credit Administration and the Banks for Cooperatives. First, they have a common interest in the success and welfare of all types of farmer cooperatives. Second, the critics of either tend to be the critics of the other. The Farm Credit Administration and the Farmer Cooperative Service are the only two Government organizations that can be relied upon to come to the general defense of farmer cooperatives. And third, these organizations have long felt a kinship to each other. What is now the Farmer Cooperative Service in the U.S. Department of Agriculture was for 20 years—1933 to 1953—the Cooperative Research and Service Division in the Farm Credit Administration. Many of the staff members of the Farm Credit Administration and the Farmer Cooperative Service had worked together on many joint projects.

The Banks for Cooperatives have made wide use of the research studies and educational publications of the Farmer Cooperative Service and have collaborated in sponsoring many types of cooperative educational meetings, workshops, schools, and training sessions. From time to time, the Farmer Cooperative Service, at the request of various Banks for Cooperatives, has made special studies of the feasibility of various cooperative proposals, including new cooperatives, expansions of services, mergers, and the location of new facilities. For a discussion of the Farmer Cooperative Service years in the Farm Credit Administration, see "Farmer Cooperative Service on FCA Team" in Chapter 26 and "Financing Food for Freedom" in Chapter 28.

Farmers Home Administration

The Farmers Home Administration is the descendent of the Farm Security Administration and its ancestor, the Rural Rehabilitation Administration— created by an Executive Order of President Roosevelt— born in the Great Depression years of the 1930s, much as the Farm Credit Administration had been a year or two earlier. However, the Rural Rehabilitation Administration (RRA) had no basic laws to govern its actions. It was headed by Rexford Tugwell, who was a very imaginative, glamorous friend of President and Mrs. Roosevelt and was frequently in the public eye with new, unusual projects such as three or four low-rent "green towns" on the far outskirts of cities, and government loan programs for smaller farmers—programs that typically involved getting the borrowers to agree to operate their farms

under new farming plans drawn up by the county RRA representative.
This approach to farm lending was quite different from that of the
Farm Credit System's "business" type loans that were dependent for
their financing largely on the sale of their securities to investors without any government guarantee.

In the early days of the Rural Rehabilitation Administration, and
the broadened Farm Credit System, the differences in philosophies of
the two agricultural lending organizations produced people who often
were critical of the other's organization. Some members of Congress
were also critical of some of RRA's suggestions and later of its successor, the Farm Security Administration (FSA). Some people also suggested merging the two credit systems. Myers remembers that Congressman Marvin Jones from Texas, who was chairman of the House
Agriculture Committee, suggested incorporating the Rural Rehabilitation Administration in the Farm Credit Administration. He recalls
telling Jones that business-type lending and "soft loans" should not
be handled by the same organization. Many people in the Farm Credit
System agreed with Myers.

In the early 1940s, when A. G. Black was Governor of the Farm
Credit Administration, there were newspaper stories suggesting the
Farm Security Administration might take over all or parts of the Farm
Credit System. In 1947, with support of some of the farm organizations,
Representative John Flanigan introduced a bill which would have
coordinated the FSA functions and the supervision of the Farm Credit
System in a new Agricultural Credit Agency under a full-time Agricultural Credit Board. Opposition from the Farm Credit System resulted in the proposal dying in the Senate. Eventually, Congress enacted a law to govern the Farm Security Administration which placed
some limits on its activities. The name was changed to Farmers Home
Administration (FmHA). Criticism from Congress and farm groups
subsided and people from each organization became less critical of
each other. By the mid-1970s there was considerable cooperation between the Farmers Home Administration and the various parts of the
Farm Credit System.

Some Land Banks are making joint mortgage loans with the
Farmers Home Administration—especially to young farmers and
others just starting to farm.

The Farmers Home Administration and the Farm Credit Association have an agreement whereby the Farmers Home Administration
will guarantee PCA loans. However, they cannot agree to terms
whereby the Farmers Home Administration will guarantee longer
term loans made by the Banks for Cooperatives because of their variable interest rates.

Relations with Budget Bureau—OMB

The present Office of Management and Budget (OMB) was established as the Bureau of the Budget. It in turn had succeeded the old Bureau of Efficiency after World War I. In essence, the function of the Office of Management and Budget is to coordinate the overall budget of all the Government departments for the President to present to Congress for approval. In order to carry out this function, it must judge what each Government organization actually needs to carry out the programs authorized by Congress. In fulfilling this function, the Office of Management and Budget tries to evaluate how each agency fits into the President's overall objectives and then tries to keep its budget within a certain predetermined level. Actually, the Office of Management and Budget is always concerned as to how it can save Government money. Sometimes, its evaluations of the effectiveness and importance of various programs differ with those that Congress has set forth.

The Farm Credit System has been affected at various times in its history by the decisions of the Office of Management and Budget and more particularly by its predecessor, the Bureau of the Budget.

Not long after the United States became directly involved in World War II, the then Governor of the Farm Credit Administration, A. G. Black, instituted an economy program to release manpower for essential Government and industrial projects. He also applied pressure on the district Banks and the Production Credit Corporations to do likewise. Staffs were gradually cut and vacancies were usually not filled. This program was continued under Governor Duggan. This economy program, overall, was probably well justified, because the emergency and organization period was over. As training programs had borne fruit, the Banks and Associations needed less supervision and more and more authority could be delegated to them.

However, shortly after World War II the Budget Bureau began looking for ways to reduce Government expenditures. It adopted Government-wide percentage cuts in money that could be spent and in the number of authorized positions. In addition, the Budget Bureau at times placed limits on the percentage of people who could be employed in the higher grades. Such programs naturally caused more problems for organizations like the Farm Credit Administration that had already done a conscientious job of reducing expenditures than they did in Government agencies that had plenty of "fat" in their budgets.

These Government-wide programs also affected the Intermediate Credit Banks and Production Credit Corporations because their budgets became subject to Congressional and Budget Bureau approval under the Corporation Control Act passed in 1946. That Act put all wholly Government-owned corporations under the whole Government budgeting program. As mixed ownership corporations, the Land Banks and Banks for Cooperatives were not affected. As Stokes points out, in 1947 the Budget Bureau reduced the funds for operational expenditures of the 12 Federal Intermediate Credit Banks from $1.78 million to $1.25 million.[1] This cut came just at a time when larger staffs were needed to handle credit and operating problems growing out of the changed conditions following World War II.

In addition to these problems, the Budget Bureau has from time to time endeavored to get Congress to place budget controls on the number of loans Government-owned corporations could make in any one year. In fact, it got such a bill through the House, but it failed to pass the Senate. The Budget Bureau insisted such budget controls were needed because the loans of such lending organizations increased the money supply and were, therefore, inflationary.

The Farm Credit System and the Farm Credit Administration have always insisted that the System's function was to supply whatever credit farmers and cooperatives needed and such amounts could not be accurately predicted 18 months in advance as required by the budgetary process. In fact, at times the Banks of the System have found it difficult to predict how much money they would need even one month in advance, as demonstrated by their over- or under-issuing of new bonds. They also have continually pointed out that since the System's loans are used very largely for production purposes and functions connected therewith, they are counterinflationary rather than inflationary.

By paying off the last of its Government capital in 1968, the System put itself beyond the reach of any foreseeable budgetary controls.

The Farm Credit Act of 1971 authorized the Federal Farm Credit Board to determine the budgets of the Farm Credit Administration without additional budgetary controls. However, the Senate and House Agriculture Committees, as well as the House Agricultural Appropriations Subcommittee, have expressed their desire to meet with the Chairman of the Federal Farm Credit Board and the Governor of the Farm Credit Administration annually to discuss the general agricultural credit situation and the progress of the System in serving the needs of its member-borrowers.

---

[1] W. N. Stokes, Jr., "Credit to Farmers," Federal Intermediate Credit Banks, Washington, D.C., 1973, p. 92.

Another function of the Office of Management and Budget, and its predecessor the Budget Bureau, is the approval for the President and his administration of any proposed legislation developed by any Government agency before it is sent to Congress. When such approvals are requested, they may run into considerable delay because the Office of Management and Budget refers such proposals to the various Government departments and agencies for comment. Then, too, the Office of Management and Budget may decide that the administration does not want such legislation to be enacted. In that case, proposals for legislation are bottled up. This was the case with the Farm Credit System and the Farm Credit Administration prior to the passage of the Farm Credit Act of 1953.

However, the Farm Credit Act of 1953 fortunately required the Federal Farm Credit Board to *report to Congress* on plans for replacing Government capital. The Act also specified the Board was to report to Congress on any additional legislation that might be needed.

When the Federal Farm Credit Board proposed the Farm Credit Acts of 1955 and 1956 to provide a means by which the Banks for Cooperatives and the Federal Intermediate Credit Banks and Production Credit Corporations could become completely farmer-owned, the Budget Bureau had some objections to these plans. As a result, the Federal Farm Credit Board sent its proposals to Congress with the notation that the Budget Bureau felt that some provision should be made for the Government to recover part of the earned net worth built up during the period when these organizations had Government capital invested in them.

In the hearings on these two Acts, the Federal Farm Credit Board explained to Congress that the Government investments in these organizations were made to accomplish specific objectives rather than to make a profit. In addition, it pointed out that farmers had been urged to replace the Government-owned stock in these organizations so they could become completely farmer-owned, under the assumption that the reserves or earned surplus would remain intact. The Board felt that any retroactive change in such plans would be unfair to the member-borrowers in the System. Fortunately, the Agriculture Committees in both Houses of Congress agreed with the Federal Farm Credit Board's point of view.

But the matter did not end there. The following year President Dwight D. Eisenhower, acting on the suggestion of the Budget Bureau, included in his State of the Union message to Congress the advice that some provision should be made for the Government to recover its share of such net worth reserves or surplus. Congress did not act on that proposal.

Relations with General Accounting Office

The General Accounting Office is directly responsible to the Congress. It provides an examination function to make sure that Government departments and agencies use their funds in the way Congress intended them.

Over the years, the General Accounting Office reinforced the Budget Bureau's suggestions for reducing the Government investment in the capital of the System and also in reducing the size of the revolving funds available for investment in the Banks for Cooperatives, the Federal Intermediate Credit Banks, and the Production Credit Corporations.

In more recent years, the General Accounting Office joined with the Budget Bureau, after all the Government capital had been repaid, in suggesting that the Farm Credit Administration should pay rent for the space which it occupied in the U.S. Department of Agriculture. It would, thus, become an expense that would be allocated to the Banks, along with other expenses of the Farm Credit Administration. The Farm Credit Act of 1971 omitted the requirement that the Farm Credit Administration be housed in the Department of Agriculture. At that point, the Federal Farm Credit Board arranged to rent space for the Farm Credit Administration outside the Department. It is now located in a modern, privately owned office building.

The Government Corporation Control Act provided that the General Accounting Office would audit the accounts of all wholly owned Government corporations. The Federal Intermediate Credit Banks and the Production Credit Corporations fell into that category. This caused considerable consternation within the Farm Credit System, because the Farm Credit Administration was already required to examine all parts of the System, and it seemed as though these parts of the System would be subject to dual examination. However, the General Accounting Office took a reasonable approach to the situation and agreed to examine sample Banks annually to test the adequacy of the Farm Credit Administration's examinations. Each year the General Accounting Office reported to Congress that it found the Farm Credit Administration was doing an adequate job of carrying on its examination function. For example, for the fiscal year 1947, the General Accounting Office in its report to Congress, when commenting on the audit of Farm Credit organizations, said,[2] "In the course of our survey, we observed no programs and no expenditures or other financial transactions which had been carried on or made without authority of law." Similar comments were made in succeeding years.

---

[2] Fourteenth Annual Report, Farm Credit Administration, Government Printing Office, Washington, D.C., 1947, p. 51.

PART FIVE

Farmers' Needs for Credit—
Explode After Slow
Buildup

The steam behind farmers', ranchers', and their cooperatives' needs for credit developed over a two-century period. When that energy was finally harnessed, it powered a credit organization from which they borrowed $250 billion in 60 years—one-half of that in the last 6 years.

Up to this point, the development of some of the most important underlying principles, procedures, and practices that have made it possible for the cooperative Farm Credit System to expand its capability to meet an increasingly large share of the fast-growing total credit needs of the agricultural industry have been traced. Chapters 22 to 30 outline chronologically some of the most important high points in that development.

Chapter 22

BEFORE THE LAND BANKS—1620 TO 1916

When did American farmers start having credit problems? That is hard to determine. It might have been when Priscilla and John Alden decided they wanted to live on the farm next to their parents instead of pushing the Indians farther back, hewing the trees, and building a log cabin on the edge of the Plymouth Colony on Cape Cod. Further, we might imagine their parents' neighbor may have been willing to sell out and take a mortgage as part payment—probably payable in kind or in hard labor.

There is evidence that there was a recognized need for specialized credit for farmers in colonial times. The Land and Loan Bank of the Carolinas was established at Charleston, South Carolina, as early as 1712, and is credited by some to have been the first farm credit bank in America.[1] Colonial Land Banks were later established in 12 of the 13 colonies that eventually became the original states.

American Ancestors of FLBs?

In Connecticut, the land owners bought stock and obtained mortgages from the New London Society United for Trade and Commerce from 1732 to 1762. There is even reported evidence to indicate that the cornerstone of the cooperative Farm Credit System—the Federal Land Banks—were their direct descendants and drew on the experience of these early colonial banks with nearly a two-century detour in Europe. The pattern for the Federal Land Banks drew on the German Landschaft system which began with the Silesian Landschaft in 1796.

According to Wiprud, they were inspired by observations of these early colonial land banks.[2] In the intervening years, the German Land-

---

[1] "The History of Farm Mortgage Credit in the U.S.," Federal Land Bank of Berkeley, in *Down the Road Together,* Federal Land Banks, 1967, p. 6.

[2] A. C. Wiprud, "The Federal Farm Loan System in Operation," in *Down the Road Together,* Federal Land Banks, 1967, p. 6.

schaft pattern had been copied by France, Denmark, and other European countries.

New Land in West—Less Pressure for Credit

However, farmers' credit problems did not begin to become generally critical for about a century and a half after those colonial land bank experiments were discontinued. When a farmer and his family had trouble—financial or otherwise—they could pick up and go west in search of rich prairie land. In the years following 1848, there was also the lure of gold to be dug in California. Then came the 1860s. There was a Civil War to be won by northerners or midwesterners and southerners, many of whom stayed home to help whip those "damn Yankees." Those who stayed home in the north could reap rich harvests of ever more plentiful dollars from higher and higher priced farm products. But the War—by whatever name—was over in 1865. Food was still in short supply for a few years, especially in the South, as battlefields gradually were reconverted to corn fields, wheat fields, pastures, and orchards.

Farm Prices—Down, Down

The farm picture started to change. Food began to become more plentiful. The big push westward was increasing the flood tide of farm products moving to eastern and foreign markets as more and more virgin prairie land was broken to the plow—spurred on by the availability of land for the claiming under the Homestead Act of 1862. Farm and other prices went on their 25-year toboggan. The supply of farm and industrial goods grew faster than the supply of gold required to back American dollars.

Farmers and rural communities far from the city money centers suffered most. Their displeasure spawned the midwestern-based Populist Party's campaign for the printing of "greenbacks" not backed by gold. In his three unsuccessful Democratic campaigns for the Presidency, silver-tongued William Jennings Bryan demanded, in his "Cross of Gold" speeches, that silver be added to the standard for U.S. currency—since silver was much more plentiful than gold.

The banking panic of 1896 generated a campaign for banking reforms. The Panic of 1907 heightened the cries for overhauling the banking system. Over a two-year period—1914 to 1916—the United States was to see the establishment of the Federal Reserve Bank System and the laying of the cornerstone for the cooperative Farm Credit

System—the Federal Land Banks and their local Associations. These local cooperatives became the main footings for the modern banking structure 60 years later.

Pressure for Credit Increases

With the Homestead Act, land free for the settling no longer available, the beginnings of farm mechanization, and the accompanying specialization, farmers' needs for credit were on the increase. Money for any kind of loans in most rural areas was scarce. Money, when it was available, was usually concentrated in the big cities.

Farm leaders, farm politicians, and the farm press naturally were in the forefront of the battle for banking reform. They also wanted a system of credit that was especially adapted to the needs of farmers, rather than one that compelled them to use loans that were designed to meet the needs of other businesses.

Country Life Commission Points the Way

In 1908, President Theodore Roosevelt appointed a Country Life Commission headed by Liberty Hyde Bailey,[3] Dean of Agriculture at Cornell University. The Commission was given a broad charter to investigate the needs of farmers and rural Americans. It held hearings in 40 states and estimated the total attendance at 12,000. The Commission's report was a comprehensive one. It included recommendations that were prophetic of what was yet to come. These recommendations included a rural free delivery system, increased educational efforts that were the forerunner of the Extension Service, development of more cooperatives, and a cooperative agricultural credit system.

Farm Papers Press for Credit for Farmers

One of the leaders of the farm paper campaign for the reform of the banking system, and particularly the establishment of cooperative credit facilities, was Herbert Myrick, editor and publisher of the Orange Judd chain of farm papers. The chain, headquartered in Springfield, Massachusetts, with offices in other cities such as New York and Atlanta, included the *New England Homestead* and *Southern Farming*.

---

[3] See "Leaders with Vision and Ability," Chapter 9 for more information about Bailey.

The intensity of Myrick's campaign is illustrated in the November 16, 1912 edition of *Southern Farming*. In that edition, he reprinted a three-column open letter to each state Governor outlining what he thought the Congress and each state should do about the banking laws. He also was taking applications for a newly formed Cooperative Finance League and carried an advertisement for a new book which he had written entitled "Cooperative Finance."

In his letter to the Governors of the states, Myrick called for the Federal and state chartering of "People's Little Cooperative Banks" (credit unions). He pointed to the success of the credit union his employees had organized under the Massachusetts Act which had been passed in 1909—the first state to do so. He also asked for the states to charter cooperative building and loan associations and for Federally and state-chartered land banks. He wanted a national land bank in each state.

President and Congress Interested

Also in 1912, President William Howard Taft had asked his ambassadors in Europe to investigate farm credit systems there. That same year, all three political parties—Republican, Democratic, and Progressive—called for the establishment of a farm credit system.

Two Commissions Go to Europe

By 1913, two commissions had been appointed to go to Europe to study what had been done in various countries. The American Commissions came as the result of action taken at a meeting of the Southern Commercial Congress, which had heard a report from David Lubin, a visionary California merchant who had been named the first U.S. delegate to the International Institute of Agriculture at Rome. He outlined in some detail the farm financing methods used in European countries, including the highly successful, 100-year-old Landschaft system in Germany. The U.S. Commission, authorized by Congress and appointed by President Wilson, included seven people. The two commissions had joined forces in studying the experience of European countries. In their joint report, they recommended including small independent Federally chartered land banks with a minimum of $10,000 in capital, Federally chartered joint stock or cooperative land banks, or local associations with a central association to buy the mortgages.

Cooperative Credit Idea Given a Chance

By this time, Congress was convinced of the need and ready to find a way to satisfy it. In the 63rd Congress, 70 rural credit measures were introduced. In general, these proposed bills fell into three classes. One advocated direct loans to farmers from Government funds. A second group believed that the job should be given to Federally chartered, but investor-owned joint stock land banks, which would finance their loans by issuing bonds backed by the mortgages given for their loans. The third group wanted to establish a cooperative system where groups of farmer-borrowers through local associations would borrow from their district Federal Land Banks, which would be initially capitalized by the Federal Government.

There was such a difference in views that a joint committee of Congress was appointed to study the problem of rural credit. The solution suggested by this committee, and ultimately passed as the Farm Loan Act of 1916 (known as the Hollis[4] bill in the Senate), was a compromise. It provided both for land banks to be ultimately owned by farmers through their local National Farm Loan Associations (now Federal Land Bank Associations) and for joint stock land banks to be owned by private investors.

Short-Term Credit Needs Passed Over

There also was concern in Congress over the need for short-term operating credit. However, its Subcommittee on Personal Rural Credits did not report out a bill. That need was to wait another 6 years before it was seriously tackled—when the Federal Intermediate Credit Banks were established—and another 10 years before a real solution was reached—the formation of Production Credit Associations.

President Wilson Sees Need and Signs

In signing the Federal Farm Loan Act on July 17, 1916, President Woodrow Wilson[5] told the assembled Senators, Congressmen, and

---

[4] Senator from New Hampshire.

[5] President Wilson used two pens to sign the Act. He gave one to Senator Duncan Fletcher of Florida who was Chairman of the Government commission that had gone to Europe to study their farm credit systems. (It was later given to the Farm Credit Banks of Columbia.) The other went to Herbert Myrick of Massachusetts, the farm paper publisher who had led the campaign for finding a solution to this farm problem. (It is currently on display at the Farm Credit Banks of Springfield on loan from the Myrick family.)

farm leaders:

> Farmers, it seems to me, have occupied, hitherto, a sin-
> gular position of disadvantage. They have not had the same
> freedom to get credit on their real estate as others have had
> who were in manufacturing and commercial enterprises and,
> while they have sustained our life, they did not in the same
> degree with some others, share in the benefits of that life.
>
> Therefore, this bill, along with the very liberal provisions
> of the Federal Reserve Act, puts them upon an equality
> with all others who have genuine assets, and makes the
> great credit of the country available to them.
>
> I look forward to the benefits of this bill not with ex-
> travagant expectation, but with confident expectation that
> it will be of very wide-reaching benefit and, incidentally, it
> will be of advantage to the investing community, for I can
> imagine no more satisfactory and solid investment than this
> system will afford to those who have money to use.

Thus, President Wilson had "laid the cornerstone" of the cooperative Farm Credit System. Like a cathedral, it has been under construction for 60 years. Who can say when needs will stop growing
and changing, so the final stone will be put in place?

Land Bank Birth Pains

Within three weeks after President Wilson had signed the Act,
he had appointed the members of the Federal Farm Loan Board,
with Secretary of the Treasury William G. McAdoo serving as
ex officio chairman. But already there was a mountain of work to be
done. The Board met on August 7 and found thousands of letters
from farmers inquiring about how to obtain loans from the newly
authorized Federal Land Banks.[6] These letters had come to the
Treasury Department, the Department of Agriculture, the White
House, and various other bureaus and departments, including the
Census Bureau and the Library of Congress.

Dividing Up the Country

Congress had left it to the Board's discretion as to what the
territories of the 12 Land Banks should be and where they should

---

[6] First Annual Report of Federal Farm Loan Board, Government Printing
Office, Washington, D.C., 1918.

be headquartered. Within 2 weeks the Board's organization began holding hearings to determine the actual farm loan needs. In 9 weeks it held 53 hearings in 44 states; it traveled over 20,000 miles.

In its first report to Congress, the Board listed nine factors it took into consideration in drawing the territories for the Federal Land Banks. The nine factors considered were as follows: (1) total land area; (2) area of land in farms; (3) area of improved land in farms; (4) number of farms mortgaged at the present time; (5) amount of outstanding mortgage indebtedness; (6) value of farm land and buildings; (7) gross value of farm products; (8) total population; and (9) rural population.

The Board had modified the averaging of these factors by two other considerations—first, whether the prevailing rate of interest in the state under consideration was such that it would be likely to lead to a rapid shifting of farm loans from existing holders to the Federal Land Banks, and secondly, whether the proposed district was fairly well developed agriculturally or still largely undeveloped.

The Board also kept in mind the advisability of creating districts which would not be one-crop districts. It felt that it would be dangerous to create districts that would be homogeneous—i.e., dependent on the same crops. The Board feared that a one-crop district might result in the Land Bank's suffering from a crop failure which would produce an undue proportion of foreclosures.

Locating the Banks

The Board had many requests to locate Land Banks in particular cities. Its decisions were based on the following factors: (1) a reasonable approximation to the geographical center; (2) prompt and frequent train and mail service; (3) a climate that would not impair the efficiency of the force; and (4) a congenial environment. The Board said:

> We felt that it was undesirable that the Banks whose principal function was to serve the farm loan needs of the country should be located in such centers of population as New York or Chicago. Other things being equal, we felt that it was preferable to select cities where there was already an aroused interest in agriculture, which had manifested itself in the formation of committees or other bodies that were doing practical and efficient work along the lines of agricultural development; where there was sympathy and appreciation of the needs and problems of the farmer; and where the Bank and its officers would have the benefit of the advice and cooperation of interested and representative citizens.

Selecting First Directors

The Federal Farm Loan Board had another job, and that was selecting the first temporary board of directors for each Federal Land Bank. Where mathematically possible, the Board chose a representative from each state in a Federal Land Bank district. It did this in order to avoid the feeling that if loans were refused in the state, or if a low valuation was placed on certain classes of land, such action was due to the fact that the state was not represented on the Board of the Bank. The second reason was that the Bank itself needed the benefit of the personal knowledge of the director as to the classes of land and types of agriculture and the character of the population in his state.

Even in its First Annual Report, the Board reported that, unfortunately, in a few cases, these directors apparently misconstrued the situation and thought part of their duty was to look after the interests of their state. The Board had to remove some of the directors of two of the Banks. In those early days the directors and officers, in some cases, were the same people. Later this practice was discontinued.

Farmers Organized NFLAs Rapidly

The last Federal Land Bank was chartered on April 3, 1917. By November 30, farmers had organized 1,839 National Farm Loan Associations and another 1,985 Associations were in the process of being organized. Already 18,000 farmers had received loans for a total of $30 million—out of applications for $200 million.

Desirable Size of NFLAs

Among the problems the Federal Farm Loan Board enumerated in this First Annual Report was the question of the most desirable size for an Association as to number of members, amount of loans, and extent of territory covered. It also was concerned about the compensation of the secretary-treasurer and the members of the loan committee; the amount and terms of surety bonds; the eligibility of borrowers; separation of Associations on lines of race,[7] creed, or character of agriculture; overlapping of territory; the furnishing of abstracts of title; and the propriety of proposed charges for appraisal or determination of title. In addition, the Board considered the problems of work-

---

[7] Some early Associations were made up entirely of blacks.

ing out proper relations between the Banks and the Farm Loan Board, as well as the relations between the Banks and the Associations.

Decisions of Board Created Later Problems

Hindsight tells us that in some cases the Board was feeling its way in its early years, making some of the right decisions and making several others that proved to be mistakes. As already mentioned, one of the most worrisome mistakes that had to be handled at a later date[8] was allowing overlapping of NFLA territories. By November 30, 1919, there was a total of 4,018 National Farm Loan Associations, and this number was to grow to 5,000 in the 1930s.

---

[8] In the 1930s and 1940s. See "Associations Small, Overlapping Territories" in Chapter 15.

Chapter 23

LAND BANK PROBLEMS GROW WITH DROP IN FARM INCOME—1917 TO 1933

The Land Banks had started doing business in the World War I period—an era of high prices for farm products and farm land. One of the World War I slogans was "Food Will Win the War." Immediately following the war, President Wilson sent Herbert Hoover to Europe to organize a program to save the wartorn countries from famine, so food was much in demand. By 1920–21, however, the United States experienced a sharp recession. The general economy revived quickly and the business boom of the roaring 1920s, off to a slow start, picked up momentum as the decade progressed. It was the era of stock market speculation and overnight fortunes—on paper.

But the country cousins out on the Nation's farms did not fare well at all. Prices of farm products had fallen precipitously from their wartime highs in that general steep recession. After some recovery, they started on a slow decline that was to last for more than a decade. European farm production had recovered and foreign demand for farm products plummeted. Farm prices and farm income kept falling, while the storm of farm unrest kept rising. The farm bloc in Congress searched for farm relief measures. A variety of bills was introduced yearly. Congress twice passed a bill to provide a domestic allotment plan that would have subsidized grain and cotton exports at world prices. Each time the President vetoed it in order to avoid dumping U.S. surpluses on world markets.

During this long agricultural depression, the business of the Federal Land Banks slowly declined. By 1929, only 17,000 farmers borrowed a total of $64 million, down from a 1922 high of 74,000 farmers who borrowed $234 million. Each year more farmers got behind on their Land Bank loans. The number of delinquent loans—due for more than 30 days—and the number of farmers who abandoned their farms increased each year. So did the number of foreclosures.

Then came the stock market crash in October of 1929. Everything, except unemployment, went down. But farm prices had a head start—they went down further and faster than anything else.

Rural banks closed almost everywhere, for all sources of credit in rural areas had dried up. School teachers went without pay. Farms were sold weekly for back taxes. In the cities, many people stood in long bread lines while others jumped out of windows.

The Federal Land Banks were dependent upon installment payments on their loans to pay interest on their bonds. The Banks' financial condition was so poor they didn't think it wise to try to sell more bonds and assume liability to pay more interest on Land Bank bonds. Therefore, by 1932 only 7,000 farmers borrowed only $28 million from the Land Banks. There were thousands more who wanted loans that year, when the last of the original Government-owned stock in the Land Banks was being paid off. However, the situation was so critical that Congress appropriated $125 million to invest in capital stock of the Land Banks all over again. This time, it was to enable the Banks to extend the loans of farmers who were unable to meet their scheduled repayments. Congress was in the process of trying to stop the rising tide of farm foreclosures.

The extent of the financial difficulties of the farmer-borrowers and the resulting financial problems of the Federal Land Banks can be seen by looking at the consolidated financial statements as of December 31, 1932. At that time, the Banks had gross mortgage loans outstanding, totaling $1.129 billion, as compared to $115 million of delinquent installments, extensions, real estate and sheriff certificates, and judgments in connection with foreclosures. Against these items, the Land Banks had set up valuation reserves totaling $22 million.

This was the situation within the Land Banks just three months before they were to be asked to take on the job of refinancing hundreds of thousands of other farmers who were in dire financial shape, with a large proportion of them faced with foreclosure.

Federal Farm Loan Board Had Other Problems

The ever-worsening economic situation and the disastrous effects on agriculture and the Federal Land Banks gave the Federal Farm Loan Board many problems to try to solve in addition to other less pressing important matters that needed to be considered. Russell C. Engberg, Economist for the Federal Farm Loan Board and now retired Director of Research and Information of the Farm Credit Administration, recalls the heroic efforts of Paul Bestor, Land Bank Com-

missioner for the Farm Loan Board in this period, in trying to help
the Land Banks find answers to their many problems in this period.[1]

Direct Borrowers an Answer to Inactive NFLAs

Foreshadowing a situation that was to grow into a major, almost
insoluble problem for the Land Banks in the 1930s, the Federal Farm
Loan Board in its Fifth Annual Report to Congress pointed out that
in some instances a few farmers had organized a National Farm Loan
Association to get loans for themselves and then had lost interest;
consequently, their Association had practically ceased functioning. As
a result of this, the Board suggested to Congress that the Federal Land
Banks be allowed to make loans directly to farmers in areas where
there were not enough interested farmers to form a local National
Farm Loan Association. Congress reacted by authorizing the Federal
Land Banks to make loans directly to farmers where there was no
active National Farm Loan Association available. The interest rate on
such loans was one-half percent higher.

The authority to make direct loans to farmers, although not widely
used by the Land Banks, was of some importance during the emergency refinancing period of the 1930s in areas where there were no
active National Farm Loan Associations.

Joint Stock Land Bank Competition

As early as 1922, the Farm Loan Board cited the fact that the
number of joint stock Land Banks had increased during the year from
23 to 63. It also mentioned that the loans made by the joint stock
Land Banks had jumped in that same year from 881 loans for $9 million
to 16,000 loans for $139 million. The Board raised the question with
Congress as to whether this private competition was healthy and
suggested the possibility of ultimately making "the System entirely
mutual.'

In the years 1923, 1925, and 1926, the joint stock Land Bank loans
just about equaled or exceeded those of the Federal Land Banks with
$190 million, $131 million, and $123 million in loans, respectively.
However, the joint stock Land Banks were soon to be in deep trouble
as the agricultural depression of the 1920s became the Great Depression of the 1930s. Even before they were all placed in liquidation

---

[1] Bestor later headed the farm mortgage loan department of a large life insurance company for many years.

in 1933, many had become inactive, five were in receivership, and several had chosen voluntary liquidation.

While some of the joint stock land banks were really interested in serving farmers, many were organized by promoters who thought they saw a chance for a quick profit.

Chapter 24

THE FICBSs BEGIN OPERATIONS—
1923 TO 1933

When Congress passed the Farm Loan Act of 1916 creating the Federal Land Bank System, it chose to ignore the problem of also providing farmers with a source of operating credit even though there was such a problem. As previously mentioned, the joint committee that was studying the matters in 1916 failed to make a report.

During World War I, the War Finance Corporation, which had been established to facilitate the war effort, provided a source of agricultural loans.

The financial crisis of 1920–21 emphasized the difficulty farmers had in obtaining short-term operating credit. At such a time the money supply in rural banks was even less than usual. The decline in farm prices made it even more difficult for farmers to pay off their loans when called by commercial banks who were feeling the general pinch on their resources. Farmers were also frightened by the declining farm prices.

At this juncture, Congress called the War Finance Corporation back into operation and in August of 1921 authorized it to discount agricultural loans and make advances to banks, trust companies, and cooperative associations which had made loans for agricultural purposes. Commercial banks in rural areas were often short of cash. This was merely a temporary emergency answer to a long-standing, basic problem. Commercial banks, dependent on deposits for their lending funds, made loans for 30 to 90 days. Crops and livestock took longer to produce. Farm loans were expected to be renewed. However, if a bank's loan funds were short, the bank had the legal right to demand payment. Such demands often came at times when farmers just did not have the money.

Earlier that year, on June 7, 1921, Congress had created the Joint Commission of Agriculture Inquiry to make recommendations on credit and other important agricultural problems. The Commission, recognizing that commercial banks depended on demand deposits for available funds, pointed out the lack of a dependable source of short- and intermediate-term credit for farmers on terms suited to the farming business.

Several Alternatives Proposed

One of the Commission's recommendations was to have the Land Banks expand their field of operations following the pattern of the War Finance Corporation. They would be authorized to discount agricultural paper for other lending agencies. The proposal included the investment of additional Government capital in the Land Banks to support this new program. This proposal evolved into a revision that provided for 12 new Federal Intermediate Credit Banks that would be separate and distinct from the Federal Land Banks but would have the same board of directors and officers.

In 1922 the hearings before the Banking Committees in both Houses of Congress produced additional proposals which included making use of existing credit facilities, creating new ones, and lending Government funds directly from the Treasury.

Following President Warren G. Harding's recognition of the need for some type of legislation in his State of the Union message, many bills were introduced in Congress. After considerable jockeying, Congress compromised by including elements of three different bills in the Agricultural Credits Act of 1923.

Congress Compromises Again

One part of this Act provided for the establishment of a system of national agricultural credit corporations which would be chartered under Federal law and authorized to issue debentures and discount their loans with the Federal Reserve Banks, with their capital coming from commercial banks and individuals. Later, an amendment to the Act provided for discounting such paper with the Federal Intermediate Credit Banks. Only three such corporations were ever chartered. Farmers, already in weak financial condition, did not have the money to capitalize such corporations.

The Act also provided for the establishment of the 12 Federal Intermediate Credit Banks by amending the Federal Farm Loan Act of 1916. The capital for these Banks was provided by U.S. Treasury investments in their stock.

There was no provision in the law establishing the Federal Intermediate Credit Banks for the users to ever become the owners and thus replace the Government capital therein—that had to wait until 1956. The Federal Intermediate Credit Banks were authorized to discount agricultural paper of agricultural credit corporations, livestock loan companies, commercial banks, and savings institutions, as well as to make direct loans to farmer cooperatives on the security of livestock or warehouse receipts or shipping documents for staple agricultural commodities. Loans secured by livestock or warehouse receipts were limited to 75 percent of their market value.

The law provided that the Federal Intermediate Credit Banks could discount paper that had maturities from 6 months to 3 years. However, the authority to go beyond 1-year maturities was not used until the 1950s and then was soon amended to provide such financing up to 5 and finally 7 years.

The Banks were prohibited from discounting loans where the lender charged his customers more than 1½ percent above the discount rate of the Bank unless approved by the Farm Loan Board. The discount rate of the Banks was not to exceed 1 percent of its last issue of debentures.

First Flow of Credit Only Trickles

It was expected that the Federal Intermedite Credit Banks would provide a new flow of funds from the money markets to rural commercial banks. However, this role never really materialized. In 1932, the discounts for commercial banks were just under $2 million, or about 2.4 percent of the total financing being supplied by the Federal Intermediate Credit Banks. Only 246 commercial banks had used the facilities of the Banks since their organization, and only 28 of them still had active accounts.[1]

In some areas, agricultural credit corporations and livestock loan companies did make substantial use of the Banks, but this did not provide credit to farmers on a nationwide basis. Some of the agricultural credit corporations were subsidiaries organized by commercial banks; others were affiliated with farmer cooperatives. Farmers generally did not have the money to capitalize their own agricultural credit corporations. They made little use of the small fund Congress made available to the Secretary of Agriculture to loan to farmers to invest in such corporations.

---

[1] W. N. Stokes, Jr., "Credit to Farmers," Federal Intermediate Credit Banks, Washington, D.C., 1973, p. 131.

Co-op Use of FICBs Also Disappointing

Although farmer cooperatives' use of the Federal Intermediate Credit Banks until 1932 equalled in total amount almost that of other organizations, the Banks were not used to the extent that many people had hoped. Such people attributed much of the farm problem to the fact that farmers were forced to sell their products shortly after harvest because they needed the money. They expected these Banks to provide the financing that would enable farmers to reap rewards from holding back their products and gradually feeding them into the market.

Unfortunately, Congress had not authorized the Intermediate Credit Banks to make loans to cooperatives to supply working capital or for financing facilities. The Banks were not permitted to make even commodity loans to farm supply cooperatives, as a result of an interpretation and ruling by the Farm Loan Board. Neither the Federal Intermediate Credit Banks nor the Farm Loan Board made any strong efforts to promote business from cooperatives. As Stokes[2] points out, "Their attitude appeared to be to accept only when offered, and then on their own terms." He also commented that many cooperatives preferred to continue their contacts with commercial banks because of the convenience and as a safeguard for stabilizing a permanent source of funds. In addition, the Credit Banks' terms were not only complicated but they also caused delay and were inconvenient and expensive.

---

[2] *Ibid.*, p. 16.

Chapter 25

FINANCING COOPERATIVES BEFORE 1933

Early efforts on the part of farmers to buy better quality supplies at lower cost and to capture some of the "middlemen's" profits for themselves led to ever-increasing efforts by farmers to organize and build cooperatives from the low farm price years of the 1880s onward. Thousands of local cooperatives were started in all parts of the country. Many were successful—a few eminently so—but many others fell by the wayside, particularly in the earlier years. Among the causes of failure or "withering on the vine" were more zeal and enthusiasm—and the resulting overoptimistic expectations—than "know-how"; the inability to recognize and pay for capable management; fierce attacks from their adversaries that were threatened by the potential competition; and lack of sufficient financing.

Most early cooperative efforts had to depend largely on farmer-members' own financial resources. These were frequently too small to provide sufficient capital. Others who had the resources were reluctant to invest heavily enough to make their new enterprises successful. The more successful cooperatives that grew and made highly significant achievements for their members were those that were able to "put it all together"—good member investment and loyal use of their cooperatives, enlightened leadership, knowledgeable boards of directors, capable management, and outside financing. Among the highly successful pioneers of this era were the California Fruit Growers Exchange—a federation of cooperative citrus packing cooperatives—dating back to 1896 and now known as Sunkist Growers, Inc., and other California commodity organizations.

However, generally the growth and development of early cooperatives were severely handicapped by the cooperatives not being able to borrow sufficient amounts of money. There was the natural reluctance for local banks to finance new ventures owned by farmers who lacked experience in running businesses beyond their line fences. And even in cases where cooperatives were relatively successful or had good potential for becoming successful, the cooperatives' local competitors were often on the local banks' boards of directors. This did not help. Local bankers usually could see cooperatives' highly apparent weaknesses, but since they were organized and run differently from most businesses, it was natural that bankers did not understand their problems or strengths.

Declining Farm Prices Again Increased Cooperative Efforts

After the severe 1921 recession—as it is now called—farmers and ranchers saw their "city cousins" prospering in the midst of a fast booming national economy. Most businesses were prospering and fortunes were being quickly made in the stock market—at least on paper. But prices of farm products which had risen to high levels in the World War I years recovered some, but not fully, after the 1921 collapse. Then, as surpluses began to pile up, prices continued to drift downward for 20 years.

As farm incomes shrank in this period, farmers increased their efforts to build more effective cooperatives. A large number of today's most effective large centralized cooperatives and regional federations of local cooperatives grew out of their modest beginnings in the 1920s and the early 1930s when farm prices hit bottom in the Great Depression. Those were the years when many regional cooperatives got started—Land O'Lakes Creameries, Farmland Industries, Cenex, Agway, Inc., Southern States Farmers Cooperative Exchange in North Carolina, Goldkist, Oceanspray Cranberries, Midland, and the Midwest Farm Bureau-affiliated state farm supply organizations such as Landmark in Ohio, Indiana Farm Bureau Cooperative, FS Services—then only in Illinois—and many more.

The marketing cooperatives were searching for ways to return a greater proportion of the consumer's dollar. Many of them concentrated on providing a constant supply of high quality products marketed and merchandized under well-publicized consumer trademarks. They prided themselves in measuring up to, or surpassing, the highest USDA grades which they pioneered in using.

Most regional purchasing cooperatives were organized to search for or produce farm supplies that measured up to the recommendations of their Land Grant colleges and to reduce the cost of their farm and home supplies. Members of more and more cooperatives discovered relatively painless ways to capitalize cooperatives. Members agreed to let their marketing cooperatives—for various periods of time—retain a small per unit amount from the sale of their products to provide the capital needed to run and expand their operations. Members of farm supply cooperatives agreed to have them charge at prevailing market prices—instead of starting price wars—and then have them pay part or all of their patronage refunds in stock or other evidences of equity, with the promise they would start paying off the oldest in cash as soon as possible. But these methods of increasing farmers' equities in their cooperatives could not be used to their full potential unless they could be supplemented by borrowed capital.

After 1922, the development of marketing cooperatives was speeded up by the removal of a serious deterrent. Usually at the instigation of buyers of farm products, many farmers who organized marketing cooperatives had been called into court, or even put in jail, on charges of violating the antitrust laws. The Capper-Volstead Act of that year, which President Warren G. Harding supported and signed, made it clear that the farmers could join together to market their products without being in violation of the antitrust laws.

The organization of the American Institute of Cooperation and what is now known as the National Council of Farmer Cooperatives in the 1920s, together with the earlier organized National Milk Producers Federation, were all factors in increasing farmers' interests in the development of cooperatives.

Farm Board Provides Credit to Cooperatives

The rising tide of interest in developing strong marketing cooperatives picked up additional pressure in 1929. President Herbert Hoover, as Joseph G. Knapp points out in his *Advance of American Cooperative Enterprise—1920-1945*,[1] in 1924, while serving as Secretary of Commerce, had become interested in developing nationwide commodity cooperatives as a means of increasing farmers' income. As the new President, he proposed and Congress passed the Agricultural Marketing Act of 1929, setting up the Federal Farm Board to engage in stabilizing farm prices and financing and promoting the development of cooperatives. Congress set up a $500 million revolving fund to accomplish these aims. This was Hoover's farm relief alternative to the McNary-Haugen Bill that President Calvin Coolidge had twice

---

[1] Knapp was the Administrator of the Farmer Cooperative Service in the U.S. Department of Agriculture from 1953 to 1966 and Associate Chief of its predecessor, the Cooperative Research and Service Division of the Farm Credit Administration from 1948 to 1953. He started his career in that Division in 1934. He is the author of eight books on the history of cooperatives.

vetoed. That bill would have established a domestic allotment plan and exported farm surpluses at world prices.

The Federal Farm Board was given broad powers to stabilize farm prices and to promote the development and provide financing for large agricultural commodity cooperatives. While it made loans to smaller cooperatives, it was chiefly interested in building large centralized cooperatives from "the top down" that could "effectively market" a commodity. Cooperatives were also authorized to join together in commodity stabilization corporations formed to work with the Board in preventing surpluses from driving down the prices of farm products.

The Farm Board with Alexander Legge, former President of International Harvester, but a strong advocate of cooperatives, as Chairman, was soon in disrepute. The Board was charged with the responsibility of stabilizing farm prices, without any tools to control production, just before the worst stock market crash in history which touched off the Great Depression of the 1930s. It could not have picked a worse time to be asked to embark on an almost impossible task. However, considering the general state of the national economy, the Farm Board record for financing farm cooperatives was relatively good. Those losses totaled only about $10 million. Its experience in this field proved cooperatives could be good credit risks and laid the foundation for the building of the Banks for Cooperatives. It also put to rest the issue that divided cooperative leaders during the 1920s as to whether it was best to build cooperatives from the "top down" or "up from the grassroots." The top-down theory and its accompanying hypothesis that cooperatives could control the marketing of an individual commodity had been proclaimed from coast to coast by a brilliant lawyer and orator—Aaron Shapiro. The idea had been given a good opportunity to prove itself, but lost. However, the Board still had—even after Congress had given away $197 million of its supply of cotton and wheat in donations to the American Red Cross and sustained huge losses on price stabilization efforts—enough to amply capitalize the 13 Banks for Cooperatives.[2] It also left a legacy of experience in lending money to cooperatives that was to prove valuable to its successors—the Banks for Cooperatives. They were fortunate to have been able to learn from the successes and mistakes of the Farm Board without having to experience them themselves.

---

[2] First Annual Report of the Farm Credit Administration—1933, Government Printing Office, Washington, D.C., 1934, pp. 56–57 and 121–140.

Chapter 26

SYSTEM ENLARGED IN AN EMERGENCY— 1933 TO 1934

By the fall of 1932, the need to get credit to farmers and rural communities was a major national problem. Farm prices had hit all-time lows. Farmers were in dire circumstances. Hundreds of thousands of farmers were finding it impossible to produce enough net income to pay their debts. They were either being foreclosed or were facing that possibility. A pall of despair and hopelessness hung over the whole country. Unemployed city cousins were "coming home"—fleeing the bread lines of the cities.

Angry and threatening mobs of farmers at frequent tax and foreclosure sales were common occurrences. Banks were closing all over the country—especially in rural areas—which compounded the problem and intensified the confusion and despair. Business in rural America was at a standstill. All sources of credit had dried up because virtually no one had any money.

Banks that had not already closed had nothing but frozen assets—bad debts. Insurance companies were also confronted with possible bankruptcy.

It is small wonder that Governor Franklin D. Roosevelt won the November 1932 Presidential election by a record landslide. But in those days he had 4 months—until March 4, 1933—to worry, fret, and plan how he was going to tackle the mess, if the country didn't completely collapse before he got started.

It was under these emergency conditions that the basic concepts, design, and guiding principles of the permanently expanded cooperative Farm Credit System and the Farm Credit Administration as its supervisory agency were developed and set in place.

Developing Plans to Solve Farmers' Credit Problems

Shortly after his election, Roosevelt sent his then New York State Conservation Commissioner, Henry Morgenthau, Jr., to Washington to begin to lay plans for meeting the farm problem. Morgenthau turned to George W. Warren, the head of the Agricultural Economics Department at Cornell University, for help. Warren suggested that W. I. Myers, then Professor of Farm Finance, go to Washington with him instead.

The Morgenthau-Myers team soon found that Roosevelt had also asked various other people to make proposals for solving the farm problem. As a result, Myers and Morgenthau began to concentrate their attention on how to solve the financial problems of farmers. They held several meetings with farm leaders and agricultural representatives in Congress, and they interviewed officials in the various Government departments who were concerned with extending credit to farmers.

There was agreement that farmers needed financial help and lots of it—immediately. But there was not too much agreement beyond that point. When it came to how to solve the problem, opinions varied widely.

The Morgenthau-Myers survey of the situation found the following:

The Federal Land Banks were still open for business, although they had been shaken by the large number of their borrowers who were unable to meet the payments on their loans, by the inability to sell bonds because of their own weak financial condition, and by a general lack of confidence of the few investors who had any funds available. Thus, they were making very few new loans—they reached an all-time low of $27 million for the entire year of 1932.

On the short-term operating credit side, there were two emergency sources of funds.

In 1932, the Reconstruction Finance Corporation was charged with the job of meeting emergency credit situations throughout the economy. It had set up 12 regional agricultural credit corporations through which they made operating loans available to farmers, and particularly to ranchers.

Secondly, Congress in 8 of the 12 years between 1921 and 1932 had appropriated funds for emergency crop production and seed loans. These funds were made available to farmers through the Secretary of Agriculture. The average-sized loan in 1932 was $126. Even with Depression prices, such loans were so restricted and so small that they were not sufficient to finance a year's operations.

The Federal Intermediate Credit Banks had a good reputation among investors, but they were wholesalers of lending funds with very few retailers that were using their services.

When it came to the financial needs of farmer cooperatives, there were two sources of funds. One was the commodity loans from the Federal Intermediate Credit Banks. The second source was the Federal Farm Board's revolving fund.

Myers as early as December 1932 had come up with an outline of plans for handling farmers' financial problems, and after discussing it with Morgenthau, they went to Albany to present their ideas to President-elect Roosevelt. He gave them the go-ahead sign, and they proceeded to work out the details in numerous drafts after conferring with farm and Congressional leaders.

The Morgenthau-Myers plan fell into the following two general categories:

1. Have the Government give the Land Banks the necessary tools for them to tackle the tremendous emergency farm refinancing job that was so urgently needed.
2. Create a well-rounded, complete cooperative credit system for agriculture by adding to the Federal Land Banks and Federal Intermediate Credit Banks, new organizations to channel FICB funds to farmers and to provide a decentralized method of financing farmer cooperatives.

Complete Farm Credit System Created

As soon as President Roosevelt was sworn into office on March 4, 1933, he began to put the plans for providing loans to farmers into action. He immediately appointed Henry Morgenthau, Jr., as Chairman of the old Federal Farm Board. On March 27 he issued an Executive Order effective on May 27 unless Congress rejected it by that date. The Executive Order made the Chairman of the Federal Farm Board the Governor of the newly created Farm Credit Administration. The Order also consolidated within the Farm Credit Administration all the functions, powers, and funds of existing Federal agencies dealing primarily with agricultural credit. It abolished the price stabilization functions of Hoover's Federal Farm Board.

The functions and powers transferred to the Farm Credit Administration included:

Function	*From*
Federal Land Bank, National Farm Loan Association and Federal Intermediate Credit Bank supervision	Federal Farm Loan Board in Treasury Department
Loans to cooperatives from Agricultural Marketing Revolving Fund	Federal Farm Board
Regional Agricultural Credit Corporations supervision	Reconstruction Finance Corporation
Crop Production and Seed Loan Offices (later called Emergency Feed and Seed Loan Offices) supervision	Secretary of Agriculture
Fund for Investments in Stock of Agricultural Credit Corporations	Secretary of Agriculture

By May 12, 1933, Congress passed and the President signed the Emergency Farm Mortgage Act. Myers, commenting on the significance of that Act, said: [1]

> [It] was a great day in the history of farm finance, and especially of the Farm Credit Administration. It assured the continuation of the Federal Land Banks and provided adequate Government funds to supplement Land Bank mortgage loans in order to refinance excessive debts of good farmers.
>
> Since no other mortgage agency was able to make loans at this time, this Act placed enormous responsibility on the Land Banks to expand operations fast enough to meet the national crisis. The ensuing six months was the greatest crisis in the history of the Land Banks.
>
> Strong leadership and high courage were required to meet this challenge successfully. Morgenthau accepted this responsibility and deserves the credit for the wonderful record made by the Land Bank System. This great success gave the Farm Credit System a national reputation and made possible the establishment of the Production Credit System.

Land Banks Start Emergency Refinancing

The Emergency Farm Mortgage Act of 1933 gave the Federal Land Bank Associations powerful weapons and plenty of ammunition to attack farmers' emergency credit problems. The drive to halt the wave of farm foreclosures by refinancing their debts was on. The Act's provisions included:

1. Reduction of interest rates to 4½ percent on new and outstanding loans for 5 years to be reimbursed by the Land Banks from the Treasury.

---

[1] W. N. Stokes, Jr., "Credit to Farmers," Federal Intermediate Credit Banks, Washington, D.C., 1973, p. 29.

2. Treasury subscriptions to the paid-in surplus of the Land Banks equal to the amount of loan extensions and 5-year principal deferments granted to borrowers not otherwise in default on their loans.

3. A Government guarantee of interest on new Land Bank bonds issued within 2 years to facilitate their sale to investors.

4. A $200 million fund for the Land Bank Commissioner to use in making first and second mortgage loans through the Land Banks up to 75 percent of their normal value. (Land Banks were limited to 50 percent on land and 20 percent on the insured value of buildings.)

The program launched by this Act was based on the theory that prices of farm products would return to their normal levels. It provided the Land Banks the direction and means for assisting its own borrowers—most of whom were having plenty of difficulty in meeting their obligations. It also provided the means by which the Land Banks would undertake the huge debt refinancing program which hundreds of thousands of farmers so badly needed.

With the Land Bank and Land Bank Commissioner refinancing program on the books, President Roosevelt, Morgenthau, and Myers soon told farmers on network radio broadcasts to write or wire Washington if their farms were threatened by foreclosure. The response was an avalanche of wires, letters, and phone calls which rose to 373 per day for a total of 43,000. The Farm Credit Administration rushed to ask creditors to wait long enough to see if they could be refinanced.

The Farm Credit Administration hired a large technical staff to answer such responses. It also had to rapidly expand its appraisal staff assigned to the Land Banks. In early 1933, there were only about 200 appraisers. By year's end 5,000 had been recruited and trained.

Each Land Bank was inundated with loan applications. For a while the Banks, even with their staffs working long hours, got further behind each day. But they recruited and trained hundreds of new people and by December 1933 loaned more money that month than they had in the entire year 1932. By then the rate of closed loans had caught up with the rate of new applications. But they were still gearing up for more new records in the year ahead.

More Money Available for Loans
from Government

Early in 1934, with this $200 million Land Bank Commissioner loan fund nearly exhausted, Congress established the Federal Farm Mortgage Corporation. Congress capitalized this Corporation with the $200 million Land Bank Commissioner fund—mostly already invested in farm mortgages. The Corporation was authorized to issue Government-guaranteed bonds up to 10 times its capital—$2 billion. The Corporation was also authorized to assist the Land Banks by buying their bonds.

Farmers' Debts Scaled Down

Realizing that there would have to be widespread scaling down of farmers' debts by their creditors to bring them within the limits of a reasonable mortgage loan, Morgenthau in 1933 had appealed to the Governors of all the states. Hoping to get creditors to agree to scale-downs of what farmers owed them, he asked the Governors to appoint state and county debt adjustment committees to be mediators between farmers and their creditors.

A total of 2,700 such committees that served without compensation were formed in the Nation's 3,000 counties. Only three States did not have such committees. These committees were able to get debts written down for 20 percent of the farmers obtaining Land Bank and Commissioner refinancing loans. The write-downs averaged about 30 percent of their debts for a total of about $200 million. Many creditors needed or wanted money so badly they were glad to settle for immediate liquid assets.

In the period from May 1, 1933, through December 31, 1935, Land Bank and Land Bank Commissioner loans totaled $1.9 billion. Hundreds of thousands of farmers were saved from foreclosure on their farms in the 1933–35 refinancing period. But many other segments of the economy benefited from this refinancing that unfroze their assets.

Nearly 89 percent of these loan funds was used to refinance existing debts. Of this amount, 23 percent was used to pay commercial banks, 14 percent went to insurance companies, and 48 percent to other creditors.

Refinancing Job Completed

By the end of 1935, the Land Banks had virtually completed their refinancing job that looked almost impossible less than three years earlier. They had appraised more than 900,000 farms—about one-seventh of the total mortgaged farms in the Nation. They held—on their own behalf and that of the Federal Farm Mortgage Corporation—48 percent of the farm mortgage debt. And along with that debt they had the undying gratitude of thousands of farm families who, into the second and third generations, were to remember and appreciate the Land Banks.

Loans outstanding for the Banks and the Commissioner had jumped from $1.229 billion to $2.867 billion with loans on over 1 million farms compared to 400,000 in 1932.

Summary of Land Bank Refinancing Job
1933 to 1935

| | Applications | | Loans Made | | | | | |
| | | | Land Bank | | Land Bank Comm'r | | Total | |
	No.	Amt.	No. Loans	Amt.	No. Loans	Amt.	No. Loans	Amt.
	thous.	mill.	thous.	mill.	thous.	mill.	thous.	mill.
1933	502	$2,065	39	$152	44	$ 71	79	$ 211
1934	403	2,044	190	730	306	553	497	1,284
1935	163	811	60	59	91	196	150	445
Total	1,068	$4,920	289	$941	441	$820	726	$1,940

PCAs and BCs Authorized in 1933 Also

While the Land Banks were doing an excellent refinancing job in 1933–35, and this saved farmers from losing their farms, it would do little good if they didn't have short-term operating credit to run those farms.

By June 16, Congress had passed and President Roosevelt had signed the Farm Credit Act of 1933, rounding out and completing the structure of a permanent Cooperative Farm Credit System. It established the 12 Production Credit Corporations, whose job it was to capitalize and supervise and train local Production Credit Associations. It also established the 12 district Banks for Cooperatives and the Central Bank for Cooperatives.

Production Credit System Gets Started

The first job to be done in getting the Production Credit System into operation was for the Farm Credit Administration to work with the district Farm Credit Boards to help them organize and staff the 12 Production Credit Corporations. It was imperative that these new corporations have a staff who knew and understood farming and ranching in their districts. The staff also had to have the background to analyze farmers' financial problems. But that was not all. The staff also needed to be able to explain new concepts to local PCA boards of directors, their managing secretary-treasurers, and other PCA staff members.

Teams of FCA representatives took to the field to help the 12 Production Credit Corporations get started. They then teamed up with the new PCC officers to organize the local Production Credit Associations.

The first Production Credit Corporation was chartered and organized in St. Louis in September 1933. By September 19, 1933, it had organized the first Production Credit Association at Champaign, Illinois. By April 1934, the Production Credit Association at Rifle, Colorado was chartered, thus completing the organization of over 600 Production Credit Associations that covered the 48 States and Puerto Rico.

In general, the aim was to get PCA service as close and as accessible to farmers and ranchers as possible—in the days before fast automobiles, good state roads, and superhighways—and also have an Association territory large enough to generate sufficient business to have an economical operation. Branch offices had not yet been thought of. They came later.

Time was to prove that this rush organizing effort was done relatively well, although understandably adjustments by way of mergers and territorial changes had to be made either because of originally unrecognized problems or because of changing conditions. By the mid-1970s there were only 430 Associations, but business had grown to the point where they needed and could support nearly 1,700 offices. So PCA service is actually closer and more convenient for farmers today than originally visualized.

In those early days, there were proponents for setting up Production Credit Associations on a commodity rather than a geographic territory basis. This idea, along with the proposal to tie Production Credit Associations to the membership of individual marketing or farm supply cooperatives, was rejected. However, separate Associations were established to serve large fruit growers in Florida and in the Baltimore district. In recent years these have been merged with local Associations. Several statewide livestock Production Credit Associations were organized in the western states for large ranchers. Some of these still operate.

BCs Reorganized Financing of Cooperatives

The ideal of providing specialized financing for farmers' cooperatives was not new in 1933. The Banks for Cooperatives inherited that job from Hoover's Federal Farm Board. And the Banks were capitalized out of funds remaining in the Board's Agricultural Marketing Revolving Fund.

But the concept of how cooperatives were to be financed was new and the organizational pattern to do the job was completely changed.

First, purchasing cooperatives were put on an equal basis with marketing cooperatives. Then, instead of concentrating on building large national cooperatives from the top down from a single Washington office, the main job was given to the 12 district Banks for Cooperatives to build up cooperatives from the ground level with grassroots support and their accompanying equity financing.

The Central Bank for Cooperatives was to make loans primarily to national and large regional cooperatives, although for some years it continued to finance some of the smaller cooperatives that had received loans from the Farm Board. Until 1953 this Bank was largely staffed by officials of the Cooperative Bank Division of the Farm Credit Administration. Homer G. Smith, President of the Central Bank for Cooperatives from 1956 to 1974, in his history of that Bank,[2] says that this at times put the Farm Credit Administration in the awkward position of supervising the Bank, which it ran, in its relationships with the district Banks which it also supervised.

One of the most important contributions the Banks for Cooperatives was to make to the building of strong, useful cooperatives was counseling and advising them on a wide variety of their problems. Such service became an integral part of the Banks for Cooperatives' lending process from their very beginning. This specialized service has been particularly important when cooperatives have gotten into financial difficulty. The Banks for Cooperatives have an excellent record of helping their member-borrowers pull through financial illnesses. They have not been afraid to advance more money in order to help cooperatives get back on their feet. But their firm discipline in such times has also been helpful. Some of today's largest, strongest, and most useful cooperatives at some time in their history had financial troubles that would have caused most lenders to withdraw their

---

[2] Homer G. Smith, "The 13th Bank, Central Bank for Cooperatives," Denver, Colorado, 1976.

financing, but the Banks for Cooperatives stayed in and helped them recover, thus providing better service and savings for their farmer-members.

Farmer Cooperative Service on FCA Team

Going almost hand in hand with such service from the Banks for Cooperatives was the work of what is now known as the Farmer Cooperative Service of the U.S. Department of Agriculture. This organization started in the U.S. Department of Agriculture as the Cooperative Marketing Division, as a result of the Cooperative Marketing Act of 1926, although its roots went back as early as 1916 when the then Office of Markets in the U.S. Department of Agriculture began to give attention to farmers' cooperative problems. In 1929 it was transferred to the new Federal Farm Board. There it was directly involved with lending and co-op promotion programs of the Board. In 1933 it became part of the Farm Credit Administration when the Farm Board merged with the Farm Credit Administration.

The Farm Credit Administration was fortunate to have a staff of experienced cooperative specialists who already were well acquainted with farmer cooperatives and their problems. From their work with the Farm Board, these specialists were well informed regarding the financial condition of many cooperatives. Some of them helped organize the district Banks for Cooperatives and, particularly in the early days of the Farm Credit Administration and the Central Bank for Cooperatives, some staff members helped analyze many loans.

Once the new BC staffs were fully organized and had acquired more experience, these specialists became the separate Cooperative Research and Service Division and spent most of their time providing research, education, and technical services to cooperatives.

When the Farm Credit Act of 1953 again made the Farm Credit Administration an independent agency, this division stayed in the U.S. Department of Agriculture. One of the reasons for this change in relationship was the fact that this division was the only part of the Farm Credit Administration that was operating on Congressionally appropriated funds.

Both while in the Farm Credit Administration and since its separation, the work of the Farmer Cooperative Service has provided research, operational studies, and educational publications and programs that have been highly important to the successful operation of the Banks for Cooperatives and the cooperatives they have financed. In fact, the Banks for Cooperatives and now the Farmer Cooperative

Service of the U.S. Department of Agriculture have jointly sponsored and cooperated on many projects throughout the years. The Farmer Cooperative Service frequently has made studies suggested by the Banks for Cooperatives.

Organizations Liquidated

Three of the major credit programs turned over to the Farm Credit Administration in 1933 by President Roosevelt's Executive Order did not fit into the plans for the permanent cooperative Credit System. One of these was the supervision of the joint stock land banks which Congress by the Farm Credit Act of 1933 placed in liquidation.

RACCs Phased Out

The emergency-oriented 12 Regional Agricultural Credit Corporarations (RACCs) organized by the Reconstruction Finance Corporation in 1932 were placed in liquidation by the Farm Credit Act of 1933, when their function was taken over by the Production Credit Associations. They were organized to make operating loans to farmers and ranchers whose sources of credit had completely dried up. About 30 percent of their loans were taken over by the Production Credit Associations by the end of 1934. However, they continued for a time to finance some farmers and ranchers who could not get financing elsewhere. (Western ranchers found this financing particularly needed.) From October 1932 to May 1, 1934, they loaned $261 million. By the end of 1937, the total had risen to $322 million.

The 12 Regional Agricultural Credit Corporations and their 21 branches—which were gradually consolidated into 1 Regional Agricultural Credit Corporation in Washington, D.C.—were called upon to handle other specialized lending programs.

Starting in 1941, a branch office was opened in Wenatchee, Washington, to finance orchardists who had accumulated such heavy debt loads they could not get financing elsewhere. Beginning in 1943, loans were made to finance production of foods and fibers especially needed in the World War II effort.

In 1949, Congress authorized loans to fur farmers for 5 years. Until the Regional Agricultural Credit Corporations were transferred to the Farmers Home Administration on April 19, 1949, they had loaned a total of $662 million.[3]

---

[3] Annual Report of the Farm Credit Administration, Government Printing Office, Washington, D.C., 1948–1949, pp. 38–39 and 176.

Crop and Feed Loans to Farmers' Home

Emergency crop and seed loans, later called Emergency Crop and Feed loans, were first provided by Congress through the Secretary of Agriculture in 1918 and in 8 of the years between 1921 and 1931 to finance farmers in various areas that had suffered unusual hardships such as droughts and floods who could not obtain credit from other sources.

Starting in 1931, loans were made on a nationwide basis, but only if other credit was not available. Congress continued to make appropriations for these loans on a yearly basis until 1937, when it authorized future loans to be made from funds collected from 1937 loans and those made in previous years.

These loans usually were limited to $400, although in later years the Governor of the Farm Credit Administration could authorize larger loans in distressed areas certified as such by the Secretary of Agriculture. When these loans were transferred to the Farm and Home Administration in 1946, a total of 4.1 million loans had been made for $504 million, and 80 percent of them had been repaid. North and South Carolina, which ranked third and first in number of loans with 316,000 and 351,000, respectively, had the highest repayment records—94.3 and 93.4 percent. With loans averaging only about $125, the lending and collection costs in most years exceeded the interest collected. However, in years when farm income was satisfactory, many repayments were made years after the crops financed had been sold.

FCA Given Job of Starting Credit Unions

Congress, in 1934, in an effort to ease the acute financial problems of workers throughout the country, authorized the chartering of Federal credit unions because many states had not made provision for doing so. It looked around for a supervisor who was friendly to, and understanding of, the problems of cooperatives and mutual endeavors. Congress gave the job of chartering, examining, and supervising Federal credit unions to the Farm Credit Administration because of its experience with credit cooperatives. Myers and the Farm Credit Administration had their hands full with emergency work but took on the job in good spirit. To head this work, Myers recruited Claude R. Orchard who, as Personnel Director of Armour and Company, had a great deal of experience in organizing and running credit unions. He was a practical idealist who was devoted to promoting the credit union idea as a way of promoting thrift and reducing the cost of credit to small borrowers.

Orchard soon recruited a modest staff who enthusiastically began answering requests for help to organize credit unions. By 1941, just before the responsibility for supervision and examination of the Federal Credit Union Section was transferred to the Federal Deposit Insurance Corporation, there were 4,245 Federal credit unions in 47 states, the District of Columbia, and the Territory of Hawaii. They had 1.4 million members whose savings accounts totaled $105 million and loans made totaled $130 million during the year. Compared to 1975, these are indeed modest figures, but the Federal credit union movement had gotten off to a good start under FCA auspices.

Chapter 27

THE SYSTEM BUILDING PERIOD—
1935 TO 1940

With the emergency refinancing program nearly out of the way and the organizational pains subsiding in the new parts of the cooperative Farm Credit System, the System began to focus attention on shoring up the structurally weak spots for the long haul in what was hoped would be a long period of relatively "normal" agricultural conditions.

FLBs Turn Attention to NFLAs

Starting in November 1935, the Land Banks embarked on a program of improving the organizational pattern of the National Farm Loan Associations and providing them with additional income by paying them for servicing loans. Up until that time most of their income had come from fees for closing new loans. During the refinancing period the Associations and their secretary-treasurers, if they were working on a percentage basis, did very well. Previously, the Associations did not have sufficient income to build up reserves to cover losses arising from their loan endorsements on their defaulted loans.

Fewer Associations and Offices

Most of the Land Banks began urging their Associations to eliminate overlapping territories and to employ joint management or consolidate their organizations. The Land Banks also offered to enter into agreements with their Associations to reimburse them for servicing their outstanding loans and farms acquired through foreclosure or abandonment.

By the end of 1940, the number of National Farm Loan Associations had been reduced from nearly 5,000 to 3,635 operating Associations. Of this number 3,589 had entered into allowance plans and they were operating out of only 1,648 offices.

Along with encouragement to the National Farm Loan Associations to employ group management, the Land Banks were working with the Associations to develop "well-managed, soundly financed credit institutions, owned and controlled by farmers."[1]

Difficulties Arise from Heavy Debt Load

The tremendous refinancing program the Land Banks carried on from 1933 to 1935 had given thousands of farmers another chance to try to hold on to their farms, but the extreme drought years of 1934 and 1935 that produced the "dust bowl" problems in the plains states and much of the Midwest, plus lower prices for some farm products in 1938 and 1939, made it very difficult for thousands of farmers to carry their heavy debt loads.

The Land Banks in this period emphasized their policy of staying with their member-borrowers as long as there was a reasonable chance that they could eventually pay out. This policy was followed if borrowers were doing their best, were taking proper care of security, and were applying a fair share of their income above living and operating expenses to their mortgage debt.

Reamortizations and Foreclosures

The Land Banks reamortized many loans to lower the annual payments. The Banks experimented with variable payment plans where the Bank agreed to take a certain share of the crop after taxes were provided for. However, in the face of these efforts, the Land Banks by 1939 had accumulated an inventory of 25,000 farms acquired by foreclosure and voluntary deeds. From 1936 to 1939 they had acquired 44,000 farms, and through strenuous programs to sell farms to tenants and former owners under favorable sales contracts, they had sold 52,000 farms.

In this connection, Fred Gilmore, former Vice President of the Omaha Federal Land Bank, former Deputy Governor and Director of the Land Bank Service of the Farm Credit Administration, recalls his days in the real estate department of the Omaha Land Bank. He says much of his time was spent begging member-borrowers to stay on their farms rather than hand over the deed and leave their farms.

---

[1] Seventh Annual Report of the Farm Credit Administration, Government Printing Office, Washington, D.C., 1939, p. 34.

Fortunately, as the war in Europe progressed, the prices of farm products began to rise and with them farm income. Thus, the number of delinquent loans declined. Once again, the vast majority of farmers proved they will pay their debts if they have the money available to do so.

Future Payment Funds Initiated

In order to help farmers keep their loans in current condition in years of low income, Congress in the Farm Credit Act of 1937 authorized the Land Banks to accept conditional payments in years when farmers have extra income. These conditional payments are held in a Future Payment Fund to be used to meet future scheduled payments on loans. The Land Banks pay their members the interest on the money held in the Future Payment Fund.

Farmers Build Stronger PCAs

In the 1935–40 period the Production Credit Associations emphasized trying to serve more farmers and increasing their operating efficiency so they could give better service and pay all their expenses out of operating income. To the extent they were successful, they were building up much needed net worth reserves. By 1940 eight Production Credit Associations had built their net worth reserves to the point they were able to pay dividends on members' capital stock.

Cash Loan Funds Started

Production Credit Associations in their first few years had to get approval of the Federal Intermediate Credit Banks to accept a loan for discount before they could make a loan. They had no funds of their own to finance any loans the Federal Intermediate Credit Banks would not accept. This caused considerable delay. Gradually, they built up a cash loan fund from their own money and by borrowing directly from their Intermediate Credit Banks. These cash loan funds enabled them to give prompt service to members in cases where they felt relatively sure the Bank would accept the loan for discount. In cases where such loans were actually refused by the Federal Intermediate Credit Banks, the Production Credit Associations had to retain them in their own cash loan fund. This, of course, reduced the amount available to make future loans from the fund.

Field Offices Opened

In order to bring service closer to farmers, Production Credit Associations began appointing field representatives and in cases where it appeared economically feasible, they started opening field offices. By 1940 they had 261 full-time field offices and 544 part-time field offices.

Training for Decentralization Starts

The Production Credit Corporation training programs had progressed to the point that they could decentralize more and more responsibility and authority to the Production Credit Associations, and they in turn to their branch offices. By 1975 standards, they had not gone far in this direction, but the trend had been started.

Member Advisory Committees Organized

The first PCA member advisory committees were organized in this period. Similar district PCA advisory committees were also formed to counsel with their Production Credit Corporations and Intermediate Credit Banks on mutual problems.

Banks for Cooperatives Help Lay Foundation for Strong Cooperatives

In this latter half of the 1930s the Banks for Cooperatives began their much needed programs to help cooperatives improve their financial and organizational structures, adopt sounder credit policies, improve their record keeping, have more complete audits, and develop increased director and member interest and understanding. All these programs proved to be important in laying the foundation for the strong, effective cooperatives of today.

Urge Strong Local Support

The Federal Farm Board had emphasized large national or regional cooperatives and given relatively little attention to developing a strong, loyally supported underpinning needed for continued success. From the very beginning the Banks for Cooperatives reversed the emphasis. They stressed, urged, and helped develop strong regional cooperatives based on informed and interested farmer-members, whether through equally strong federations of local cooperatives like Farmland Industries, Land O' Lakes Creameries, Farmers Union Grain Terminal Association, Cenex, Sunkist Growers, Gold Kist, Landmark FS Services, and Far-Mar-Co. or through direct membership in centralized regional cooperatives such as Southern States, Agway, Inc., and Ocean Spray Cranberries.

Controversy and Politics Rear Their Ugly Heads

In the spring of 1939, President Franklin D. Roosevelt dropped a bombshell on the cooperative Farm Credit System that started a controversy that was to last, in varying intensity, for 14 years. Roosevelt issued an Executive Order ending the independent agency status of the Farm Credit Administration that he had created by Executive Order six years previously. The Order, effective July 1, 1939, placed the cooperative Farm Credit System's supervisory agency in the Department of Agriculture.

Why all the fuss? Wasn't it logical to have an agricultural lending function as part of the U.S. Department of Agriculture? Shouldn't there be fewer Government organizations? The cooperative Farm Credit System preferred the independent status for the Farm Credit Administration.

The controversy was whether the System would get involved in politics—either farm or party politics. It was the subject of several front page news stories and editorials in the newspapers in Washington and Farm Credit district headquarters cities, as well as in the farm and co-op press.

The underlying reasons behind the difference of opinion were soon to be revealed. Many people believed that the farm price and related agricultural programs or their opponents were politically motivated. Henry Wallace, then Secretary of Agriculture, had long been involved in those debates. And the two political parties frequently divided on the subject, as they have ever since. The cooperative Farm Credit System did not want to risk its usefulness to farmers by getting involved in such issues.

When Congress held hearings to decide whether to void the President's Executive Order—1939 Reorganization Plan Number 1—Wallace testified he had not been consulted before the Order was issued. Circumstantial evidence indicated that if he had not, at least his most politically motivated close associates knew it was coming, because they took little time in arranging for the transfer.[2]

Years before, Wallace had tried to get the Farm Credit Administration to require farmers to sign up for the farm program production controls and price supports in order to be eligible for loans from Production Credit Associations. The Farm Credit Administration, under Governor Myers, had insisted that the Farm Credit System should and did leave management decisions to its borrowers. After several discussions that extended over a period of months, eventually the Farm Credit Administration agreed to ask the Production Credit Associations to encourage their members to comply with the farm program rather than require it.

The national farm organizations, being generally upset over the change in the FCA status, asked former Governor Myers to discuss the matter with President Roosevelt on their behalf and see what could be done. According to reports that circulated around Washington, Roosevelt agreed that he would announce that the Farm Credit Administration was to remain autonomous within the Department of Agriculture. Whereupon, Myers suggested that it would be easier on Wallace to let him make such an announcement. Roosevelt agreed and asked Myers to write the release for Wallace.

The Farm Credit Administration received a few copies of such a release from the Office of Information in the Department of Agriculture. However, even though the controversy had been front-page news in many papers in various parts of the country, this news did not appear. About two weeks later, Ralph Foster, then Director of Information for the Farm Credit Banks of Wichita, sent out a release in which the General Agent of those Banks said he had received word of Wallace's announcement. That release—two weeks after they supposedly had received the news—appeared in newspapers throughout Kansas, Oklahoma, Colorado, and New Mexico. Apparently Wallace's release was sent only to the Farm Credit Administration.

A few months later, Wallace said he found it was impossible to be in a position where he could be held responsible for actions of an autonomous part of his Department.

By early January 1940, Governor F. F. Hill, as a result of disagreements with Wallace over basic policies, had resigned effective in March. Land Bank Commissioner Albert S. Goss was soon to follow.

---

[2] Paul H. Appleby, later to become Under Secretary of Agriculture, was in charge of the transition arrangements.

Farmer Ownership and Control Threatened

Goss's resignation was triggered by the fact he had not been consulted before the Wheeler-Jones bill had been introduced in Congress at Wallace's request. This bill, if it became law, would have completely changed the basic concepts involved in the FLB's ownership and control structure. It would have retired at par all the farmer-owned stock in the National Farm Loan Associations (now Federal Land Bank Associations) and reimbursed past farmer-borrowers for their losses on stock in Associations that had been retired. All past and present borrowers would soon have received a check in an election year. Borrowers would still have been "members" but without any share in the ownership.

At this point the whole cooperative Farm Credit System was threatened. There was a good chance that the proposed bill could have been hurried through. The House Agricultural Committee supposedly was evenly divided until a fatal error was committed by its proponents.

In order to try to get popular support for the bill, the new Governor, Albert G. Black, who came to the Farm Credit Administration from the Department of Agriculture, ordered the Federal Land Banks to send their 600,000 member-borrowers his memorandum, enclosing one to him from Secretary Wallace expressing concern over the plight of farmer-members of the Land Bank System and vaguely suggesting that something should be done about it. At the time, the Land Banks on their own behalf and on behalf of the Land Bank Commissioner held 25,000 farms they had taken over by foreclosure or as a result of abandonment, and about 30 percent of their loans were past due. The stock of a large proportion of the National Farm Loan Associations was impaired.

Under these circumstances, some people in the Farm Credit Administration were talking about employing 60 people to answer the expected 60,000 replies. One employee with some experience in direct mail, noticing the vagueness of the request for a reply, suggested they would be lucky to get 6,000 replies. Only 1,900 arrived and about three-quarters of those vigorously protested tinkering with the Farm Credit System.

Congress Dropped the Idea

When Congress heard about this venture, it was incensed at the use of the Government frank to attempt to lobby for a bill being considered by Congress. The Wheeler-Jones bill died quickly. The threat of transforming the Farm Credit System from a cooperative to a Government-owned system was over. Wallace, who had been trying to stir up support for the Democrats to nominate him for President if Roosevelt decided not to break tradition and run for a third term, was soon nominated for Vice President and lost interest in the Farm Credit System.

Getting off to this kind of start in the Department of Agriculture, it is little wonder that many of the System's leaders and influential farm and co-op organization friends remained wary of its influences— and all politically oriented interest in the System. These leaders sometimes probably saw motives that were not there. However, this continuing attitude was largely responsible for the Farm Credit Administration's again being made an independent agency insulated from political influence by the Federal Farm Credit Board in 1953, thus bearing out Governor Black's comment that he learned that an organization that knows where it is going has more effect on the man than the man has on the organization.

Chapter 28

THE DEPARTMENT OF AGRICULTURE
YEARS—1940 TO 1953

Even before the United States entered World War II in December 1941, the farming picture began to change and the cooperative Farm Credit System found itself having to recognize the new roles it would be called upon to assume.

Trying to Hold Farm Land Prices Down

In 1941, Governor Black called a conference of organizations making loans to farmers—primarily long-term mortgage lenders—but not exclusively. When the conferees met in Washington, Governor Black, recalling the World War I boom in farm land prices and the resulting decline throughout the next 13 years, suggested the mortgage lenders try to avoid making heavy loans that would help generate another fast rise in farm land prices. The meeting resulted in the formation of the National Agricultural Credit Committee which continued to meet three times a year. The Committee included representatives of the leading farm organizations, the American Bankers Association, the Mortgage Bankers Association, large life insurance companies, the Board of Governors of the Federal Reserve System, and the Farmers Home Administration.

The Farm Credit Administration carried on a publicity program throughout the war period urging farmers not to pay too much for land and reminding farmers of the World War I aftermath.

How much, if any, effect the campaign had on land prices is questionable. They rose 68 percent from 1941 to 1946. However, looking back, the agricultural economists at some of the Land Grant colleges who commented later that farmers probably should not have taken the Farm Credit Administration's or some Land Banks' advice and put off buying more land—although many college economists

253

were saying the same thing—proved to be right. The farm land price downslide after World War II never materialized. In fact, the prices of farm land increased 141 percent in the 5 years 1947 to 1952. The Land Banks themselves may well have lost business they otherwise would have had. "Hindsight is always better than foresight"—especially when history does not repeat itself!

Farmers Reduce Debts to Land Banks

Farm income rose due to the war-induced short supply of food and the resultant rise in prices of farm products. With the Farm Credit Administration and the Land Banks wisely urging farmers to reduce their depression-produced heavy debt load, and with a shortage of things to buy with their increased income, farmers did substantially reduce their farm mortgage debts. The total mortgage debt of all farmers declined from $12 billion in 1940 to $8 billion in 1945. The Land Banks and Land Bank Commissioner outstanding loans dropped from $2,400 million in 1940 to $946 million—its low point— in 1949. The percentage of the total farm mortgage debt held by the Land Banks and the Federal Farm Mortgage Corporation dropped from its depression peak of more than 48 percent to 16 percent. In contrast, by 1976, the percentage had gradually risen to 30 percent.

Drive Toward Farmer Ownership Begun

During this period, farmers, in order to avoid any possible new threats of the System becoming Government-owned rather than farmer-owned, made a determined effort to pay off the Government capital.

Land Banks Complete the Job

The Land Banks, starting in 1944, initiated a program to pay off all their Government-owned capital by May 1, 1946, except St. Paul whose paid-in capital was impaired. By June 1945, five of the Land Banks had completed that job—Houston, Louisville, Springfield, St. Louis, and Spokane. The other Land Banks, except St. Paul, completed paying off all their Government capital in 1946. The last, St. Paul, did so in 1947.

PCAs Start to Repay

During this period, the intensity of the Production Credit System's drive to achieve complete farmer-ownership of their capital greatly increased. Individual Production Credit Associations with much encouragement from their district Production Credit Corporations developed campaigns to get their members to purchase Class A, nonvoting stock in their Associations in addition to their Class B stock required investments—5 percent of their loans. By 1953, farmers had voluntarily purchased $18 million of Class A stock under these programs. By 1944, the Production Credit Association in Kewanee, Illinois, became the first Association to achieve the goal of complete farmer-ownership. By 1953, a total of 283 of the 499 Production Credit Associations were completely farmer-owned. At that date the Government-owned stock was down from $79 million in 1943 to $5.5 million. The farmer-owned stock plus net worth reserves had increased from $55 million in 1943 to $178 million.

BCs Study Ways to Achieve Goal

Starting in the mid-1940s, the Banks for Cooperatives were studying possible ways to change the provisions of their law to make it possible to gradually return their Government-owned capital.

Financing Food for Freedom

During the World War II years, Production Credit Associations and the Banks for Cooperatives were called upon to finance crops that were in short supply. The Production Credit Associations had only a modest increase in their total financing during the war years, however, because so much needed farm equipment was in short supply. Farmers and ranchers borrowed only 20 percent more in 1945 than they did in 1940.

In the case of the Banks for Cooperatives, their volume of business increased much faster—110 percent. Cooperatives were expanding their businesses because many farmers found them better able to provide the farm supplies that were hard to find. Apparently cooperatives either had more success in fighting priority battles than other businesses, or they were not tempted by larger profits available in other directions.

The Cooperative Research and Service Division of the Farm Credit Administration devoted much of its time during the war period to trying to help cooperatives present their cases as the representatives of farmers before Government war agencies. They were relatively successful in their endeavors to get the needed priorities for farmer cooperatives.

Wartime Appraisals and Disposals for Government

During World War II, the Land Banks appraised the farm, ranch, and forest lands acquired by the Government for such uses as training camps, artillery ranges, air bases, highways, waterworks, ammunition dumps, and warehouses. When the War was over, the Land Banks smoothly handled the disposal of 1¾ million acres of such surplus land on delegation of authority from the War Assets Administration and other agencies through the Secretary of Agriculture and the Governor of the Farm Credit Administration. The return of surplus land to peacetime uses involved a complex system of priorities involving Federal, state, and local governments, former owners, tenants, veterans, owner-operators, and nonprofit institutions.

Looking Ahead to Things to Come

As the period when the Farm Credit Administration was part of the Department of Agriculture drew to a close, Governor Duggan began calling attention to the need for share-the-risk plans because of the increasing size of credit exposures. He also began to point out that farmers needed loans for more than one year to finance increasing large investments in such capital improvements as heavy farm machinery. At the time, the Production Credit System thought its practice of renewing portions of such financing each year was adequate to do the job. The change to 3-, then 5-, and then 7-year loans was not to take place until policy-making for the Farm Credit Administration became the function of the Federal Farm Credit Board.

The beginnings of a future broad program of credit-related services was inaugurated in 1952 when Production Credit Associations began making group credit life insurance available to their members. The Land Banks soon followed.

Chapter 29

THE EARLY FEDERAL BOARD YEARS— 1953 TO 1968

During most of the 14 years the Farm Credit Administration was part of the U.S. Department of Agriculture, a national farm organization credit policy committee considering the problems of the cooperative Farm Credit System was at work. The committee included representatives of the National Grange, the American Farm Bureau Federation, the National Council of Farmer Cooperatives, and at times, the National Farmers Union, and the National Milk Producers Federation. The committee's first chairman was Albert Goss, Master of the National Grange and former FCA Land Bank Commissioner. At his death in 1950 he was succeeded by Herschel Newsome, the new Master of the National Grange.

A large share of this committee's efforts went into discussing various proposals for insulating the Farm Credit Administration from any possible political influence. At one point, the committee proposed a full-time policy-making board only nominally in the U.S. Department of Agriculture. However, this proposal did not meet with unanimous System approval.

After the National Farm Loan Associations and Production Credit Associations organized national committees for the same purpose, the two groups began working together.

In 1952 a bill to establish a policy-making board for the Farm Credit Administration went through one House of Congress.

With the encouragement of Dwight D. Eisenhower's Presidential campaign endorsement of the Federal Board concept at Omaha, the farm organization committee and those from within the System, the Farm Credit Act of 1953 was enacted and signed October 4, 1953. It again made the Farm Credit Administration an independent agency in the Executive branch of the Government under a part-time policy-making Federal Farm Credit Board with the power to appoint the Governor to administer its policies.

Board Establishes Communications Channels

The new Federal Farm Credit Board immediately realized the need for two-way communication with many groups in order to discharge properly its responsibility to keep the policies of the Farm Credit Administration, as the Farm Credit System's supervisory agency, responsive to the rapidly changing needs of the System's current and potential member-borrowers. In order to maintain two-way communications with the district policy-making bodies—the district Farm Credit Boards—the Board members immediately started to attend district Farm Credit Board meetings on a regular basis and have continued to do so. They attend such meetings to report on Federal Board actions and the reasons therefor. They also want to keep informed of the operations of the System in their home districts and of any problems that are arising.

The Federal Board also annually schedules one or more of its bimonthly meetings in connection with a district Farm Credit Board meeting. In addition, it attends and participates in the annual National Farm Credit Directors' Conference.

Shortly after it organized, the Federal Board set up a systematic method for channeling information and ideas from local Associations to the Board.

In order to be sure that means were provided for transmitting ideas from the local level on an organized basis, the Federal Board annually schedules as part of one of its regular meetings, a session with the National Committees of Federal Land Bank Associations, Production Credit Associations, and cooperatives borrowing from the Banks for Cooperatives. These committees in the case of the Federal Land Bank Associations and the Production Credit Associations are made up of the Federal Board's counterparts—the local policy-makers—members of the boards of directors.

The Federal Board periodically includes on its agendas meetings with representatives of the national farm and cooperative organizations to discuss mutual interests, to get their views on matters affecting credit, and to keep these organizations' leaders up-to-date as to Farm Credit policies and problems. From time to time it also meets with financial leaders such as representatives of the Federal Reserve Board and other lending groups as well as security dealers.

It also started coordinating Board meetings with the annual meetings of the National Council of Farmer Cooperatives and the American Institute of Cooperation so Board members could become better acquainted with the leadership of other cooperatives and their problems and activities.

Congress Asks for Plans for Complete
Farmer-Ownership

In the Farm Credit Act of 1953 setting up the Federal Farm Credit Board, Congress asked it to submit plans for farmers to become the complete owners of the cooperative Farm Credit System. This necessitated replacing Government-owned capital with farmer-owned capital, either in the form of capital stock investments or equities built up and retained from operations of the organizations .involved.

Tackling Farmer-Ownership

Almost immediately after taking office, the Federal Board asked the Farm Credit Administration to work with the parts of the System that still had Government capital to develop plans for replacing it with farmer-owned capital. As already covered in some detail, the following is a list of the milestones occurring in the 1953 to 1968 period:

1955—Farm Credit Act provided a plan by which farmer cooperatives could gradually reach full ownership of the Banks for Cooperatives. But Congress rejected the Federal Farm Credit Board's proposal for the Production Credit Association's attaining ownership of Production Credit Corporations.[1]

1956—Farm Credit Act merged the Production Credit Corporations into the Federal Intermediate Credit Banks and provided a plan for the Production Credit Associations to achieve full ownership of them.[2]

1968—*Users Became the Complete Owners of the System.* By the end of 1968 the cooperatives using the Banks for Cooperatives and the Production Credit Associations and the other financial institutions obtaining funds from the Intermediate Credit Banks became the complete owners of the Farm Credit Banks they used. The last three Production Credit Associations also paid off their remaining Government capital. The goal of complete user ownership was finally reached

---

[1] See "Drive for Farm Ownership Spurs Action" in Chapter 14.
[2] *Ibid.*

35 years after the cooperative Farm Credit System was rounded out in the Great Depression year—1933.

Farmers, ranchers, their cooperatives, the boards of directors, and officers of all the credit cooperatives making up the System or using it could be justly proud of achieving complete ownership of what Marvin Briggs, Chairman of the Farm Credit Board in 1956, had declared to be the largest cooperative organization in the world. No one had ever challenged his claim!

This great cooperative Farm Credit System achievement put the capstone on the 15-year career of Robert B. Tootell as Governor of the Farm Credit Administration. It put the Federal Farm Credit Board in the position of being able to name the next Governor without asking Presidential approval and thus once more it avoided the possibility of political considerations determining the future course of the Farm Credit System.

In the 15 years of its existence, the Federal Farm Credit Board had created the climate and provided the leadership under which this team effort could reach the long-sought goal of thousands of farmers and ranchers.

Loan Service to Users Grows Rapidly

Under Federal Board-adopted policies, the System's rate of growth soon started to increase at a more rapid rate, both as to the number of farmer-members and cooperatives served and as to the amount of financing in use. Between 1953 and 1968 the number of members and the amount of loans they had outstanding increased as shown in the accompanying table.

Increased Use of System—1953–1968

	1953		1968		Average Annual Rate of Percentage Increase in Amount[1]
	Borrowing Members	Amount	Borrowing Members	Amount	
		(millions)		(millions)	
Federal Land Banks	316,000	$1,135	399,000	$5,973	28
Production Credit Associations	249,000	768	323,000	4,097	29
Banks for Cooperatives	2,024[2]	319	3,036[2]	1,454	24

[1] Total percentage increase for period divided by 15 years.
[2] Number of cooperatives with loans outstanding June 30.

Other Milestones

Several other important changes were made in the period of these first 15 years under the leadership of the Federal Farm Credit Board, but they have already been discussed under their appropriate headings.

Chapter 30

SYSTEM MODERNIZED FOR MODERN FARMING—1969 TO 1975

The repayment of the last of its Government capital placed the cooperative Farm Credit System in a new stance. It then was only dependent on Government for its Federal charter and its resulting supervision and examination. The Board having chosen a new Governor—E. A. Jaenke[1]—agreed it was time to take stock of what kind of credit service agriculture was going to need in the years ahead and how well the System was geared to meet its prospective needs. In 1967–68, Dr. John Brake, while on leave from Michigan State University, had projected a possible growth in the System's loan volume from $10.7 billion to $32 billion by 1980 and from 21 percent of the total credit used by agriculture—farmers and their cooperatives—in 1967 to 30 percent by 1980[2]

Commission on Agricultural Credit

On the recommendation of Governor Jaenke, the Farm Credit Board appointed the Commission on Agricultural Credit in May 1969 to take a broad but in-depth look at where the System stood and what changes might be required to meet the fast-changing credit needs of the Nation's producer-owned food production and marketing system. The 27-member commission, formed in May 1969, included representatives of the national farm and cooperative organizations, farm communicators, a young farmer leader, the agricultural representative on the Board of Governors of the Federal Reserve System,

---

[1] See "Leaders with Vision and Ability" in Chapter 9 for details on Jaenke's background.

[2] Adjusted to include debts of cooperatives to creditors other than Banks for Cooperatives based on proportions in most recent Farmer Cooperative Service, USDA estimates.

and representative policy-makers—members of district Farm Credit boards and administrators—Bank presidents—from the Farm Credit System.

The Commission's report made several basic recommendations for broadening and modernizing the cooperative Farm Credit System. Under the keen, broad-minded, always diplomatic chairmanship of Julian Thayer,[3] a Middlefield, Connecticut, farmer, the Commission over a 10-month period held seven working sessions. It conferred with farmers, economists, cooperative leaders, bankers, Farm Credit Bank staff members, and officials of the Farm Credit Administration.

In answer to a public request for interested individuals and groups to submit ideas and suggestions, it received more than 360 thoughtful letters.

An open forum attended by more than 400 people was held in Champaign, Illinois—as part of the program of the American Institute of Cooperation—where individuals expressed their viewpoints.

Thayer, in his letter of transmittal of the Commission's report[4] to the Federal Farm Credit Board, pointed out that it was the general view of the Commission as a body, even though some of the Commission members disagreed with certain points in the recommendations. In closing his transmittal letter, Thayer said:

> The Commission is mindful of the fact that these suggestions are advisory in nature. It remains for the Farm Credit Administration, its policy-making Federal Farm Credit Board, the Congress, and the Farm Credit System—boards, Banks, Associations and member-borrowers—to consider and implement them as deemed appropriate.,

The Commission's report suggested a general statement of objective for the System, 12 goals in major areas of interest, with broad recommendations under each with short comments thereon.

As an overall objective the Commission recommended:

> Recognizing that a prosperous, productive agriculture is essential to a free Nation, it is the objective of the farmer-owned, cooperative Farm Credit System to improve the income and well-being of American farmers and ranchers by

---

[3] Thayer was a former member of the Farm Credit Board of Springfield, former Chairman of the Federal Farm Credit Board, and former Chairman of the Executive Committee of Eastern States Farmers Exchange, now Agway, Inc.

[4] "The Farm Credit System in the 70's—The Report of the Commission on Agricultural Credit," Farm Credit Administration, Washington, D.C., 1970.

furnishing adequate and constructive credit and closely related services to them, their cooperatives, and selected farm
related businesses necessary for efficient farm operations.

The goals in 12 major areas suggested by the Commission were:

Area	Goal
Serving Farmers	Extend to farmers adequate credit to meet their total needs where a sound basis for such credit exists.
Serving Young Farmers	Provide greater opportunity for competent young farmers to obtain adequate amounts of credit consistent with sound lending practices while recognizing the well-being of the applicant and reasonable protection for the lender.
Serving Cooperatives	Serve the total credit needs of cooperatives which help meet farmers' supply, marketing, and processing needs. Provide such service in a manner that will promote the growth and development of cooperatives and thus the general well-being of farmers.
Serving Farm Related Businesses	Make credit available for selected farm related businesses which provide services directly to farmers necessary for efficient production, processing, and marketing of farm products.
Credit Standards	Employ credit standards which enable the System to fully recognize management ability and earnings potential in providing maximum availability of credit to member-borrowers.
Credit Related Services	Assure the availability to member-borrowers of credit related services necessary for a successful farming business.
Serving Rural America	Take a broader view of serving credit needs than in the past. Meet the projected credit needs of farmers, their cooperatives, and farm related businesses which will require consideration of the development needs of rural communities as well as the direct credit needs of the farm business.
	Strive to be ever alert for ways in which it can contribute directly to the well-being of rural residents and rural communities in the future and be receptive to suggestions as to

Area	*Goal*
Serving Rural America (Continued)	how it might share either its knowledge of credit or organizational structure for helping solve the serious credit needs of rural America.
	Assist, for example, in financing nonfarm rural homes, rural community needs, and rural cooperative utility systems. (Although the Commission does not include in this report specific recommendations as to how to achieve such services, it does urge that the System consider how and when such services might be initiated.)
Financing the System	Utilize the most reliable sources of loan funds available and obtain funds at lowest possible cost.
Organization and Functions of the Banks and Associations	Provide the best possible credit service to farmers and their cooperatives through the cooperation of the units of the Farm Credit Service and through the coordination of the units' functions.
Policy-making	Maintain boards of directors who are sensitive to the particular credit needs of farmers and alert to the constantly changing agricultural economy.
Role of the Farm Credit Administration	Develop and promote the strongest possible Farm Credit organization with which to serve farmers, their cooperatives, and the Nation through the Farm Credit Administration.
External Relations	Maintain communications with others concerned with financing American agriculture. Cooperate at all levels on activities which will best serve agriculture and the Nation.

Farm Credit Act of 1971 Enacted

The Commission's recommendations were discussed at meetings of managers and boards of local Associations. A questionnaire was sent to System members. Then, after discussion of the Commission's report by the Federal Farm Credit Board and Governor Jaenke with district Farm Credit Boards and the presidents of the Farm Credit Banks, the Federal Board made the necessary policy decisions and asked Governor Jaenke to have the necessary legislation prepared.

Controlling legislation for the Farm Credit System then was included in scores of laws and separately adopted amendments dating back to 1916. This had resulted in many variations between the provisions regulating the operations of various parts of the System, usually without any apparent well-founded reasons. In general, the Farm Loan Act of 1916, even with its many amendments, having been the pioneer legislation for the Land Banks and Associations, was considerably more restrictive and less flexible than the laws relating to other parts of the System. That Act had many limitations and specifications that were not included in the laws governing the Production Credit Associations and Banks for Cooperatives. In most cases the need for them had evaporated, as Fred Gilmore, Deputy Governor and Director of the Land Bank Service, frequently had pointed out.

As a result of this situation, it was decided to have Howard Campbell, General Counsel of the Farm Credit Administration, recodify existing law, and in the process, eliminate limitations that experience had proven were no longer needed. He—after conferring with the Farm Credit district General Counsels and particularly with Fred Knutsen, President of the Federal Land Bank of Spokane[5]—provided greater consistency between the three parts of the System and much more flexibility in the law. The proposed bill left to the Federal Board the responsibility for keeping regulations up-to-date rather than providing narrow specifications in the law that would need frequent changes.

After many discussions with concerned groups within the System—both at the district and Association level—the proposed legislation went to Congress. After some amendments and a few compromises, the Farm Credit Act of 1971 was passed by Congress and signed by the President. The Farm Credit Act of 1971 provided an updated charter for the System.

The new charter in effect delegated many authorities and responsibilities from Congress to the Federal Farm Credit Board. In turn, provision was made for assigning many of its former powers to district Farm Credit Boards. The local Associations also received more powers that were formerly held by district Boards. The Federal Board was given additional authority to delegate to the Farm Credit Banks and their district Farm Credit Boards. The district Boards were also

---

[5] Knutsen had also served as General Counsel of the Farm Credit Administration in the transition period after the passage of the Farm Credit Act of 1953, again making the Farm Credit Administration an independent agency under the Federal Farm Credit Board. Knutsen also had long served as General Counsel of the Farm Credit Banks of Spokane.

given authority to delegate additional powers to the Federal Land Banks and Production Credit Associations and their boards of directors.

1971 Act Broadens Systems Ability to Serve

System's Services Broadened

The Farm Credit Act of 1971 also gave the Farm Credit System the authority to considerably broaden its services to meet the growing needs of farmers, ranchers, their cooperatives and rural America.

Limit on Land Bank Loans Raised

One of the most important of all the provisions in the Act were those that enabled the Land Banks to use more credit judgment in making farm mortgage loans and thus greatly increasing their ability to serve the modern credit needs of farmers and ranchers. For years the Land Banks were not allowed to make loans for more than 65 percent of the *normal* appraised value of the farm or ranch—plus the amount needed to buy stock in the borrower-member's Federal Land Bank Association.

With years of continued inflation, normal values always lagged behind current prices. The 65 percent limitation made it impossible for the lender to give consideration to any special factors surrounding the loan such as the unusual financial strength of the borrower, his above-average management ability, or any outside income that might be available. It had often been said the Land Banks were purely collateral lenders.

The new Act allows the Land Banks to lend up to 85 percent of the market value of the property. While the Land Banks are not expected to lend up to that limit in most cases, that change gives them the authority to do so when the circumstances warrant it. Consequently, each loan involves a careful credit analysis to determine how far the Land Bank should go with each individual applicant. There is much more room to make credit judgments.

Additional Areas and Kinds of Service

The Farm Credit Act of 1971 also for the first time gives the authority to the Land Banks and Production Credit Associations, under certain restrictions, to make loans to nonfarm rural home owners.

This is a service that was much needed as demonstrated by the fact that by the end of 1975 a total of nearly 26,000 rural residents had $558 million in such loans.

The Act of 1971 also broadened the field of service of the System to include loans to commercial fishermen. In 1975 they borrowed $37 million. The Act authorized loans to businesses providing farm-related services. It also broadened the System's authority to provide credit-related services. This is an authority that will probably grow in importance as farm businesses continue to grow more complex.

BCs Can Lend to More Co-ops

In the field of cooperatives, the Federal Board had asked Congress to let district Farm Credit Boards decide what percentage of farmer-members a cooperative had to have to be eligible for loans from the Banks for Cooperatives within the range of 65 to 90 percent. Because of the objections of two district Farm Credit Boards, Congress came up with a compromise of 80 percent. In the 1974 and 1975 sessions of Congress, the Federal Board asked that district Farm Credit Boards be allowed to reduce this eligibility requirement in the case of cooperatives acting as a public utility—such as electric and telephone service—to 60 percent. In early 1976, Congress gave the authority to make such loans to cooperatives that had 70 percent or more farmer-members.

The number of members served by the System and the total amount borrowed from all parts of the Farm Credit System have increased substantially since the passage of the Farm Credit Act of 1971. Some of the increase is undoubtedly due to inflation, but the dramatic increase in number of borrowers from the Land Banks is an indication that the greater flexibility provided by the Act is enabling them to serve many more farmers and ranchers, even after allowing for their loans to nonfarm rural home owners. In the 1975 fiscal year the number of new loans was double that of 1971—up from 36,936 to 74,901—higher than any year in the Land Bank's history except for 1934. Only 12,000 of the 1975 loans were to rural home owners. The money borrowed from the Land Banks in fiscal year 1975 was 259 percent more than in 1971—up from $1.3 billion to $4.6 billion.

System's Share of Financing Increased

In commenting on the fact that the proportion of the total farm mortgage debt accounted for by the Federal Land Banks rose from

22.9 percent in 1970 to 28.9 percent by 1975, the Economic Research Service of the Department of Agriculture said,[6] "The rapid shift in market share and the increase in funds provided by the Federal Land Banks are dramatic evidence of the changes in lending policies which were the result of the Farm Credit Act of 1971. This shift also reflects the inability of insurance companies to increase their allocation of funds to agriculture in a time of rising demand for loan funds."

A Single Farm Credit Regulations Manual

As a result of the recodification of legislation governing the co-operative Farm Credit System, the Farm Credit Administration, after consulting with committees made up of district bank representatives, developed and issued a single Manual of Regulations to cover the operations of all 37 Farm Credit Banks, in place of several former manuals. This laid the groundwork for more consistent supervision and made it possible for the district Farm Credit Banks and Associations to work together in closer harmony.

FCA Reorganized on Functional Lines

The Farm Credit Administration staff until 1972 had operated on a line basis. Each type of credit—land bank, production credit, and banks for cooperatives—had its own Presidentially appointed Commissioner until 1953. The Commissioners were then replaced by Deputy Governors who were in charge of supervising their type of credit.

In 1972, Governor Jaenke, with Federal Board approval, adopted a functional type of organization with a deputy governor and division director in charge of credit, and another in charge of operations and finance. Thus, all three groups of Banks were placed under the same supervision.

In late 1974, Governor Harding, in order to reduce the number of people contacting district bank officers, while continuing the functional approach, put one deputy governor in charge of an Office of Credit and Operations, another in charge of an Office of Finance and Research, and a third in charge of an Office of Administration. In 1976, he appointed a Deputy Governor in charge of the Office of Examinations and made the General Counsel a Deputy Governor.

---

[6] "Balance Sheet of Farming Sector 1975," Economic Research Service, U.S. Department of Agriculture, Washington, D.C., 1975.

Getting More Money at Lowest
Possible Cost

The cost of borrowing money to lend is greater by far than all other Farm Credit System costs combined—currently ranging from a low of 76 percent of total costs in 1972 to 86.7 percent in 1971. Interest rates the System paid for newly borrowed money averaged much higher in the 10 years 1966 to 1975—6.97 percent—than in any previous period. In the preceding 10 years—1956 to 1965—the average was only 3.9 percent. The range of fluctuations in the average annual cost of new money borrowed by the System also became wider in the 1966–1975 period. The low average was 5.26 percent in 1972 and the high of 8.66 was for 1974—which dropped to 6.88 percent in 1975—while in the previous 10 years the annual average cost ranged from a low of 2.74 percent in 1958 to a high of 4.48 percent in 1959.

Also the need to examine all available sources of lending funds to meet the System's rapidly expanding loan demands became essential. Thus the importance of exploring all alternative sources of funds has greatly increased.

Flowing out of the recommendations of the Commission on Agricultural Credit, a Finance Advisory Committee of financial specialists was appointed in 1970. That Committee suggested further study of various supplementary ways of obtaining lending funds. As one result of these recommendations, the System developed a discount note program that started operating January 1, 1975.

These discount notes are issued for periods from 5 to 150 days. In the first year of this program the System sold $3.8 million of such notes at an average cost of 5.97 percent compared to the 6.89 percent average rate paid on Banks for Cooperatives' six-month bonds issued during the same period. The possibility of issuing Farm Credit bonds backed by all 37 Banks, as suggested by the Commission on Agricultural Credit and the Finance Advisory Committee, to supplement or replace separate issues of consolidated bonds for each banking group, was continuing to be explored in 1976.

FarmBank Services

After considerable investigation and discussion, the 37 Farm Credit Banks, effective January 1, 1975, established a service organization—FarmBank Services—located at Denver, Colorado, to provide services that can be arranged for more efficiently or more effectively on a joint basis than on a single Bank basis. These services may include national advertising, training and management development programs, employee benefits such as insurance and pensions, and others. One of the first services it started handling was that of providing computerized management information under the name of FarmBank Research and Information Service.

Financing Young Farmers

The Federal Land Banks and Production Credit Associations have long helped many young farmers get established in farming and then build sizable farm operations. However, following a Young Farmer Financing Conference in 1974, several of the Farm Credit districts have developed special loan programs aimed specifically at helping young farmers who lack sizable equities, but have good management ability, to build viable farm businesses.

In this connection, starting in the early 1970s, the Land Banks have made some loans jointly with the Farmers Home Administration to farmers who lack the equities usually considered necessary. The largest group of prospects for such loans is young farmers.

Use of System Continues to Climb

Members' use of the cooperative Farm Credit System continues to increase rapidly, as illustrated in the following table.

Increase in Service to Members [1]

Farm Credit System	1969	1971	1973	1975
Federal Land Banks				
Number Borrowers				
(000)	404	406	414	460
% Increase	2.5	0.5	2.0	11.0
Amount Borrowed (bill.)				
(outstanding)	6.6	7.6	10.1	15.4
% Increase	24	15	33	52
Production Credit Associations				
Members Served [2]				
(000)	371	367	384	393
% Increase	−0.8	−1.1	4.6	2.3
Amount Borrowed (bill.)				
(outstanding)	4.6	5.4	7.5	10.8
% Increase	25	17	39	44
Banks for Cooperatives				
Number Borrowers				
(000)	2.96	2.91	3.11	3.17
% Increase	−2.0	−1.7	5.1	1.9
Amount Borrowed (bill.)				
(outstanding)	1.6	2.0	2.7	3.4
% Increase	23	25	35	26
System Total				
Amount Borrowed (bill.)				
(outstanding)	13	16	21	30
% Increase	30	23	31	43

[1] Percentage increases are for 2-year periods.
[2] Members having a loan outstanding sometime during the year.

Chapter 31

SUMMARY AND A LOOK TO
THE FUTURE

The availability of financing from the cooperative Farm Credit System has been a major factor in making possible the rapid development of the highly efficient, modern food production and the farmer-owned marketing system that the United States has today. It has helped make it possible for family farm operators to compete with large farming corporations.

Both farm owners and tenant operators have borrowed money from Production Credit Associations. Many of the tenants who built up equities in their businesses have gone on to buy farms of their own with loans from the Federal Land Banks.

The Banks for Cooperatives by the right mixture of providing specialized financing and advice and counsel have been a major factor in helping develop a growing national network of strong cooperatives that provide farmer and rancher members with an ever-widening number of supply and marketing services that reach further and further back to the basic resources needed in farming and carry farm products nearer to the consumer.

Even more important than the highly significant reductions in the cost of credit the System has provided to its members, and through competition to other farmers, has been the availability of a constantly adequate supply of funds on terms suited to the need of individual borrowers to finance soundly based operations. That availability has made it possible for the System's borrowers to continually develop more efficient farm, ranch, and cooperative operations. In the process, farmers and their cooperatives have borrowed money from it in ever-increasing amounts. The total for its 60 years of operation is $250 billion. Of this total, one-half of it has been borrowed in the last 6 years.

But even more important than the amount of money supplied

by the Farm Credit System is the ever-increasing number of farmers it has served either directly or indirectly through their marketing and farm supply cooperatives. The exact number is not possible to estimate, but it probably now totals considerably more than half the total number of farmers.

The System has tried many approaches and methods of meeting problems and providing service. It has made its share of mistakes but has usually learned from them.

It is often said the Farm Credit System has been fortunate to have operated in a period of rising farm prices that has buried many of its mistakes. However, not to be overlooked are the testings the System and its member-borrowers have endured. It has come through two world wars and several lesser conflicts, the deepest depression the country ever had, years of droughts and floods, including the record-breaking dust bowl years of the 1930s. While the general trend in farm prices has been upward, there have been many years in which a large share of its members have had to contend with surpluses and low prices for their particular products. There have been many periods of cost-price squeezes.

The System's innovations in the field of farm finance have been many and varied. They have helped all farmers and cooperatives who borrow money, because, as the pacesetter, the System's terms are soon imitated by other lenders.

Equal to Challenges Ahead

There are many challenges ahead for farmers, their marketing, supply and business service cooperatives, as well as for the cooperative Farm Credit System. Just what those challenges will be is hard to imagine with any degree of accuracy. But parts of history are likely to be repeated. The weather hazards of floods, droughts, and frosts are likely to continue. Periods of low prices for various farm products and high costs will come again but, hopefully, wars will not. These challenges the System has faced before and past history—mistakes and victories—points the directions to future successful courses of action.

The System must ever be alert to keep up with the constant changes in agriculture and must seek answers to new problems even before they arrive.

Financial Strength Highly Important

The System has built good reserves and a strong financial base, but with ever-rising costs and the accompanying larger number and amount of loans, the System must continue to watch its financial base to make sure its strength grows fast enough to bear the weight of the loan structure it has to support.

Recruiting Top People and Training Will Bring Continued Success

The Farm Credit System has hired and trained and is continuing to train a highly competent and imaginative staff that is determined to help its member-users meet the ever-changing conditions that lie ahead. However, staffs are not static. People move on, retire, or die. Loans continue to grow larger and more complex. Other problems do too. The best people available need to be hired now. They need to be well trained and given opportunities for continued development. They need to be well paid and have advantageous fringe benefit programs.

Training, development, and fringe benefits can best be provided on a cooperative basis. All are needed to hold good people who will stay with the System and be available to take positions of greater responsibility. The best people also need to see many opportunities for new challenges and advancement ahead. If people can move easily from Association to Association; from Associations to Banks; from Bank to Bank; from district to district; and from district to the Farm Credit Administration and back, the horizons and opportunities will be vastly increased. Wider experience will make good people better people. Today's loss for one organization made possible by greater mobility may be its gain tomorrow.

The increasing amount of cooperation between all parts of the Farm Credit System bodes well for the future. Working together for the mutual benefit of all can accomplish great things in the drive toward more and better quality service for farmers and ranchers at lower cost—the System's ultimate aim.

Intersystem Cooperation Increasing

The opportunities for even more cooperation through FarmBank Services are almost endless for Banks, Associations, and members. And the System's renewed interest in finding more and better ways to serve young farm families and in getting them involved in running the System is highly important. Today's members and boards of directors will soon be gone. The System needs a new crop coming on.

Member Relations Build Loyalty

Good member relations and communications programs have played important parts in building a strong, democratically run System made up of loyal, well-informed members. The future health of the System will be greatly dependent on how well these programs are maintained, expanded, and improved.

Given all these important elements, farmers, ranchers, fishermen, and nonfarm rural home owners can look to the System with confidence that it will serve their needs for generations to come!

APPENDIX

Federal Farm Credit Board Members

Springfield District

Luther W. Jennejahn, Hilton, N.Y.	1973–
Jonathan Davis, Sterling Junction, Mass.	1967–1973
Julian B. Thayer, Middlefield, Conn.	1961–1967
Harlan B. Munger, Byron, N.Y.	1953–1961

Baltimore District

Galen B. Brubaker, Rocky Mount, W.Va.	1974–
J. Homer Remsberg, Middletown, Md.	1968–1974
William T. Steele, Jr., Richmond, Va.	1962–1968
Glen B. Boger, Allentown, Pa.	1956–1962
J. D. Anderson, Morgantown, W.Va.	1953–1956

Columbia District

David C. Waldrop, Silverstreet, S.C.	1975–
T. Carroll Atkinson, Jr., Marion, S.C.	1969–1975
Lorin T. Bice, Haines City, Fla.	1963–1969
Marshall H. Edwards, Bartow, Fla.	1953–1963

Louisville District

Marvin R. Bradley, Indianapolis, Ind.	1976–
Kenneth N. Probasco, Worthington, Ohio	1970–1976
Marion A. Clawson, Eaton, Ind.	1964–1970
Marvin J. Briggs, Indianapolis, Ind.	1953–1964

New Orleans District

Ernest G. Spivey, Jackson, Miss.	1970–
R. Watkins Greene, Abbeville, La.	1965–1969
J. Pittman Stone, Coffeeville, Miss.	1959–1965
Elbert J. Hodge, Andalusia, Ala.	1953–1959

St. Louis District

Melvin E. Sims, Liberty, Ill.	1972–
R. D. Pennewell, Palmyra, Mo.	1966–1972
L. C. Carter, Stuttgart, Ark.	1960–1966
L. V. Ritter, Marked Tree, Ark.	1953–1960

St. Paul District

Alfred Underdahl, Hebron, N.D.	1973–
Millard F. Dailey, Red Lake Falls, Minn.	1967–1973
Joe B. Zeug, Walnut Grove, Minn.	1961–1967
George P. Daley, Lewiston, Minn.	1955–1961
Clark L. Brody, Lansing, Mich.	1953–1955

Omaha District

Dennis S. Lundsgaard, Cherokee, Iowa	1974–
C. Everett Spangler, Omaha, Neb.	1968–1974
J. B. Fuller, Torrington, Wyo.	1962–1968
Sam H. Bober, Newell, S.D.	1955–1962
Raymond Sayre, Ackworth, Iowa	1953–1954

Wichita District

Ralph N. Austin, Westcliffe, Colo.	1975–
James H. Dean, Hutchinson, Kan.	1969–1975
Kenneth T. Anderson, Emporia, Kan.	1963–1969
George W. Lightburn, Capron, Okla.	1957–1963
H. W. Clutter, Holcomb, Kan.	1953–1957

Houston District

William Dale Nix, Canadian, Tex.	1976–
E. G. Schuhart II, Dalhart, Tex.	1970–1976
David G. Gault, Manor, Tex.	1964–1970
Frank Stubbs, Corpus Christi, Tex.	1958–1964
C. H. Mathews, Eagle Lake, Tex.	1953–1958

Berkeley District

Earl S. Smittcamp, Clovis, Calif.	1971–
Paul A. Dobson, Exeter, Calif.	1967–1971
Ralph K. Cooper, Buckeye, Ariz.	1965–1966
Glen R. Harris, Richvale, Calif.	1959–1965
Golden F. Fine, Yuba City, Calif.	1953–1959

Spokane District

E. Riddell Lage, Hood River, Ore.	1972–
A. Lars Nelson, Seattle, Wash.	1966–1971
Robert T. Lister, Prineville, Ore.	1960–1966
Earl H. Brockman, Caldwell, Ida.	1953–1960

Representative of Secretary of Agriculture

Elton R. Smith, Lansing, Mich.	1973–
R. Edward Bauer, Van Meter, Iowa	1969–1973
Arthur J. Smaby, Minneapolis, Minn.	1965–1969
Murray D. Lincoln, Columbus, Ohio	1961–1965
Francis W. Peck, St. Paul, Minn.	1953–1961

Farm Credit Administration Governors

W. Malcolm Harding	Nov. 1, 1974–
Edwin A. Jaenke	March 1, 1969–Oct. 31, 1974
Robert B. Tootell	April 1, 1954–Feb. 28, 1969
Carl R. Arnold	July 16, 1953–March 31, 1954[1]
Ivy W. Duggan	June 22, 1944–June 30, 1953
Albert G. Black	March 27, 1940–June 21, 1944
Forrest F. Hill	Sept. 21, 1938–March 26, 1940
William I. Myers	Nov. 17, 1933–Sept. 20, 1938
Henry Morgenthau, Jr.	May 27, 1933–Nov. 16, 1933

[1] Acting Governor as of December 4, 1953.

Springfield

FEDERAL LAND BANK

Howell Hughes	1975–
Gordon Cameron	1960–1975
Myron C. Peabody	1952–1960
Harlan B. Munger	1947–1951
Macdonald G. Newcomb	1944–1946
Edward H. Thomson	1919–1944
Leonard G. Robinson	1917–1919

FEDERAL INTERMEDIATE CREDIT BANK

Howell Hughes	1975–
Gordon Cameron	1960–1975
Myron C. Peabody	1952–1960
Harlan B. Munger	1947–1951
Bernard A. Colby	1942–1946
Allen L. Gillett	1934–1942
Edward H. Thomson	1923–1933

BANK FOR COOPERATIVES

Howell Hughes	1975–
Gordon Cameron	1960–1975
Myron C. Peabody	1952–1960
Harlan B. Munger	1947–1951
George W. Lamb	1933–1946

PRODUCTION CREDIT CORPORATION

Myron C. Peabody	1952–1956
Harlan B. Munger	1935–1951
Van B. Hart	1934–1935

PRESIDENTS OF FARM CREDIT BANKS

Baltimore

FEDERAL LAND BANK

E. G. Fouse	1970–
Warren R. Fankhanel	1963–1970
Hugh S. Mackey	1958–1963
J. Thomas Vandenburg	1950–1958
E. Paul Crider	1947–1950
Howard Vaughan	1942–1947
Charles S. Jackson	1932–1942
Vulosko Vaiden	1919–1932
George H. Stevenson	1917–1919

FEDERAL INTERMEDIATE CREDIT BANK

E. G. Fouse	1970–
Warren R. Fankhanel	1963–1970
Hugh S. Mackey	1933–1963
Charles S. Jackson	1932–1933
Vulosko Vaiden	1923–1932

BANK FOR COOPERATIVES

Jack R. Cobb	1967–
Richard B. Jones, Jr.	1958–1967
Samuel M. Thomson	1943–1958
Franklin B. Bomberger	1933–1942

PRODUCTION CREDIT CORPORATION

J. Thomas Vandenburg	1950–1956
E. Paul Crider	1948–1950
M. O. Wilson	1936–1948
J. K. Doughton	1935–1936
George H. Stevenson	1933–1934

F FARM CREDIT BANKS

Columbia

FEDERAL LAND BANK

Robert A. Darr	1965–
D. M. Dowdell, Jr.	1962–1965
Rufus R. Clarke	1954–1962
Julian H. Scarborough	1934–1954
Frank H. Daniel	1929–1934
Howard C. Arnold	1924–1928
David A. Houston	1918–1924
F. J. H. Engelken	1917–1918

FEDERAL INTERMEDIATE CREDIT BANK

Robert A. Darr	1954–
Rufus R. Clarke	1948–1954
J. E. Cagle	1933–1948
Frank H. Daniel	1929–1933
Howard C. Arnold	1924–1928
David A. Houston	1923–1924

BANK FOR COOPERATIVES

Richard W. Bonney, Jr.	1968–
Robert H. McDougall	1961–1968
J. D. Lawrence	1948–1961
Rufus R. Clarke	1944–1948
L. G. Foster	1939–1944
Virgil R. Judson	1936–1938
Alfred Scarborough	1933–1936

PRODUCTION CREDIT CORPORATION

Robert A. Darr	1951–1956
Julian H. Scarborough	1945–1950
W. Arthur Minor, Jr.	1941–1945
Frank J. Towles	1940–1941
S. M. Garwood	1939–1940
Rufus R. Clarke	1939–1939
Ernest Graham	1933–1939
Frank H. Daniel	1933–1933

PRESIDENTS OF FARM CREDIT BANKS

Louisville

FEDERAL LAND BANK

Paul F. Bachman	1971–
E. V. Landers	1959–1970
M. S. Kennedy, Jr.	1946–1959
E. Rice	1935–1946
Frank D. Rash	1934–1935
E. Rice	1933–1934
A. G. Brown	1930–1933
George M. Wilbur	1930–1930
James B. Davis	1922–1930
Walter Howell	1917–1922

FEDERAL INTERMEDIATE CREDIT BANK

Donald B. Roark	1974–
E. Glenn Sanderfur	1973–1974
J. Walter Brown	1971–1973
Homer C. Hayward	1957–1971
J. B. E. La Plante	1934–1957
A. G. Brown	1930–1933
George M. Wilbur	1930–1930
James B. Davis	1923–1930

BANK FOR COOPERATIVES

Thomas N. Farr	1970–
Wilson A. Orr	1966–1970
J. Kenneth Ward	1952–1966
John E. Brown	1934–1952

PRODUCTION CREDIT CORPORATION

Homer C. Hayward	1955–1956
Howard Gerlaugh	1954–1955
F. Leonard Kerr	1942–1954
Walter Gahm	1933–1942

PRESIDENTS OF FARM CR

New Orleans

FEDERAL LAND BANK

Olin B. Quinn	1969–
John L. Ryan	1955–1968
R. L. Thompson	1938–1955
Norman Monaghan	1937–1937
Edward B. Green	1935–1937
R. A. Beeland, Jr.	1934–1935
R. B. Clark	1931–1933
T. F. Davis	1917–1930

FEDERAL INTERMEDIATE CREDIT BANK

F. Vernon Wright	1970–
William E. Ulmer	1966–1969
Stephen Voelker	1961–1965
J. E. Kelly	1951–1961
J. M. Magruder	1933–1951
R. B. Clark	1931–1933
T. F. Davis	1923–1931

BANK FOR COOPERATIVES

W. C. Verlander, Jr.	1966–
N. F. Pendleton	1961–1966
E. F. Chavanne	1956–1961
H. O. Pate	1940–1956
J. J. Watson	1933–1940

PRODUCTION CREDIT CORPORATION

Stephen Voelker	1952–1956
Jesse B. Hearin	1933–1952

PRESIDENTS OF FARM CREDIT BANKS

St. Louis

FEDERAL LAND BANK

Glenn E. Heitz	1970–
Ralph E. Nowlan	1964–1969
Wm. A. Dickison	1961–1963
Walter H. Droste	1943–1961
F. W. Niemeyer[1]	1942–1943
W. L. Rust	1933–1942
Wood Netherland	1929–1933
H. Paul Bestor	1922–1929
Herman W. Danforth	1917–1922

[1] Acting President

FEDERAL INTERMEDIATE CREDIT BANK

Harry B. Chlebowski[2]	1976–
T. R. McGuire	1969–1976
S. A. Morrow	1957–1969
Joseph R. Cosgrove	1933–1956
Wood Netherland	1929–1933
H. Paul Bestor	1923–1929

[2] Acting President

BANK FOR COOPERATIVES

Harry B. Chlebowski	1970–
W. Russell Boniface	1964–1969
David M. Hardy	1934–1963
Joseph R. Cosgrove[3]	1933–1933

[3] Acting President

PRODUCTION CREDIT CORPORATION

S. A. Morrow	1956–1956
W. S. Brock	1938–1956
F. M. Niemeyer	1934–1938
J. M. Huston	1933–1934
S. M. Garwood	1933–1933

PRESIDENTS OF FARM CREDIT BANKS

St. Paul

FEDERAL LAND BANK

Albert C. Mohr	1973–
Hans T. Hagen	1963–1973
Marion D. Avery	1945–1963
Frank W. Peck	1938–1945
Roy A. Nelson	1933–1938
Fred H. Klawon	1928–1933
Herbert K. Jennings	1925–1928
Edward G. Quamme	1917–1925

FEDERAL INTERMEDIATE CREDIT BANK

Howard C. Richards	1973–
Andrew Lampen	1957–1973
Marshall H. Nugent	1953–1956
Fred H. Klawon	1928–1953
Herbert K. Jennings	1925–1928
Edward G. Quamme	1923–1925

BANK FOR COOPERATIVES

Burgee O. Amdahl	1974–
Oren R. Shelley	1969–1974
Lloyd L. Ullyot	1958–1969
Herbert M. Knipfel	1952–1958
Hutzel Metzger	1933–1951

PRODUCTION CREDIT CORPORATION

Andrew Lampen	1954–1956
George Susens	1933–1954

Omaha

FEDERAL LAND BANK

Arthur C. Buffington	1974–
Wilbur V. Erickson	1970–1974
Thomas A. Maxwell, Jr.	1958–1970
H. Arthur Viergutz	1955–1957
Edwin N. Van Horne	1942–1954
Charles H. McCumsey	1936–1942
Dennis P. Hogan	1917–1936

FEDERAL INTERMEDIATE CREDIT BANK

Donald L. Hovendick	1972–
Herman W. Frerichs, Jr.	1963–1972
Edwin J. Petrik	1956–1963
Myles E. Welsh, Jr.	1943–1956
Charles A. Stewart	1939–1943
Leonard N. Burch	1934–1939
Charles H. McCumsey	1934–1934
Dennis P. Hogan	1923–1933

BANK FOR COOPERATIVES

John A. Harling	1973–
Hugh W. Cox	1969–1973
John E. Eidam	1955–1969
Thomas F. Tobin	1944–1955
James H. Mason	1934–1944

PRODUCTION CREDIT CORPORATION

Edwin J. Petrik	1946–1956
Walter E. Anderson	1940–1946
Louis A. Christensen	1937–1940
E. R. Heaton	1933–1937

FEDERAL LAND BANK

Wm. S. May	1976–
G. A. Wiles	1973–1976
Wm. G. Plested, Jr.	1958–1973
W. E. Fisher	1948–1958
C. G. Shull	1941–1948
Roy S. Johnson	1937–1941
Hugh L. Harrell	1935–1937
L. E. Call	1934–1935
John Fields	1929–1933
Milas Lasater	1919–1929
T. J. Guilfoil	1918–1919
Dan Callahan	1917–1918

FEDERAL INTERMEDIATE CREDIT BANK

Alton B. Cook	1975–
Kenneth M. Lyon	1959–1975
Grover Hill	1946–1959
Frank Butcher	1934–1946
John Fields	1929–1933
Milas Lasater	1923–1929

BANK FOR COOPERATIVES

James R. Williams	1960–
Fred R. Merrifield	1948–1960
Ralph E. Snyder	1934–1948

PRODUCTION CREDIT CORPORATION

A. J. Troup	1948–1956
David L. Mullendore	1934–1947

PRESIDENTS OF FARM CREDIT BANKS

Houston

FEDERAL LAND BANK

George W. Cunningham	1973–
Herbert H. Decker	1968–1972
Hal Weatherford	1960–1967
Sterling C. Evans	1941–1959
A. C. Williams	1933–1940
M. H. Gossett	1917–1932

FEDERAL INTERMEDIATE CREDIT BANK

Jack H. Barton	1976–
W. H. Calkins	1971–1976
W. N. Stokes, Jr.	1956–1971
W. J. McAnelly	1947–1956
Tazewell P. Pridde	1941–1947
Dwight P. Reordan	1933–1940
M. H. Gossett	1923–1932

BANK FOR COOPERATIVES

Jack P. Hughes	1976–
Murrell M. Rogers	1969–1975
John Rhein	1963–1968
W. J. McAnelly	1956–1962
W. N. Stokes, Jr.	1947–1956
W. J. McAnelly	1941–1947
Sterling C. Evans	1934–1940

PRODUCTION CREDIT CORPORATION

Sam N. Hardy	1956–1956
Virgil P. Lee	1937–1956
Tully C. Garner	1934–1937
A. C. Williams[1]	1933–1934

[1] Acting President

Berkeley

FEDERAL LAND BANK		FEDERAL INTERMEDIATE CREDIT BANK		BANK FOR COOPERATIVES		PRODUCTION CREDIT CORPORATION	
George P. Bloxham	1972–	George M. Anderson	1969–	William C. Pendered	1974–	W. F. Mixon	1946–1956
Arvin E. Boerlin	1968–1972	Herbert E. Barker	1962–1969	Bernard H. Schulte	1969–1974	T. P. Coats	1945–1946
Wallace E. York	1961–1967	Charles W. Hudner	1947–1962	Walter A. Rubin	1966–1969	Samuel P. Applewhite[1]	1943–1945
Walter C. Dean	1947–1961	Willard D. Ellis	1923–1947	Lindsay A. Crawford	1947–1966	T. P. Coats	1933–1942
Willard D. Ellis	1943–1947			Daniel G. White	1946–1947		
Chas. Parker	1934–1943			Ellis A. Stokdyk	1933–1946		
Willard D. Ellis	1920–1933						
W. H. Joyce	1917–1920						
Burrell G. White	1917–1917						

[1] Vice President and President pro tem

PRESIDENTS OF FARM CREDIT BANKS

Spokane

FEDERAL LAND BANK		FEDERAL INTERMEDIATE CREDIT BANK		BANK FOR COOPERATIVES		PRODUCTION CREDIT CORPORATION	
A. W. Neel	1973–	Wm. F. Barratt	1970–	M. J. Carter	1962–	E. E. Henry	1935–1956
Fred A. Knutsen	1955–1973	Carl H. Nieberg	1967–1970	A. C. Adams	1935–1962	John A. Schoonover	1933–1934
Henry Matthew	1948–1955	Paul F. Matson	1949–1967	John A. Scollard	1933–1935		
R. E. Brown	1940–1948	Werner E. Meyer	1934–1949				
E. M. Ehrhardt	1927–1940	E. M. Ehrhardt	1927–1934				
George C. Jewett	1925–1927	George C. Jewett	1925–1927				
D. G. O'Shea	1917–1925	D. G. O'Shea	1917–1925				

Central Bank for Cooperatives Presidents

Bernard H. Schulte	1974–
Homer G. Smith	1956–1974

BIBLIOGRAPHY

Agricultural Finance, Amer. Inst. of Banking, Amer. Bankers Assn., New York, 1969. 311 pp.

Annual Reports of the Farm Credit Administration and the Cooperative Farm Credit System, Farm Credit Admin., Govt. Printing Office, Washington, D.C., 1933–1975.

Arnold, C. R., *Farmers Build Their Own Production Credit System—Organization and First 25 Years,* Cir. E-45, Farm Credit Admin., Govt. Printing Office, Washington, D.C., 1958. 89 pp.

Baird, Freda and Brenner, Claude L., *Federal Intermediate Credit Banks,* Brookings Institution, Washington, D.C., 1933. 416 pp.

Banks for Cooperatives—How They Operate, Cir. 40, Banks for Cooperatives, Washington, D.C., 1973. 12 pp.

Baum, E. L., Diesslin, Howard G., and Heady, Earl O., *Capital and Credit Needs in a Changing Agriculture,* Iowa State University Press, Ames, Iowa, 1961. 406 pp.

Butz, Earl L., *The Production Credit System for Farmers,* Brookings Institution, Washington, D.C., 1944. 104 pp.

Characteristics of Federal Land Bank Loans, 1973, Stat. Bul. 8, 1974, Farm Credit Admin., Washington, D.C., 1974. 20 pp.

(The) Cooperative Farm Credit System—Its Functions, Organization and Development, Cir. 36, Farm Credit Admin., Washington, D.C., 1974.

Cooperative Farm Mortgage Credit—1916–1936, Cir. A-8, Farm Credit Admin., Govt. Printing Office, Washington, D.C., 1937.

Down the Road Together, Federal Land Bank System, Washington, D.C., 1967. 33 pp.

Duggan, I. W. and Battles, Ralph U., *Financing the Farm Business,* John Wiley & Sons, Inc., New York, 1950. 354 pp.

Eliot, Clara, *The Farmer's Campaign for Credit,* D. Appleton and Company, New York, 1927. 312 pp.

Engberg, Russell C., *Financing Farmer Cooperatives,* Banks for Cooperatives, Washington, D.C., 1965. 168 pp.

(The) Farm Credit System in the '70s—The Report of the Commission on Agricultural Credit, Farm Credit Admin., Washington, D.C., 1970. 36 pp.

Farmers' Need for Intermediate Term Credit, Bul. CR-6, Farm Credit Admin., Govt. Printing Office, Washington, D.C.,

(The) Farmers' Own Credit System, Cir. A-4, Farm Credit Admin., Govt. Printing Office, Washington, D.C., 1936.

Federal Land Banks—How They Operate, Cir. 35, Federal Land Banks, Washington, D.C., 1974.

(The) Federal Land Bank System—A Half Century of Service to Agriculture, Cir. E-43, Farm Credit Admin., Govt. Printing Office, Washington, D.C., 1967. 32 pp.

Financing Farm Adjustments in the Southern Piedmont, Bul. CR-7, Farm Credit Admin., Govt. Printing Office, Washington, D.C.,

Financing the Farm Credit System, Report of the Advisory Committee on Finance, Farm Credit Admin., Washington, D.C,. October, 1970. 12 pp.

Five Years of Progress in Cooperative Credit, Cir. A-14, Farm Credit Admin., Govt. Printing Office, Washington, D.C., 1939.

Herrick, Myron T. and Ingalls, R., *Rural Credits—Land and Cooperative,* D. Appleton and Company, New York, 1928. 519 pp.

(The) History of Farm Mortgage Credit in the United States, Federal Land Bank of Berkeley.

Hoag, W. Gifford, Sunbury, B. Benjamin, and Puhr, Marie, *Banks for Cooperatives—A Quarter Century of Progress,* Cir. E-47, Farm Credit Admin., Govt. Printing Office, Washington, D.C., 1959.

Holt, W. Stull, *The Federal Farm Loan Bureau—Its History, Activities and Organization,* Inst. for Govt. Research, Washington, D.C., Service Monograph No. 34, The Johns Hopkins Press, Baltimore, Md., 1924. 160 pp.

Horton, Donald C., Larsen, Harold C., and Wall, Norman J., *Farm Mortgage Credit Facilities in the United States,* Misc. Pub. 478, Bur. Ag. Econ., USDA, Govt. Printing Office, Washington, D.C. 262 pp.

Jaenke, E. A., *Cooperatives: The Clear Alternative,* Address, National Symposium on Cooperatives and the Law, The University of Wisconsin, Madison, April 23, 1974. Published by the Farm Credit Admin., Govt. Printing Office, Washington, D.C., 1974.

Johnson, E. C., *Federal Farm Mortgage Corporation—Its Operations and Achievements,* Cir. E-46, Farm Credit Admin., Govt. Printing Office, Washington, D.C., 1959. 18 pp.

Jones, Lawrence, A. and Durand, David, *Mortgage Lending Experience in Agriculture,* a study by the National Bureau of Economic Research, New York, Princeton University Press, 1954. 223 pp.

Larmer, Forrest M., *Financing the Livestock Industry*, Inst. of Economics, Carnegie Corporation, The Macmillan Company, New York, 1926. 327 pp.

Lee, Virgil P., *Principles of Agricultural Credit*, McGraw-Hill Book Company, Inc., New York, 1930. 405 pp.

Manion, Leo E., *Land, Men and Credit—It's Land That Makes Men Free*, Island Press, New York, 1947. 61 pp.

Monson, Daniel L., *Farm Credit Act of 1971 and Its Relationship to Cooperatives*, Address, National Symposium on Cooperatives and the Law, The University of Wisconsin, Madison, April 23, 1974. Published by the Farm Credit Admin., Govt. Printing Office, Washington, D.C., 1974. 16 pp.

Morgan, Dick T., *Land Credits—A Plea for the American Farmer*, Thomas Y. Crowell Company, New York, 1915. 299 pp.

Murray, William G., *Farm Appraisal*, Iowa State College Press, Ames, Iowa, 1947. 278 pp.

Myers, W. I., *Farm Credit Administration*, Amer. Inst. of Banking, Amer. Bankers Assn., New York, 1934. 478 pp.

Myrick, Herbert, *Co-Operative Finance*, Orange Judd Company, New York, 1912. 328 pp.

Myrick, Herbert, *The Federal Farm Loan System*, Orange Judd Company, New York, 1916. 239 pp.

Nelson, Aaron G. and Murray, William G., *Agricultural Finance*, 5th ed., Iowa State University Press, Ames, Iowa, 1967, (includes bibliography).

Norton, L. J., *Financing Agriculture*, The Interstate Printers & Publishers, Inc., Danville, Ill., 1938. 321 pp.

Production Credit Associations—How They Operate, Cir. 37, Federal Intermediate Credit Banks, Washington, D.C., 1974.

Puhr, Marie, *Years of Progress with the Cooperative Land Bank System— 1917–1957*, Cir. E-43, Farm Credit Admin., Govt. Printing Office, Washington, D.C., 1957. 54 pp.

Quereski, Anwar Igbal, *Agricultural Credit—A Study of Recent Developments in Agricultural Credit Administration in the United States of America*, Sir Isaac Pittman & Sons, Ltd., London, 1936. 176 pp.

Schwartz, Carl H., Jr., *Joint Stock Land Banks—A Financial Study*, Washington College Press, Takoma Park, Md. (Washington, D.C.), 1938. 208 pp.

Sparks, Earl Sylvester, *Agricultural Credit*, Thomas Y. Crowell Company, New York, 1932. 476 pp.

Stokes, William N., Jr., *Credit to Farmers*, Federal Intermediate Credit Banks, Washington, D.C., 1973. 171 pp.

U.S. Country Life Commission Report, L. H. Bailey, Chairman, with transmittal message from President Theodore Roosevelt, Senate Doc. 705, 60th Congress, 2nd Session, Govt. Printing Office, Washington, D.C., 1909. 65 pp. Also reprinted in "American Farmers and the Rise of Agribusiness" Series, Arno Press, New York, 1975. 150 pp.

Wiprud, A. C., *The Federal Farm Loan System in Operation*, Harper & Brothers, New York, 1921. 280 pp.

Wright, Ivan, *Bank Credit and Agriculture—Under the National and Federal Reserve Banking Systems*, McGraw-Hill Book Company, Inc., New York, 1922. 340 pp.

Wright, Ivan, *Farm Mortgage Financing*, McGraw-Hill Book Company, Inc., New York, 1923. 343 pp.

CPSIA information can be obtained
at www.ICGtesting.com
Printed in the USA
BVOW08s1148250318
511523BV00023B/563/P